POST-FORDISM AND SOCIAL FORM

Capital and Class
General Editor: Simon Clarke

The Conference of Socialist Economists (CSE) was founded in 1969 to provide a non-sectarian and internationalist forum for Marxist theoretical debate. Much of the most fertile intellectual work on the left over the last two decades has had its origins in the working groups and annual conference of the CSE, and has first been published in the CSE's journal *Capital and Class*. This series makes these fundamental debates available to a wider readership, by bringing together published and unpublished papers with an editorial introduction, in order to inform the renewal of socialist thinking in the 1990s.

Werner Bonefeld and John Holloway (*editors*)
POST-FORDISM AND SOCIAL FORM

Simon Clarke (*editor*)
THE STATE DEBATE

Andy Friedman (*editor*)
THE LABOUR PROCESS

Sue Himmelweit (*editor*)
GENDER

Simon Mohun (*editor*)
VALUE THEORY

Hugo Radice (*editor*)
THE INTERNATIONALIZATION OF CAPITAL

Post-Fordism and Social Form

A Marxist Debate on the Post-Fordist State

Edited by
Werner Bonefeld
Department of Politics
University of Edinburgh

and

John Holloway
Department of Politics
University of Edinburgh

M

First published 1991

Published by
MACMILLAN ACADEMIC AND PROFESSIONAL LTD
Houndmills, Basingstoke, Hampshire RG21 2XS
and London
Companies and representatives
throughout the world

British Library Cataloguing in Publication Data
Post-Fordism and social form: a Marxist debate on the post-Fordist state.
1. Politics. Theories
I. Bonefeld, Werner II. Holloway, John
320.01
ISBN 978-0-333-54393-1
ISBN 978-0-333-54394-8 pbk

Contents

Notes on the Contributors

Werner Bonefeld works at the Department of Politics, University of Edinburgh.

Simon Clarke is Senior Lecturer in the School of Sociology, University of Warwick.

Richard Gunn is a Lecturer in the Department of Politics, University of Edinburgh.

Joachim Hirsch is Professor of Politics at the University of Frankfurt-am-Main.

John Holloway is a Lecturer in the Department of Politics, University of Edinburgh.

Bob Jessop is Professor of Sociology at the University of Lancaster.

Eloína Peláez is a Research Fellow in the Research Centre for Social Sciences, University of Edinburgh.

Kosmas Psychopedis is Professor of Politics at the University of Athens.

1 Introduction: Post-Fordism and Social Form

Werner Bonefeld and John Holloway

In the last few years, the focus of attention in Marxist discussion has shifted from the issue of capitalist *crisis* to the question of the *restructuring* of capitalism.

The argument that the international crisis which began in the late 1960s and early 1970s was a crisis of a pattern of capitalist social relations referred to as 'Fordism', and that we are now on the way to a new pattern called 'post-Fordism' (or sometimes 'neo-Fordism') has gained widespread acceptance, both in Marxist and non-Marxist circles. The old pattern is generally seen as having been characterised by mass production based on the assembly-line principle adopted so successfully by Henry Ford, by rising wages which provided the basis for a new articulation between mass consumption and mass production, by large factories, and by a high degree of state intervention based on Keynesian principles, the development of the welfare state and a central role for the trade unions both in institutionalising collective bargaining and in the formulation of state policies. The new pattern of post-Fordist capitalism is said to be characterised by new methods of production based on microelectronics, by flexible working practices, a much reduced role for trade unions in society, a new individualism, a reduction of state intervention, and a new relation between production and consumption.

This argument, which we may call the 'Fordism thesis', originated with the work of Palloix, Aglietta and other authors in France in the mid-1970s, but it has since been taken up in many parts of the world and has acquired the status of an international theoretical movement, with its own regular newsletters and international conferences. Most of the work done in this area has been done by people who have been trained as, and regard themselves as, economists. Although the issue of state intervention and the nature of the Keynesian and post-Keynesian state is of central importance to the whole development analysed by the Regulation theorists, little attention has been devoted to the systematic discussion of the state by the main stream of regulationist analysis.

The issue of the state and of the relevance of the concepts of Fordism and post-Fordism for our understanding of the state has been developed not by the French Regulation School but by a theoretical current with a rather different theoretical tradition. The concept of the 'Fordist state' was first developed by Joachim Hirsch in West Germany in the early 1980s, but the approach has since been developed by other authors in West Germany and elsewhere, notably by Bob Jessop in Britain. Despite the richness of these contributions, the specific debates on Fordism and the reformulation of state theory have not received the same international attention as the main stream of regulationist analysis.

The purpose of this book is twofold: to introduce the debates on the reformulation of state theory around the notions of Fordism and post-Fordism and also to develop a theoretical and political critique both of the specific reformulation of state theory and of the regulation approach in general.

The Reformulation Approach has its theoretical roots in the state derivation debate, which originated in West Germany in the early 1970s, but has had considerable influence in international Marxist discussion.

The basic aim of the state derivation debate was to understand the limits and determinants of state action through an analysis of the relation between the state and capital, or, more precisely, to understand the state as a particular form of the capital relation. This approach has often been criticised as being functionalist, as a 'capital-logic' approach, which effectively interprets state action as a simple expression of the requirements of capital. While this is true of some of the contributions to the state derivation debate, other authors, such as Hirsch, were concerned to emphasise that the fact that the state was a *particular* form of the capital relation meant that state actions could not be understood as a direct response to the requirements of capital: both capital accumulation itself and the development of the state could only be conceptualised in terms of class struggle (Hirsch 1974/78; Holloway 1980).

One implication of the conclusion that the development of the state could only be understood in terms of class struggle was that the discussion of the capitalist state had to proceed beyond theoretical generalities and become more historically specific. This does not mean, of course, that theory was abandoned or that the nature of the relation between state and capital ceased to be central. The question was rather how to develop a theoretically informed understanding of the development of the state. It is this issue which has been at the heart of discussions of the state in recent years.

For Hirsch, moving on from the state derivation debate meant in practice an effort to refine the tools of conceptual analysis. This involved firstly a turning towards concepts developed by Gramsci and Poulantzas to discuss the different types of state apparatus and the constitution and process of state power, particularly in his contributions to the debate on the development of the West German state and the so-called 'Modell Deutschland' at the end of the 1970s. The turn towards Poulantzas might be considered surprising considering Hirsch's rejection of the idea of the 'relative autonomy of the state' in his contribution to the state derivation debate: however, it can be argued that a tension between functionalism and the historical process of class antagonism was already built into Hirsch's contribution to the state debate (Holloway/Picciotto 1978 and Holloway's contribution in ch. 5 of this volume), and that the attempt to incorporate Poulantzas' concepts into his analysis merely reinforced functionalist tendencies that were there from the beginning. In Britain, Jessop followed a fairly similar development, seeking to combine the conclusions of the state derivation debate with some of the ideas of Poulantzas, and trying to approach the study of the state through a process of conceptual refinement: this led, for example, to his analysis of corporatist strategies in Britain during the 1970s as comprising a 'corporatist state' (Jessop 1978).

A different line out of the state derivation debate was taken by others, such as Holloway and Picciotto, who sought to go beyond the prevailing functionalism and structuralism by emphasising that the development of capitalism and the capitalist state does not follow pre-given objective laws of capitalist development, but rather that these laws are themselves forms through and in which class antagonism exists. The London Edinburgh Weekend Return Group (1979, 1980) discussed the development of the state in terms of the changing patterns of class struggle and class domination. Thus, the state at any particular time could be understood as part of a specific, form-determined *mode of domination*, a specific pattern of defining, repressing and integrating the working class. The institutional form of the state was thus seen as the historical mode through which and in which the class struggle was expressed within the state (Holloway 1980, 1982).

There are thus two different lines of development out of the state derivation debate: one seeking to proceed through the refinement of general concepts and the development of intermediate concepts which would provide a basis for operationalising the general theoretical framework, the other emphasising the importance of understanding capital as a relation of class struggle, and the state as moment of a mode of domination.

The article by Hirsch included in this volume is a good example of his work on the reformulation of state theory and development of the concept of the Fordist state. The article was written under the impact of the conservative shift to power in West Germany in 1982. Its aim is to understand conceptually the significance of this shift as a new departure in the way in which the social relations of production are politically regulated within the overall pattern of the crisis-ridden development of capitalist accumulation. He develops the regulationist analysis of Fordism in his analysis of the Fordist state, as the political form appropriate to the Fordist regime of accumulation. The crisis of Fordism is thus also the crisis of the Fordist political system: as the development of capital accumulation undermines the social relations appropriate to the previous forms of reproduction, it leads to social instability and the rise of new social movements, destroying the class compromise institutionalised in the Fordist form of the state. Hirsch sees the state as responding to the social distintegration inherent in the crisis of accumulation by penetrating even more deeply into civil society in order to restructure social relations into forms appropriate to the emergence of a new, post-Fordist regime of accumulation. This 'statification' of society in the crisis is expressed in the concept of the 'Fordist security state', which is seen as giving way to the 'post-Fordist state', in which state regulation is achieved not through Keynesian-inspired modes of political integration appropriate to Fordism, nor through directly repressive mechanisms of the transitional phase, but through the state-regulated commodification of civil society. According to this approach, the post-Fordist state does not involve a withdrawal of the state from economic regulation, but offers new, highly differentiated and flexible forms of state regulation, appropriate to the segmentation of the working class and the greater flexibility of production characteristic of post-Fordist accumulation.

The rest of this book is concerned principally with the discussion of the theoretical bases of the theories of post-Fordism and the post-Fordist state. The two principal critiques are contained in the articles by Bonefeld and by Clarke. While Clarke concentrates on the general critique of regulation theory, Bonefeld's article is a presentation and critique of the reformulation of state theory. Both articles argue that the approaches criticised disarticulate the internal relation between 'structure' and class struggle and that they reduce the class struggle to a 'but also' position quite separated from the 'objective laws of capitalist development'. Both articles argue that what is needed to achieve an understanding of capitalist development is a Marxist analysis which dwells on the historical and conceptual priority of class struggle.

The issue of the relation between struggle and structure is taken up by Jessop in his reply to Bonefeld. Jessop argues that both the regulation approach and the reformulation of state theory do give proper weight to class struggle and criticises Bonefeld for having an 'essentialist' and 'workerist' approach. The argument is then taken one step further in Holloway's reply to Jessop, in which he relates the disarticulation of structure and struggle criticised by Bonefeld in the theory of the Fordist state to Hirsch's earlier work in 1970s. In a second contribution, Jessop takes issue with Holloway's reply and Clarke's critique of the regulation approach. On the basis of an analysis of *Capital*, Jessop criticises Holloway's assertion that capital is class struggle. He contrasts Holloway's allegedly 'workerist approach' with Clarke's critique of the regulation approach which, he argues, rests on a 'form-analytical account of class domination'. Jessop argues that the regulation approach shares the same conceptual starting point and that the criticisms by Holloway and Clarke are misplaced. In his response to Jessop, Holloway reasserts that capital *is* class struggle. He argues that Jessop reifies structures by dismissing the power of labour in and against capital and emphasises the political implications of Jessop's approach, in particular the theoretical suppression of struggle in Jessop.

The selection of articles included in this volume is completed by three articles criticising other aspects of the post-Fordist thesis. Peláez and Holloway focus on the issue of technology and suggest that there is a technological determinism underlying the assumptions of the post-Fordist argument. The article by Psychopedis assesses critically the methodological assumptions of structural Marxism and the reformulation of structural Marxism in the regulation approach and the debate on (post-)Fordism. He suggests that the regulation approach and the debate on (post-)Fordism pursue a 'pre-critical' analysis of capital and its development. He argues that the regulation approach and the debate on (post-) Fordism signify a crisis in theory which, in turn, is to be seen as a moment of the crisis of capitalism. The book concludes with an article by Gunn which relates some of the themes of the Fordism debate to other recent theoretical developments, most notably the theory of critical realism associated with Bhaskar, which has a number of points in common with the concerns of the reformulation of state theory, particularly in the notion that theoretical understanding can proceed through the elaboration of 'intermediate concepts' as a half-way house between theory and practice.

From this brief presentation of some of the issues discussed in the articles collected in this book, it might appear that all that is at issue is the definition of concepts with little practical importance. Nothing could be farther from the truth.

There are two crucial issues in the discussion of Fordism and the Fordist state. The first is the nature of the present crisis. Is capitalism already on the way to overcoming the international crisis and to establishing a relatively stable basis for a new period of prosperity, as the post-Fordism thesis suggests, or are we still in the middle of a prolonged and quite unresolved crisis of overaccumulation, as Clarke suggests? The answer given to this question affects dramatically how one sees the prospects of world development and the urgency of the socialist destruction of capitalism. It is important to remember that the last major crisis of capitalism was resolved only through the destruction of millions of workers, and that the possibility of this recurring, but on a far greater scale, is a very real one. While it is undoubtedly true that the working class has suffered important defeats internationally over the last ten years, it may be that these are nothing like the defeats which capital needs to inflict if it is to reestablish itself on a stable basis.

The second issue is how one understands the driving force of capitalist development. Given that there are major changes taking place in the pattern of capitalist social relations at the moment, how is one to understand these changes? As the replacement of one model by another, driven forward by the objective tendencies of capitalist development, or as a process taking place through constant, hard-fought struggle? If the former, we are confronted by a new reality, a closed structural–functionalist world which we are powerless to change, and all we can do is adapt or cry out in despair. But if the latter, we are faced with no 'reality' other than the reality of a constant struggle, a struggle of which we are inevitably part.

REFERENCES

Hirsch, J. (1974 and 1978), 'The State Apparatus and Social Reproduction: Elements of a Theory of the Bourgeois State', in Holloway/Picciotto (1978).

Holloway, J. (1980), 'State as Class Practice', *Research in Political Economy*, Vol. 3 (Jai Press, 1980).

Holloway, J. (1982), *Fundamentos Teóricos para una Critica Marxista de la Administración Publica* (Mexico: Instituto Nacional de Administración Publica).

Holloway, J. and S. Picciotto (eds) (1978), *State and Capital* (London: Edward Arnold).

Jessop, B. (1978), 'Capitalism and Democracy: The Best Possible Political Shell?', in Littlejohn (ed.), *Power and the State* (London: Croom Helm).

London-Edinburgh Weekend Return Group (1979), 'Working For and Against the State', *CSE Conference Papers, 1979* (London: CSE).

London–Edinburgh Weekend Return Group (1980), *In and Against the State* (London: Pluto Press).

2 Fordism and Post-Fordism: The Present Social Crisis and its Consequences*

Joachim Hirsch

THEORETICAL REFLECTIONS

That the economic crisis which has persisted since the mid-1970s is not a phase of the usual capitalist cycle, but is of a deeper, 'structural' nature is now accepted by economists of almost every persuasion (see the most recent structural reports of the German institutes of economic research: Schmidt *et al.* 1984; Gerstenberger 1984; DIW 1984). The diagnosis of the established economists (most of whom have now retreated from Keynesianism and moved over to the camp of the monetarists and the supply theorists) is roughly as follows: the decisive cause of the crisis is the excessive rises in wages over the years, together with an extreme expansion of 'consumptive' state expenditure (that is, welfare state expenditure in the wider sense) and of the state indebtedness which that implies; the cost of the 'labour factor' was increased further by the costly economic and social decisions of the state (such as expansion of the social security system, and legislation protecting labour against dismissal); the result of this development was rising inflation. In view of the 'lack of coordination' between incomes and budgetary policies, the fight against inflation by the central bank led inevitably to sharp economic frictions (for example, rises in interest rates, resulting in difficulties for capital); the cumulative effect of these factors has been the fall in the profitability of capital which has persisted since the late 1960s, with just a short interruption between 1975 and 1979 (Schmidt *et al.* 1984, pp. 33ff.). This fall in profitability is seen as the essential cause of the weakness of investment in the West German economy, of the falling or even negative rates of growth and of rising unemployment.

The fall in investment leads, through the ageing of the machinery and the delayed introduction of newer, technically more advanced machines, to a slowdown in the tempo of technological innovation. This is intensified by the fact that entrepreneurs are less and less ready to take risks, that they seem to be losing their Schumpeterian qualities. The stalling of innovation is also connected with a series of legal–institutional factors: fiscal obstacles to self-financing, lack of 'flexibility' of the labour force and the network of state regulations limiting the activities of firms, in the area of environmental protection, for example. As at the same time there has been a rapid advance in the industrialisation of the so-called 'newly industrialised countries', with these countries emerging ever more strongly as suppliers of industrial goods, the competitive position of the Federal Republic of Germany has been deteriorating considerably. Falling behind the USA and Japan in the sphere of high technology products, it is increasingly under pressure from the industrialising cheap-wage countries in the field of standard technologies. In view of the world-wide dimensions of the present crisis, world trade in industrial commodities as a whole is stagnating and the FRG's share in this stagnating market is falling (from 17.4 per cent in 1962 to 15.6 per cent in 1982: DIW 1984, pp. 10ff.). Only the newly industrialised countries and Japan are still able to increase their share. The present export-led boom based on the rise of the dollar can only temporarily conceal this disadvantage.

The tongs of wage costs thus grip from both sides: from the point of view of the internal *and* the external conditions, the 'demands' of the wage-earners are driving the economy into crisis. Yet the state, under pressure from the trade unions, plays a part in another way in the dangerous slowdown in the technological change of the structure of the German economy: by giving subsidies to maintain branches of industry which are no longer internationally competitive, with the aim of preserving employment, it hinders the adaptation of those branches to the changed conditions of international competition.

In essence, then, the crisis is seen as a *political* one, by which it is not individual political decisions that are meant (the 'lack of coordination' between the different actors in economic policy are unavoidable) but the whole field of activity of state policy. More precisely, it is a question of the *structure* of the social-democratic Keynesian state: powerful trade unions, wilful governments at the mercy of pressure from organised (wage-earners') interests, the powerful network of social bureaucracies and welfare pressure groups, the established 'demanding attitudes' of the broad masses. Accordingly, help is not to be expected from a simple change of government. It is a question rather of a fundamental change in the institutional structure of the socio-political system and of the relations of power crystallised within it: it is a question of forcing back the trade unions, reducing demands, changing the pattern of consumption, dismantling and restructuring the welfare state, deregulating and withdrawing from state intervention altogether, revitalising market forces.

Between these established 'bourgeois' and relevant left diagnoses of the crisis there are a number of interesting convergences and differences. The 'left Keynesian' theories close to social democracy have become largely obsolete, based as they were on the assumption that the process of economic development could be steered by state intervention, that there would be continuous full employment, relatively undisturbed growth (and hence expansion of reform policies), and that the Marxist theory of value and crisis was outdated. In the 1960s, such theories blossomed throughout the world, but they have been unambiguously disproved by the factual development. The 'crisis of Keynesianism' is obvious. This has favoured the renaissance of the 'theory of the long wave' (Mandel 1980, Altvater 1982), a theory which is based on Marxist value theory and the 'law of the tendency of the rate of profit to fall' as the decisive foundation of the capitalist crisis mechanism. Briefly, this theory says that in the process of accumulation the organic composition of capital must necessarily rise and that this rise leads to a fall in the rate of profit, overproduction of capital, stagnation and crisis, *in so far* as a number of 'countertendencies' which are also present (such as a rise in relative surplus value and a change in the composition of capital through technological development, and real falls in wages and intensification of exploitation) remain ineffective.

Crises of this sort form historical breaks in the process of capitalist development, which can be overcome only through a structural reorganisation of the technological and social conditions of production, of working and class relations. That explains the appearance of 'long' waves of capitalist development, overlaid upon the normal variations in the conjuncture and normally lasting several decades, at the turning points of which stand 'secular' crises of a worldwide scale, associated with social transformation (the great depression of the 1870s and 1880s, the world economic crisis of the 1930s and now the present crisis).

In opposition to this there is a left variant of crisis theory, which one can refer to very roughly as 'profit-squeeze theory', and which, in peculiar agreement with the 'bourgeois' theories mentioned above, sees the causes of the present crisis in the strength attained (again) by the working class, successful wage struggles and the growing resistance to the manifold forms of capitalist exploitation in the factory. This theory too has a 'secular', even if not exactly a long-term, cyclical explanation: the present crisis is the consequence of a long period of post-war prosperity, in the course of which the working class was able to recover from the defeats of fascism, war and the immediate post-war period, to strengthen its organisation and extend again its political room for manoeuvre (Bowles *et al.* 1983; O'Connor 1984; Gorz 1983; Dockes and Rosier 1978; Coriat 1984).

These different theoretical approaches have one thing in common: they each in a particular way place political-institutional relations, established social power structures and forms of socialisation at the centre of their explanation of crisis. The present crisis is seen as a structural crisis of the capitalist social formation which had developed in the post-war period. This can be taken as a point of departure in the attempt to construct a more consistent explanatory framework which avoids the different contradictions and inaccuracies of the existing approaches.

The Marxist theory of the tendency of the rate of profit to fall has the advantage of offering an explanation for the periodic appearance of 'big' crises in the history of capitalism and for the long-term cycles of capitalist reproduction. For this theory the decisive cause of the crisis lies not in historically contingent external conditions, but in the capital relation itself. That means that long waves and secular crises are unavoidable within the capital relation. However, the Marxist theory comes up against a number of difficulties. One consists in the still unresolved problem of its value-theoretical foundation (especially the so-called 'transformation problem', on which see *Gesellschaft* 13, 1979) — a weakness which can admittedly be found equally in competing theories. A second difficulty results from the construction of the theory itself: in so far as the crisis is explained in terms of a contradictory interplay of tendency and countertendencies, the implications of the theory are undefined. If one assumes the value-logical validity of the basic tendency (rising organic composition of capital), then the determination of the timing and form of appearance of a concrete crisis, that is, of a fall in the rate of profit which interrupts the normal course of accumulation, requires a statement about the conditions in which the 'counteracting tendencies' are effective. However, these cannot be 'derived' from the law of value and the general structural conditions of the capitalist mode of production, but are the expression of a historically specific complex of social, technological, political–institutional and ideological conditions (technological development, strength of the working class, state interventionism, imperialist relations of force).

Basically capital can pursue different *accumulation strategies*, according to the given social, political and technological circumstances: strategies focussing on the domestic or on the world market, 'intensive' (based on accelerated technological development and increase in the production of relative surplus value) or 'extensive' strategies (based on the subordination of new spheres or regions to the capital relation, reductions in wages, lengthening of the working day) (Aglietta 1979). The realisation of a particular strategy of accumulation or model of accumulation is always bound up with the possibility of imposing a compatible political–ideological *hegemonic structure* and an appropriate form of political system, manner of suppressing the working class and institutionalising class relations (Jessop 1983; Hirsch 1983). However, the concept of 'strategy' must not be misunderstood as implying a theory of agency: the implementation of an accumulation, and hegemonic, structure is always the result of structurally determined and contradictory class and group action, and thus a 'process without a subject'.

The character of the different formations which capitalism has formed in the course of its historical development is defined by a definite accumulation strategy, a model of accumulation and a corresponding hegemonic structure. Put somewhat simply, structural crises of capitalism occur historically when within the framework of a given model of accumulation and hegemonic structure it is no longer possible to mobilise sufficient countertendencies to the fall in the rate of profit, and when the further valorisation of capital requires a transformation of this structure, that is, the imposition of a new capitalist formation. Secular crises are thus crises of integral, coherent and structurally established social formations, crises of a 'historic bloc' in Gramsci's sense, and their function consists in 'revolutionising' this structure in such a way that the process of accumulation can proceed again on a new social basis (Hirsch 1974; Mattick 1971).

This is the basis of the theory of Fordism, which is concerned with the structural characteristics and the politico–economic mechanisms of regulation in post-war capitalism and its current crisis (Aglietta 1979; Palloix 1979; Hirsch 1980). It follows that the Marxist theory of crisis should by no means be misunderstood 'objectivistically' or 'economistically', and certainly not as a mechanistic theory of capitalist collapse. Statements based on crisis theory about the nature of crises and the course of crises always require also an analysis of the concrete social conditions, hence of accumulation strategies and hegemonic structures. Crises and the resolutions of crises are ultimately the expression of concrete class struggles, albeit struggles which always take place under 'objective' conditions which establish themselves behind the backs of the actors. The Marxist theory of crisis is a decidedly *politico–economic* theory, not an economistic or objectivist one.

The 'profit-squeeze' approach, on the other hand, founds 'structural' crisis processes not in the inner contradictory nature of the capital relation, but in the relations of distribution which result from the 'political' relations of class forces. The material successes of the wage earners in the (political) struggle over distribution and their successful resistance against the intensification of exploitation reduce the profit on capital and so produce 'weak investment', stagnation and crisis. Thus the profit squeeze theory finds itself in very striking agreement with the crisis diagnoses of the established economists. It also shares therefore some of their weaknesses. Within the framework of these assumptions it is difficult to explain, for example, that the wage quota in the Federal Republic has sunk since 1975 and that the unit labour costs have shown a remarkable stability by international standards, without this having led to a sufficient rate of profit and to a renewed 'upswing'. The explanation that the relative fall in wages has been too weak (Schmidt *et al.* 1984, pp. 40ff.) is very unsatisfactory in view of the premises of the theory. In contrast, the theory of the tendency of the rate of profit to fall has no difficulty at all in accounting for a parallel movement between falling real wages, declining profits and crisis.

If one brings together the various explanations of the crisis, it can be seen that the different factors of a complex crisis situation are weighted differently or even filtered out. Put in terms of Marxist crisis theory, both the 'bourgeois' and the profit squeeze theories concentrate on certain 'countertendencies' and the conditions of their absence (development of real wages, development of the forms of exploitation, technology). They thus point to an essential aspect of the crisis situation, but fail to understand it as a whole. One thing, however, is common to all theories: the decisive moment of 'secular' crises is seen as the contradiction between the established structure of a social formation characterised by specific class relations, socio–political institutions, interest organisations and 'values', on the one hand, and the changing valorisation requirements of capital, on the other. Secular or structural crises occur when the process of capital valorisation comes up against the limits of a historical form of socialisation, in the framework of which it originally prospered. The crisis functions as a moment of resolution and the vehicle for a 'reconstruction of society' required by valorisation. For bourgeois economists, the Keynesian welfare state form of capitalism, which developed and established itself in the 1950s and 1960s, is a purely 'external' cause of the present crisis. They have to argue in this way because they cannot grasp the contradictions of the capital relation. Their theoretical weakness is shown by the fact that they can understand the organisation of society adequate to valorisation only as a problem of political regulation (*Steuerung*). Their theory thus locates the causes of the crisis in the failure of the (democratic) political system – and comes, already on purely theoretical grounds, as it were, fatally close to authoritarian concepts and systems of every conceivable political colour. Because it is incapable of grasping the crisis fully, it responds to historical crises of the capitalist economy with a radical change in its theoretical paradigms: Keynesianism is dead, monetarism and supply theory dominate the field. The (secular) crisis of the economy produces to some extent a similar crisis of theory.

Because the Marxist theory of the tendency for the rate of profit to fall in its elaborated (that is, neither economistic nor mechanistic) form is broader and more comprehensive, we shall take that as the starting point. However, its unresolved theoretical problems should not be overlooked and it must be borne in mind that the Marxist theory of crisis in its general form provides only a framework of reference, which can help in the investigation of concrete historical formations and their crises. The Marxist theory of the tendency of the rate of profit to fall does not explain any single historical crisis, but rather the general crisis-ridden character of a social structure, which must assume historically different forms. Used in this way, however, it allows one to explain the historical development of capitalist society with its 'long waves' and 'secular crises'. It emphasises the structural necessity (that is, a necessity independent of the actions of the class actors) of periodical crises of the historical capitalist formation. It avoids 'economistic' and 'politicist' misunderstandings which break the connection between economics and politics, and, finally, it is capable of integrating relatively smoothly the partial explanations of competing theories.

STRUCTURAL FEATURES OF THE FORDIST FORMATION

By the term 'Fordism' we designate the capitalist formations which were formed from the 1930s to the 1950s in the wake of the world economic crisis and the Second World War. They were established on the basis of the dominant imperialist position of the United States and of the postwar prosperity which developed and was maintained under that dominance. The Fordist 'long wave' reached its peak in the 1960s and culminated in a new 'secular' and worldwide crisis phase in the mid-1970s. The concept of Fordism allows us to understand and to grasp analytically decisive structural features of the capitalist metropoles and thus of the world capitalist system in the phase of development which has just finished. To identify general phases of historical development of the capitalist formation does not of course mean that one overlooks the manifold national particularities and non-simultaneities, for example, the preeminent role of corporatively supported state regulation in the northern and central European countries, as compared with the United States, or the relative backwardness of Italy and France in this respect, not to mention the 'special case' of Japan. These differences are the result both of special historical circumstances and of relations of international competition and dependence within the Fordist formation itself. They do not affect therefore the validity of the analytical approach, but they do make it necessary to make differentiations and comparative investigations, which we cannot undertake here. Within the framework of the general theoretical concept, we limit ourselves essentially to an analysis of the structure and development of Federal German society. This is not, however, a special national case, but is integrated into and defined by the historical structural changes in capitalist production and reproduction, mediated through the world market.

The Fordist formation is based on a strategy of 'intensive' capital accumulation, which rests essentially on the Taylorist reorganisation of the labour process (Braverman 1974; Edwards 1979; Stearns 1980; Clawson 1980; Gartman 1979). The establishment of Taylorism signified a decisive intensification of exploitation, based on far-reaching deskilling processes, the destruction of traditional craft forms of workers' power and the introduction of efficient techniques of managerial control and supervision. The Taylorist organisation of production and the enormous increase which it brought in the productivity of labour made possible the mass production of cheap consumption goods and created thereby the precondition for the establishment of new key technologies (automobile construction, household implements, electronic means of mass communication). It also made possible a gradual and perceptible increase in real wages: that is, the mass worker created by Taylorism could become the mass consumer of industrially produced commodities. In this way the Fordist articulation of production and reproduction was created. The Taylorist reorganisation of labour processes was bound up with an accelerated capitalisation of society: industrialisation of agriculture and of the household, decline of artisanal forms of production and of traditional service occupations in favour of industrial wage labour. There was thus a tendency for the reproduction of labour power, and hence the consumption goods and the service industry, to become a decisive sphere of investment and valorisation for capital. Capitalisation, universalisation of wage labour, establishment of a comprehensive internal market and increased labour productivity formed the basis of the new cycle of accumulation (Lutz 1984). Under the hegemony of the United States, the world market which had collapsed in the world economic crisis was reestablished in the 1950s. The growing internationalisation of production changed the structure of the international division of labour, new forms of the exploitation and use of raw materials developed, dependent economies were selectively industrialised. At the same time the intensification of competition on the world market in the dominant economies led to an enormously increased pressure for rationalisation and innovation, which sent technological development leaping forward.

This Fordist model of accumulation made possible a comprehensive increase and stabilisation of the rate of profit and thus created the basis for a long period of prosperity. Its basis was the creation of new fields of investment for capital (capitalisation) and a decisive raising of relative surplus value (Taylorisation). The latter was based on the lowering of the reproduction costs of labour power made possible by industrial mass production and the massive rise in the productivity of labour. In addition there were a series of technological developments which counteracted a rapid rise in the organic composition of capital: the use of new, cheaper raw materials and sources of energy (oil), the industrialisation of the service sector, the development of new technologies of organisation, communication and transport.

The establishment of the Fordist model of accumulation had crucial consequences for the forms of socialisation and the structure of the political system. 'Pre-capitalist' forms of life and social relations, traditional cultures and milieus (above all of workers) were dissolved; forced mobility, consumer individualism and the weakening of traditional family and communal structures led to growing manifestations of social distintegration: there developed a forcibly 'modernised' mass society composed of atomised individuals, characterised by social relations mediated through money, an externally imposed division of labour and industrial economy of time, a society regulated and held together ever more by large bureaucratic organisations. Whereas capital at the beginning of industrialisation could develop by growing into and exploiting existing pre-capitalist social structures and natural resources (rural population as a reservoir of labour power, family as social insurance, nature as free productive force), it broke up and destroyed these conditions as it became established. That meant, however, that the social production of the basic conditions of production, of people and nature, had to become a matter for social — or, under capitalist conditions, essentially state — regulation.

The modern welfare and interventionist state was born under the pressures of competition on the world market, the increasing concentration of capital and social disintegration. It proves less and less possible to leave the economic and social reproduction process to the mechanisms of the market and the effectiveness of spontaneous social networks alone. Concentration of capital and social disintegration lead to a growing bureaucratisation and to an expansion of the regulating, controlling and surveillance state ('security state': Hirsch 1980). State bureaucratic regulation becomes an essential basis of the economic process and the precondition for the maintenance and direction of a labour force adequate to the new patterns of production and consumption. Technologically highly developed complexes of industrial and financial capital closely interwoven with the state administration, on the one hand, and the network of welfare bureaucracies, on the other, are thus two sides of the same coin: the expression of Fordist socialisation.

The generalisation of wage labour, complex processes of homogenisation and division of the working class, social distintegration and the increasing tertiarisation of society (expansion of the state, industrial and service bureaucracies) are the essential bases for the growth of the bureaucratised and centralised trade union apparatuses and the mass parties with socially dispersed membership and electoral support and with class-unspecific programmes. The 'Keynesian state' as a form of political regulation developed on this basis, characterised by the predominance of statified parties of mass integration and trade unions corporatistically bound into the political apparatus (Buci-Glucksmann and Therborn 1982). Its ideological basis is a broad productivist consensus on growth and progress which binds together the relevant political organisations. Social democratic (and similar) parties have a special significance in the political integration of the working class, the corporatist integration of the trade unions and the implementation of an interventionist state policy of modernisation. Continuous growth and relatively full employment were essential preconditions of this form of regulation, which institutionalised a powerful cartel of interests in favour of policies of growth and full employment, incorporating the relevant capital fractions and parts of the working class. Growth, modernity, progress, individualism, consumerism, work discipline, administrative 'feasibility', statist social reform and egalitarianism were the dominant normative values which held together this economic–political hegemonic structure of Fordism.

THE CRISIS OF FORDISM

The cause of the present crisis is that this Fordist structure of accumulation and hegemony has begun to become a *barrier* to the valorisation of capital. Although its establishment was at first the condition for a long-term stabilisation of the profitability of capital and of a relatively long period of capitalist prosperity, the economic and social structures and mechanisms associated with it have now themselves become a factor of crisis. That is to say that within the given economic, social, political and ideological structures which are knitted together in a historical social formation, the 'countertendencies' which compensate the fall in the rate of profit gradually lose their force. As a result, the fall in the rate of profit, from being a contradictory tendency, becomes empirical reality. While the context of the law of value, formulated by Marx, remains the basic cause of crisis, the conditions that trigger off the crisis and their forms of appearance must be sought in the historically specific structural features of the Fordist social formation. These determine the different elements of a complex crisis which — rooted as they are in the unity of the formation as a coherent 'historic bloc' (Gramsci) — can of course be separated only analytically.

The Crisis of the Taylorist Organisation of Work

There are indications that the reserves of productivity contained in the Taylorist organisation of work have gradually been exhausted. Increasing intensification of work, deskilling, monotony and alienation lead to forms of resistance which are unorganised, sporadic and concealed, which unfold below the level of the regulatory interest-bureaucracy, but which become all the more significant as the technologically highly developed and interwoven systems of production become more complex and vulnerable and as the high level of investment makes unproductive stoppages more and more costly: absenteeism, sloppiness and sabotage (Coriat 1984; Davis 1978; Edwards 1979; Bowles *et al.* 1983; O'Connor 1984; Gorz 1983). After Taylorism had got rid of the traditional craft worker and of the control of the immediate producers over the work process, the new unskilled 'mass worker' now appears to have become in turn a barrier to the valorisation of capital. It has become increasingly difficult to recruit workers for the monotonous, badly paid and burdensome jobs, difficulties which can no longer be overcome by the mass import of migrant workers. Rationalisation measures which are technically possible on the basis of the Taylorist organisation of work come up more and more clearly against the barriers of incalculable human risks. Thus, in the centres of industrial production, Taylorist mass work gradually ceases to be the decisive stabiliser of capitalist profit, which means that the basis of the Fordist system of production and reproduction is put in question.

The Crisis of the Corporatist Welfare State

If the structure of the Taylorist labour process leads to a crisis of productivity, then its organisational–political 'superstructure', the system of bureaucratically centralised, corporatistically integrated trade unions and the institutionalised system of social security, also shows itself ever more clearly to be a barrier to the process of valorisation. The very institutional complex which secures the Fordist integration and disciplining of the wage earners comes to be a threat to capitalist profit in the face of the growing difficulties of accumulation and declining rates of growth. The network of welfare state regulations and apparatuses implies a form of institutionalisation and legalisation of social demands and services which blocks a smooth reduction of the standard of material reproduction. The medical–

industrial complex which is incorporated into the bureaucratic welfare state develops an almost uncontrollable dynamic of rising costs while at the same time declining in effectiveness. As growth rates fall and social damage increases (unemployment, wear and tear of labour), the system of social security absorbs increasing masses of finance and becomes an essential factor in the crisis of state finances.

At the same time, the existence of centralised trade unions operating with comprehensive and unifying wage contracts secures for the wage earners at least a defensive position which prevents an abrupt and thorough reduction of real wage levels. In a sense, it is the Taylorist expansion, homogenisation and levelling of the working class itself which has created 'the objective conditions for a unified, mass representation of interests and a unified, mass struggle of the workers on a scale which had not existed previously' (Coriat 1984, p. 47; also O'Connor 1984; Buci-Glucksmann and Therborn 1982). This relative strength is reinforced by the fact that the developed Fordist production apparatus, with its susceptibility to technical failure and its intensive interconnections, has become more vulnerable to even relatively small strike actions — in so far as they can be carried out in the more difficult economic circumstances. Certainly, the corporatist, bureaucratic trade union apparatuses were not able to prevent the gradual decline of real wages, nor the growth of unemployment with its associated processes of social disintegration, but they have been able to oppose major reductions in real wages in the case of employees in the key industrial sectors and a major dismantling of the system of social security.

The Crisis of the Interventionist State

The Fordist state is an 'interventionist state' not only in the sense that it secures the maintenance, orientation and regulation of labour power. In addition, it represents an administrative–industrial complex based on a high degree of concentration and financial interlinking between firms, which is oriented towards technology and infrastructure policies designed to secure the conditions for the valorisation of capital on a world scale. The bureaucratic welfare and interventionist state does not become a factor of crisis merely because it institutionalises certain standards of material reproduction for the working class. Beyond that, it becomes more and more clear that there are limits to its ability to pursue a 'structural policy' which can promote socio–technological processes of modernisation.

A fundamental dilemma results from the necessity, under the pressure of competition on the world market, of implementing or permitting processes of structural adaptation at an ever faster pace, in order to sustain the profitability of the national 'location' for an increasingly internationalised capital, and thus to uphold growth and employment in the national area. This international competition to modernise, seen globally, is an essential factor in the stabilisation of the rate of profit, but at an increasing social cost (unemployment, marginalisation, uneven regional development, destruction of the environment) which puts in question the 'acceptability' of this policy and hence the democratic legitimacy of the state (Fröbel *et al.* 1981; Dockes and Rosier 1978; Destanne de Bernis 1978). In any case there is a growing contradiction between the imperatives of a 'growth policy' centred on the world market and a pluralist–corporatist system of mass integration based on the availability of material concessions and compensations.

A further weakness in the process of structural change results from the institutionalised connections between state apparatus and companies, which have developed above all in the area of (not only military) research and technological development. The development of research and technology complexes between state and industry and the growth in the state financing of research and technology are the expression of a pressure to innovate coming from the world market, which partially surpasses the financial and organisational capabilities of even highly concentrated individual capitals. The structures of the military industrial complex which are characteristic of the Fordist state now extend far beyond the arms sector itself. As a result, an essential part of the social potential for innovation is concentrated in a quasi-state monopoly organisational complex, which leads more and more clearly to waste of resources and weaknesses in economic innovation (Hirsch 1974). The failure of large technological projects like the nuclear and data processing programmes in the Federal Republic, or the way in which the monopolistic association between the Federal Post Office and the electronic industry institutionalises technological backwardness, can be cited as examples. There are more and more indications that, because of their inflexibility, their planning problems and transfer difficulties, the state-supported technology monopolies of big industry have become an obstacle to economic innovation oriented to the world market, and thus undermine the effect of technical progress in stabilising the rate of profit.

The Crisis of the Fordist Subject: Contradictions of the Model of Consumption and the 'Change in Values'

Those theories which suggested the possibility of an absolute 'real subsumption', or almost limitless malleability, of the subjects under the conditions of capitalist production and reproduction have proved to be clearly untenable (for example: Breuer 1978; for a critique, see Horn 1978). Rather, even the Fordist form of socialisation produces a contradictory subjectivity in manifold, and certainly not always functional, forms (Marcuse 1979). There is a contradiction inherent in the Fordist model of consumption. Because Fordism makes the reproduction of labour power and mass consumption a decisive basis for the process of accumulation and valorisation, it must aim for a tendentially unlimited expansion of consumption, it systematically institutionalises 'wish production' and it constantly extends needs. These can only be satisfied in commodity form, which produces ever new needs (D'Amico 1978; Ewen 1976; Fox and Lears 1983). The 'endlessness of needs' (O'Connor 1984) introduced with Fordist society, the limitlessness of consumer demands inherent in the Fordist model of consumption, contains an inbuilt tendency to a material 'demand inflation', which threatens to explode the valorisation nexus. The 'narcissistic' shaping of the subject (Lasch 1978; Attali 1981) binds the structure of the Fordist individual with consumerism, which may certainly be politically stabilising, but also has an economically precarious effect.

The contradiction is strengthened by the mechanism which F. Hirsch has described as 'the struggle for positional goods' (F. Hirsch 1977). If the individual use value of consumption goods is reduced precisely by the fact that they are the objects of mass consumption (for example, cars on jammed and polluted roads), so that almost always use-restricting 'external effects' of mass consumption have to be reckoned with, then it follows that a rising monetary income can go together with a falling degree of real satisfaction of needs, a mechanism that must lead to further monetary demands and thus sets in motion an apparently endless spiral.

In general it can be assumed that the Fordist form of socialisation *must* create substructures which contradict the functional standards of normality and of the discipline of work and consumption. Alienated work, the commodity form of the satisfaction of needs, commercialised social services and bureaucratic dependence strengthen the desire for individual self-activity, 'autonomous work', alternative forms of consumption, non-commercialised and non-formalised contacts and social relations. The growing dependence on large bureaucratic organisations produces the need for self-administration and autonomous interest representation. The infinity of desires postulated by consumerism, the destruction of traditional orientations and norms, the commodification of personal relations, social atomisation and narcissistic individualism contain the possibility of 'cultural liberation processes' (Ziche 1981), the effect of which is unpredictable: not *a priori* rebellious, but by no means capable of seamless integration into the Fordist sytem of values. Refusal to achieve, failure to accommodate, exploding demands and sporadic rebellions increasingly disrupt the complex network of the Fordist social formation.

The Crisis of Ecology

An essential basis of the Fordist model of accumulation is the unlimited availability of cheap raw materials and sources of energy, together with the possibility of exploiting without limit the natural bases of production and reproduction as a 'free force of production'. The imperialist control of the sources and markets of raw materials by the capitalist metropoles under the hegemony of the USA is a decisive precondition for this. But now the exploitation of raw materials and the destruction of nature and the environment have taken on such dimensions that the natural preconditions for the continuation of the relevant production processes are threatened with destruction, and the limits of acceptability are being surpassed for more and more of the interested parties. This inevitably forces regulatory intervention by the state in production and consumption, but also leads more and more to forms of production which have as their sole object the improvement of, or compensation for, damage produced. There thus arises a 'destructive growth' without any real increase in the satisfaction of needs (Gorz 1983). Even if one assumes that 'protection of the environment' can be pursued in many areas quite profitably by individual capitals, there is in any case a reduction in the general level of material reproduction and a need to change established patterns of production and consumption. This gives rise to resistance, frictions and conflicts between capital fractions, not to mention the fact that international competition and modernisation acquire a new and problematic dimension. In any case the squandering of resources and destruction of nature which underlies the Fordist organisation of production and of society proves to be more and more costly.

The Crisis of 'Global Fordism'

In addition to the creation of larger markets in the metropolitan centres (the European Community, for example), a decisive basis for the Fordist model of accumulation was the selective industrialisation of third world countries, the transfer of technologically simpler production processes to those countries and the associated super-exploitation of cheap and often female labour. This development confirms and concretises Wallerstein's thesis that capitalism depends structurally on the existence of non-proletarian wage-labour, that is, on the possibility of exploiting paid labour power below its level of material reproduction through reliance on local forms of subsistence production (the 'housewife-ing of work') (Wallerstein 1979; see also von Werlhof 1984). In fact the strategy of transferring production proved to be a cause of slow growth and unemployment in the metropoles (Schlupp 1979; Junne 1979). The profit-stabilising effect of the 'bloody Taylorism' (Lipietz 1982) based on the creation of islands of super-exploitation is just as limited as the strategy of 'peripheral Fordism', that is, the incorporation of a few 'newly industrialised countries' into the Fordist production network of the metropoles without technological autonomy, balanced internal development or social regulation (Lipietz 1982; Simonis 1979). The instability of Fordism on a global level is expressed also in the international debt crisis, which considerably limits the scope for the export of the means of production especially to some 'newly industrialised countries', and in the growing political crises and social unrest in these regions, which can be 'pacified' now only with great difficulty by the terrorist regimes supported by the imperialist powers. Just as there are limits to the exploitation of raw materials, there are limits too to the extent to which metropolitan profit rates can be stabilised by the 'external' capitalisation and dependent industrialisation of the third (and to some extent also the 'second') world.

CONTOURS OF A POST-FORDIST CAPITALISM

Whether, how and in what form a new post-Fordist capitalist social formation will emerge from the current crisis can be predicted only with difficulty. It depends on worldwide political and social struggles, the outcome of which is still open. Nevertheless, starting from the causes of the crisis of Fordism and on the basis of already visible restructuring tendencies, projects and programmes, it is possible to sketch the *possible* contours of a new accumulation model and a new hegemonic structure of capitalism. It is not a question of forecasting a general social development that is to be expected, but of indicating real and therefore contradictory tendencies which will shape the conflicts of the future. In order to determine these tendencies, it is necessary to start from the structure of the Fordist formation and its crisis.

'Hyperindustrialism': the Post-Taylorist Organisation of Work

The establishment of a new model of accumulation requires the development of product technologies which can be the bearers of a new 'growth' cycle. Apart from the still not fully foreseeable consequences of molecular and genetic technology, it is above all the new information, telecommunications and data processing technologies which could become the basis of a 'hyperindustrialisation' which could revolutionise especially the service sector. As indicated by the slogan of the 'cabling of the republic', this would have far-reaching implications for the dominant pattern of consumption and forms of socialisation.

At the same time, the 'microelectronic revolution' makes possible a deep transformation of the social relations of work. Capital is responding to the crisis of the Taylorist labour process and its politico–institutional 'superstructure' with the introduction of new information processing, planning and regulating technologies essentially based on microelectronics, which aim at a renewed historical push towards rationalisation and the reduction of living labour power, but will hardly lead to the total establishment of the workerless factory' (Kern and Schumann 1984). Rather, the reorganisation of the labour process is directed towards the establishment of new, more flexible combinations of person and machine, the creation of new hierarchies among the wage earners and a systematic individualisation of work relations. The aims are a fragmentation and diversification of the Taylorist mass worker through the labour process and the organisation of work, a reduction in the vulnerability of the production process, a rise in the utilisation of capacity (continuous production) and the undermining of collective interest organisation based on standardised working conditions.

However, it can be doubted whether — as Kern and Schumann seem to assume — this will lead to a gradual elimination of the Taylorist mass worker. The 'new labour policy' aims at the formation of a small, privileged core of highly qualified employees entrusted with complex tasks of supervision and direction. At the same time, however, it can be assumed that both in the core areas of industrial production and in the administrative and service sectors unskilled, monotonous jobs directed by others will still be retained. The new information processing, planning and regulating technologies make it possible to establish a Taylorism on a higher level. On the whole, these technologies increase decisively the freedom of the enterprise to shape processes of work. Person and machine in the production process can be separated both temporally and spatially to a degree previously unknown. That means that the use of living labour is determined less and less by technological necessity and can respond more flexibly to economic and labour calculations. This makes possible a 'flexibilisation' of work times at the same time as a transition to continuous working, a spatial uncoupling of work and machinery (new forms of computerised working at home), a radical individualisation of the work places, of wage determination and of labour-contractual conditions (Kommission 1983). The microelectronic reorganisation of Taylorism goes far beyond attempts simply to reestablish the assembly line, for example by the creation of partially autonomous groups (Coriat 1984, pp. 49ff.). Beside the skilled and relatively autonomous core workers there arises on the basis of the new technologies a *new type of mass worker*, who is precisely not spatially concentrated, unified and subject to homogeneous working conditions, but is individualised to a high degree, flexibilised and segmented. The Taylorised and deskilled mass worker will by no means disappear — especially when there is a structural over-supply of cheap labour power. 'Flexibilised', peripheral and insecure jobs, part-time, home and temporary work will not only remain but will even expand, even though there is a reduction in employment in the core sectors of material production, in administration and in services as a whole, and an increase in mass unemployment (Brandt 1981).

Dualisation and Segmentation of Society

The rationalisation drives associated with the 'post-Taylorist' changes in the labour process both in material production and in the administrative and service sector bring about a double division in society.

Within the core of the 'modern' industrial, financial and service sectors integrated into the world market, there is a growing division between 'stabilised' employees with skilled, highly paid and relatively secure conditions of employment and the 'destabilised' workers (Coriat 1984, pp. 59ff.) in the simple, fluctuating and insecure jobs, in temporary and subcontracted conditions of work without bonds to the firm (Gorz 1983; Gorz 1984), and even including quasi-employees pushed into formal self-sufficiency. At the same time a further huge increase in unemployment must be reckoned with. On the basis of unemployment, a marginalised production and service sector is developing. This marginal (or, euphemistically, 'informal') sector with its small production, craft and retail businesses and its many forms of 'alternative' services fills, as it were, the gaps and niches, which the world-market oriented process of hyperindustrialisation leaves or opens up. Alongside the computer-based rationalisation of industrial production, state and business administration and the associated industrialisation of personal services, there develops a peripheral production and service sector, which in terms of working conditions is also characterised by uncertain and badly paid jobs, mostly requiring little skill and with minimal or no provision of social security (Gorz 1984). Peripheral wage labour in the core sectors and peripheral 'enterprise' in the 'informal' production and service sectors express a complex tendency towards dualisation and segmentation, which was already present in the Fordist phase (Esser *et al.* 1980), but which could now become much broader and deeper. This development indicates a trend towards a post-Fordist layering of society, which contains elements of a new class division between 'core' and 'periphery'.

However, this will not necessarily lead to a rigid socio–political exclusion of the army of the unemployed and those employed in the 'informal' sector ('Southafricanisation'). For political and economic reasons, even the marginal sector will remain regulated, controlled and subsidised by the 'welfare state': by specific forms of promotion of small enterprises, the maintenance of a training system to absorb the unemployed at least temporarily and also by a (materially reduced) system of unemployment benefit — not least because of the need to stabilise even the marginalised social groups as recipients of mass produced industrial products and thus to keep them integrated into the post-Fordist consumption model.

In general, a tendency can be discerned towards what can be described as the 'housewife-ing' of work in society (von Werlhof

1984; Gorz 1984; Westphal-Georgi 1982). Even in the industrial core sectors there remain unskilled, insecure, badly paid part-time, temporary and home-based jobs, the 'female' jobs, as it were, in spite of the skilling and stabilisation of the core workforce; at the same time, however, wage labour in society as a whole is less and less adequate to secure the material level of reproduction. As a counter-tendency to the Fordist generalisation of the wage relation and the associated capitalisation of the sphere of reproduction, there could develop a massive extension of new forms of subsistence work: 'new self-sufficiency' and superexploitation in the 'informal' sector, increase of 'independent work' at home, as a pendant to the hyperindustrialised self-service and self-supervision society.

From the point of view of the valorisation of capital, the effect of a successful dualisation, segmentation and hierarchisation of society would consist in the lowering of the level of material reproduction as a whole (while inequalities increase). At the same time a multi-layered, tendentially over-qualified and mobile 'reserve army' would be available for the purposes of peripheral and fluctuating wage labour. The consumption and service needs arising from the process of hyperindustrialisation, from the health food shop to the bio-energy and self-discovery workshop, could be satisfied by a marginalised 'informal' sector, reproducing itself in very tight circumstances. The divided society would be held together by means of 'welfare state' and politically repressive regulation and control. All in all, this implies an extreme social (and also regional) heterogenisation *within* the capitalist metropoles, that is, the imperialist north–south gap reproduces itself again within the capitalist centres themselves.

Authoritarian Statism and Segmented Corporatism

Ultimately the question is how a politico–ideological hegemonic structure corresponding to a post-Fordist model of accumulation and society could be created, one which would bind this formation together into a coherent 'historic bloc', stabilise its contradictions and confirm its economico–social development tendencies. What form of political system can we expect to follow in the wake of the Keynesian state founded on full employment, growing material well-being, strong trade unions and a developed system of social security, with its central-corporatist mode of political regulation mediated essentially through the social democratic parties? The post-Fordist state must be based on the economic and social structures, the social divisions and fragmentations which are developing in reaction to the crisis of Fordism and it must develop forms of political regulation which make possible and even promote the establishment of a new model of accumulation and society.

Basically, it can be taken that, contrary to neo-liberal ideology, the post-Fordist and post-Keynesian state will by no means be a weak, withdrawn state which again allows unhindered free play to the 'market forces', but on the contrary a strong state, autonomised from the plurality of social interests, interventionist in many different ways and highly armed, internally and externally. This results from the global situation of the system of nation states, which is characterised by intensified internal as well as external breaks and conflicts, by an intensifying struggle (fought not least by military means) for sources of raw materials and economic zones of influence, and explosive social conflicts and divisions within the capitalist metropoles. In addition to all that there is a growing compulsion, under pressure of competition on the world market and the continuing internationalisation of production, to pursue a policy of structural adaptation, which is likely to encounter resistance internally.

The basis of the post-Fordist state is a strongly segmented and divided society. The divisions within the working class tendentially deprive the reformist social democratic parties of their electoral support (Buci-Glucksmann and Therborn 1982, pp. 264ff.), while at the same time the trade unions are in danger of finally sinking to the level of being representatives of the quasi-corporate interests of the privileged core workers (Rosanvallon 1982, pp. 72ff.). This means the collapse of the essential corner pillars of the Keynesian state, with its regulation model of a centralised, statist corporatism organising comprehensive (class) interests. Instead of that there can be discerned the origins of a sort of central, segmented social corporatism, in which corporatist cells are composed of diverging and competing professional, status and interest groups, within a 'relation of social forces that has become structure-less' (Rosanvallon 1982, p. 74).

A political system which regulates and stabilises this segmented corporatism must differ from the Keynesian–Fordist state in decisive ways. Among these differences are above all the further expansion and perfecting through information technology of the state apparatuses of repression and surveillance; but also the 'restructuring' of the welfare state, which, just as before, must at the same time confirm, deepen and bureaucratically control the social divisions. That means that it cannot simply be a question of a simple 'dismantling' of the welfare state system, but of differentiating its potential for division, integration and control, within a general context of lower material benefits. To this process belong selective privatisation strategies in favour of materially privileged groups (from refuse collection to private insurance and even to private universities), materially restricted 'help for self-help', tied to controlling conditions, for the marginalised sectors, 'deregulated' funds, poured for example into the form of a private legal foundation or otherwise freed from codified demands, designed for purposeful ideological and political intervention, the growth in the quantitative significance of social assistance, which is materially restrictive and inadequately supported by legal guarantees, at the cost of institutionalised insurance systems (in the case of unemployment, for example) and not least through the re-stratification of the education system ('promotion of elites'). The segmentation of the welfare state apparatus into privileged and legally protected sectors and the institutions of the largely discretionary 'regulation of poverty' already points this way today. 'Decentralisation', 'private initiative' and 'self-help' will thus play a double role: as pure existential necessity for those who can survive in no other way because they fall through the ever looser 'social net', and as a privileged form for those who can pay for it. The post-Fordist variation of the 'security state' will therefore be harder and more selective.

That does not mean, of course, that the relevant social processes of division and exclusion have to be established through the state administration. Loss of solidarity and depoliticisation occur automatically in the crisis and under the conditions of the discernable new model of accumulation. What is necessary for the state is the development of a political regulation apparatus which permits this development and at the same time stabilises it ideologically and politically.

A corresponding tendency can be seen at the level of the party system. The dominant mass parties seem to be changing from comprehensive 'people's parties', channelling and integrating organised interests and acting as a medium for the establishment of pluralist distribution compromises, into extremely bureaucratised, centralised and statified political machines. Their central function, in view of the declining scope for material concessions, consists in providing a discourse which harmonises ideologically a deeply divided society characterised by segmented corporatist structures. This requires the rebuilding of the party apparatuses into public relations apparatuses, efficient in their use of information technology and using commercial marketing strategies, apparatuses which are capable of developing an authoritarian–populist discourse, which runs counter to material interests but articulates the complex divisions in society (Esser and Hirsch 1984; Westbrook 1983; Dubiel 1983; Hall 1980).

The contours of this new ideological discourse can already be seen clearly: traditional 'Keynesian' values like progress, equality, solidarity, collective welfare and material security find little esteem. Instead, achievement, success, astuteness, privacy, family, sacrifice and morality are again in vogue. Corresponding to a more and more divided society which is disintegrating into competing status groups, 'elites' and excluded zones, there develop images of the world, which are composed of a mixture of the ethos of individualised achievement and an authoritarian need for security, a readiness for violence and a diffuse anxiety, a collective aggressivity and a private resignation, pseudo-liberalism and blunted morality, singles culture and synthetic family idyll. Nationalism is again useful as a cementing replacement for the material consensus of society which has disappeared. The intensifying divisions have to be pasted over with the old–new enemy-images that are there: foreigners, drop-outs, social parasites and deviants, communists, pacifists, Russians and, to be sure, also Americans.

The logic of such a development points to a profound change in the relation between political system and society, a change which could lead to a 'de-formalisation' of politics, that is, to a loss of importance of collective institutions and interest organisations, a 'de-bureaucratisation', 'de-legalisation' and authoritarian–populist depoliticisation of social conflicts. This does not mean that the ideological discourse can ignore material interests, but, in a divided and 'de-formalised' society, these can be politico–ideologically so formed, shattered, re-combined, played off against one another and re-formed that they fit into the framework of a new hegemonic structure.

The origins of post-Fordism would thus bear the marks of a 'passive revolution from below' (Buci-Glucksmann 1982). However, whether and in what particular form it is established still remains open. Capitalist development, which takes place through crisis-ridden historical breaks, is not without alternative, not even within the limits of the capital relation. The force of the crisis levels the ground for the construction of a new model of accumulation and society, but it also produces new contradictions and conflicts. The alternative cultures which have arisen in recent years and the 'new social movements' will play an important part in these conflicts.

Themselves children of Fordism and its crisis, they remain of course shaped by its contradictions. It is still not clear whether they will finally prove to be just a vehicle for the 'passive revolution from below' or whether they can so alter the social and political relations of force that humane forms of crisis resolution get a chance.

NOTE

* This article first appeared in German in the *Politische Vierteljahreszeitschrift* 1985 2. Translated by John Holloway

REFERENCES

Aglietta, M. (1979), *A Theory of Capitalist Regulation: the US Experience* (London).

Aglietta, M. (1978), 'Phases of US Capitalist Expansion', *New Left Review* 110.

Altvater, E. (1982), 'Der Kapitalismus vor einem Aufschwung? Uber Theorien der "langen Wellen" und der "Stadien"', in *Wirtschaft und Gesellschaft, Festschrift für Theodor Prager und Philip Rieger* (Vienna).

Attali, J. (1981), *Die kannibalische Ordnung. Von der Magie zur Computermedizin* (Frankfurt/Main, New York).

Bowles, S., D. Gordon and T. Weisskopf (1983), *Beyond the Waste Land. A Democratic Alternative to Economic Decline* (Garden City, New York).

Brandt, G. (1981), 'Die Zukunft der Arbeit in der "nachindustriellen" Gesellschaft', *IHS Journal*, 5.

Braverman H. (1974), *Labor and Monopoly Capital: The Degradation of Work in the Twentieth Century* (New York, London).

Breuer, S. (1978), 'Subjektivität und Maschinisierung. Zur wachsenden organischen Zusammensetzung des Menschen', *Leviathan* 1.

Buci-Glucksmann, C. and G. Therborn (1982), *Der Sozialdemokratische Staat. Die 'Keynesianisierung' der Gesellschaft* (Hamburg).

Buci-Glucksmann, C. (1982), 'Formen der Politik und Konzeptionen der Macht', in *Neue soziale Bewegungen und Marxismus. Argument-Sonderband*, AS 78 (Berlin).

Clawson, D. (1980), *Bureaucracy and the Labor Process: The Transformation of US Industry, 1860–1920* (New York, London).

Coriat, B. (1984), 'Differenzierung und Segmentierung des Gesamtarbeiters in der Serien-Industrie — Der Fordismus, der Massenarbeiter und die "Aufwertung der manuellen Arbeit", in K. Düll (ed.), *Industriearbeit in Frankreich. Krisen und Entwicklungstendenzen* (Frankfurt/Main, New York).

D'Amico, R. (1978), 'Desire and the Commodity Form', *Telos* 35.

Davis, M. (1978), 'Fordism in Crisis: A Review of Aglietta', *Review* 2.

Destanne de Bernis, G. (1978), 'Les Firmes Transnationales et la Crise', in X. Greffe and L. Reiffers, *L'Occident en Désarroi* (Paris).

Deutsches Institut für Wirtschaftsforschung (1984), *Erhöhter Handlungsbedarf im Strukturwandel. Strukturberichterstattung 1983* (Berlin).
Dockes, P. and B. Rosier (1978), 'Crise et transformation du Capitalisme', in X. Greffe and L. Reiffers, *L'Occident en Désarroi* (Paris).
Dubiel, H. (1983), 'Neue alte Politik. Falsche Antworten auf richtige Fragen — der neokonservative salto mortale', *Freibeuter* 18.
Edwards, R. (1979), *Contested Terrain: The Transformation of the Workplace in the Twentieth Century* (New York, London).
Esser, J., W. Fach, G. Simonis (1980), 'Grenzprobleme des "Modells Deutschland"', *Prokla* 40.
Esser, J., J. Hirsch (1984), '*Der CDU-Staat: Ein politisches Regulierungsmodell für* den "nachfordistischen" Kapitalismus', *Prokla* 56.
Ewen, S. (1976), *Captains of Consciousness. Advertising and the Social Roots of the Consumer Culture* (New York).
Fox, R. and T. Lears (eds) (1983), *The Culture of Consumption: Critical Essays in American History 1880–1980* (New York).
Fröbel, F., J. Heinrichs and O. Kreye (eds) (1981), *Krisen der kapitalistischen Weltökonomie* (Reinbek).
Gartman, D. (1979), 'Origins of the Assembly Line and Capitalist Control of Work at Ford', in A. Zimbalist (ed.), *Case Studies on the Labour Process* (New York, London).
Gerstenberger, W. (1984), *Strukturwandel unter verschlechterten Rahmenbedingungen. Strukturberichterstattung 1983* (IFO-Institut für Wirtschaftsforschung) (Berlin, Munich).
Gesellschaft. Beiträge zur Marx'schen Theorie (1979), 13, *Wert-Theorie* (Frankfurt/Main).
Gorz, A. (1983), *Ecology as Politics* (London).
Gorz, A. (1983), *Wege ins Paradies* (Berlin).
Gorz, A. (1984), 'Dualisierung der Arbeit am Beispiel der USA', *Links* 174.
Hall, S. (1980), 'Popular-democratic versus Authoritarian Populism: Two Ways of "Taking Democracy Seriously"', in A. Hunt (ed.), *Marxism and Democracy* (London).
Hirsch, F. (1977), *Social Limits to Growth* (London).
Hirsch, J. (1974), *Staatsapparat und Reproduktion des Kapitals* (Frankfurt/Main).
Hirsch, J. (1980), *Der Sicherheitsstaat* (Frankfurt/Main).
Hirsch, J. (1983), 'Nach der "Staatsableitung". Bemerkungen zur Reformulierung einer materialistischen Staatstheorie', in *Aktualisierung Marx. Argument Sonderband*, AS 100, Berlin.
Horn, K. (1978), 'Ein linker Konservatismus mit kritischem Gestus oder Das Veralten eines Psychoanalyseverständnisses', *Leviathan* 6, no. 4.
Jessop, B. (1983), 'State Form, Social Bases and Hegemonic Projects', *Kapitalistate*, 10/11.
Junne, G. (1979), 'Internationalisierung und Arbeitslosigkeit', *Leviathan*, 7, no. 1.
Kern, H. and M. Schumann (1984), *Das Ende der Arbeitsteilung?* (Munich).
Kommission, 'Zukunftsperspektiven gesellschaftlicher Entwicklungen' (1983), *Bericht, erstellt i. A. der Landesregierung von Baden-Württemberg.*
Lasch, C. (1978), *The Culture of Narcissism: American Life in an Age of*

Diminishing Expectations (New York).
Lipietz, A. (1982), 'Towards Global Fordism?', *New Left Review* 132.
Lutz, B. (1984), *Der kurze Traum immerwährender Prosperität* (Frankfurt/Main, New York).
Mandel, E. (1980), *Long Waves of Capitalist Development: The Marxist Interpretation* (London).
Marcuse, H. (1979), Die Angst des Prometeus. 25 Thesen zu Technik und Gesellschaft, *Neues Forum* 20/21.
Mattick, P. (1971), *Marx and Keynes* (London).
O'Connor, J. (1984), *Accumulation Crisis* (Oxford, New York).
Palloix, C. (1979), 'Die organische Krise des Kapitalismus', in C. Deubner *et al.*, *Die Internationalisierung des Kapitals* (Frankfurt/Main, New York).
Rosanvallon, P. (1982), 'Nach der Sozialdemokratie', *Freibeuter* 11.
Schlupp, F. (1979), 'Internationalisierung und Krise', *Leviathan* 7, no. 1.
Schmidt, K-D. *et al.* (1984), *Im Anpassungsprozess zurückgeworfen. Die deutsche Wirtschaft vor neuen Herausforderungen* (Tübingen).
Simonis, G. (1979), 'Die Bundesrepublik und die neue internationale Arbeitsteilung', *Leviathan*, 7, no. 1.
Stearns, P. (1980), *Arbeiterleben. Industrie und Alltag in Europa, 1890–1914* (Frankfurt/Main, New York).
Wallerstein, I. (1979), *The Capitalist World Economy* (London, New York).
Werlhof, C.v. (1984), 'Das Proletariat ist tot — Es lebe die Hausfrau?' in *Die Zukunft des Sozialstaats*, published by Landesfachausschuß Soziales und Gesundheit der GRÜNEN Baden-Württemberg (Stuttgart).
Westbrook, R. (1983), 'Politics as Consumption: Managing the Modern American Election', in Fox and Lears (1983).
Westphal-Georgi, U. (1982), 'Der Sozialstaat wird Umgebaut — Perspektiven für die Frauen', *Prokla* 49.
Ziehe, T. (1981), *Zur Verletzlichkeit des Narzißmus. Der psychische Niederschlag 'kultureller Freisetzungsprozesse'*. Ms.

3 The Reformulation of State Theory*

Werner Bonefeld

Since the conservative shift to power in the main capitalist countries the state is again at the centre of debate. Recent work on the interrelation between changes in the relations of production and the restructuring of the mode of domination has been influenced by authors such as Esser, Hirsch, Jessop and Roth. Their discussion of the development of the 'post-Fordist state' aims at a more concrete 'reformulation' of state theory in order to provide a materialist account of the changes that have taken place within the state and between the state and the economy. There are, however, differences between the authors, for example, between Jessop on the one hand and Esser/Hirsch/Roth on the other. Jessop's insistence on the historically contingent outcome of the dialectic between structure and struggle and his concern with modes of regulation appears to be slightly different from Hirsch *et al.*'s insistence on the law-determinate development of capitalism in relation to class struggle and on the centrality of the state. In what follows, I shall concentrate mainly on the German debate. On the other hand, Jessop's contribution is significant and is examined whenever possible. The difference between the authors becomes less important when the debate is discussed in general terms.

In the last few years the reformulation of state theory (hereafter: Reformulation) by the authors mentioned has emerged as an influential framework for the analysis of current changes in capitalism (Fordism/post-Fordism). This article will examine their approach to the state.

The Reformulation aims to overcome the slow-down of the state derivation debate in the 1970s (Hirsch).[1] Its major argument owes much to the French Regulation Approach of Aglietta, Lipietz and Mazier (hereafter: RA). The importance of the RA for the Reformulation lies in its claim to relate value transformations to changes in the social and political sphere. However, its analysis of the state and changing patterns of the mode of domination is incomplete since it is mainly restricted to the historical transformation of value production and regulative forms of value realisation. The regulation of domination, the historically changing patterns of class disorganisation and capital organisation (power bloc) are hardly taken into consideration.

The Reformulation aims to develop an analysis of the crisis-ridden development of capitalism, the transformation of capitalist relations and the transformation of the articulation between accumulation and state functions. The key issue for those participating is not to reject the state derivation debate but to subsume it into a theory of capitalist development. In this way, the perennial theme of Marxist controversy — that is, the question of the relation between object and history, structure and struggle and objective laws and subjective forces — is discussed more concretely in the context of contemporary developments. The Reformulation adopts a combined analysis of the interrelations between changes in the relations of production, accumulation and state forms. It thus intends to go beyond the Poulantzian influence on the debate over power relations, which very much influenced Hirsch (1976; 1977). As such, it aims to give a more elaborated account of the contradictions and developments of today's 'enchanted world' (Marx 1971, p. 830) of capitalism. The debate aims at a conceptualisation of an 'intermediate' concept of 'state': the Fordist or post-Fordist state as distinctively different modes of capitalist domination. Both, the RA and Reformulation, use the concept of Fordism to analyse capitalist development from the 1920s onwards. 'Fordism' has to be distinguished from its former meaning in industrial sociology. It conceptualises a complex and contradictory articulation of a distinct type of production and value realisation (a regime of accumulation) and the corresponding forms of social and hegemonic regulation/domination (see De Vroey, 1984).

Since the crisis of Fordism, in the late 1960s/early 1970s, we are said to be experiencing a period of transition towards a transformed structure of capitalist reproduction. The conservative shift in power in the main capitalist countries during the last ten years is regarded as a historical break which indicates the development of a new corresponding mode of regulation referred to as neo- or post-Fordism. Thus, Thatcherism is seen as leading to post-Fordism within the national development pattern of Great Britain (Jessop 1986).

The implications of the much broader application of 'Fordist' concepts for socialist policy in Britain are significant. The debate on Fordism/post-Fordism, in this broader application, assumes the emergence of a new predominant mode of accumulation and class domination which necessitates a reassessment of the strategy for socialism. Parts of the British left use this debate in such a way as to condemn militancy (for example, the miners' strike) and to abandon 'ambitious demands'. Their reassessment of the road to socialism treats supposedly 'unrealistic' working-class resistance as supporting the conservative policy. They proclaim the moderation of socialist policy, and the need to accommodate it to the new reality of capitalism. Hence, new unionism (Carter 1986), the new consensus in new factories (for critique, see Holloway 1987), the support for the politics of fashion and populist socialism (see *Marxism Today*). In Britain this analysis of the new realities of post-Fordist capitalism has been put forward most consistently by *Marxism Today* (see Holloway 1987b).

These political conclusions differ from those drawn by the Reformulation theorists themselves. Although their intention is mainly analytical, the Reformulation theorists are either searching for new emerging areas of resistance (Hirsch/Roth) or dwelling on the notion of the contingent outcome of class struggle (Jessop). Despite these differences between the determinist use of the concepts of Fordism by parts of the British left and that of the theorists presented here, I shall argue that it is the ambiguity, and the disarticulation of structure and struggle, in the concept of Fordism which leaves it open for the argument that struggle is not possible in the present situation.

In this paper I shall introduce the literature of the Reformulation and discuss the application of the concepts to concrete analysis. The following is the order of presentation: the brief introduction of the RA[2] concentrates on relevant arguments for the Reformulation. There then follows a partly immanent critique which charges that the Reformulation misemploys its own concepts — which concepts are themselves problematic and subject to criticism in their turn. Both, the presentation and the critique, should provide an understanding of the conceptual framework within which the concepts of Fordism and post-Fordism can be discussed. After this presentation I consider the validity and the weakness of the debate on Fordism and post-Fordism. I shall come back to the political implications in my paper's final part. My presentation is restricted to the arguments which concentrate on issues relevant to the state.[3]

THE REGULATION APPROACH (RA)

The RA is concerned with understanding how the reproduction of the capital–labour relation is historically realised and regulated and how capitalism is prevented from collapsing.

It is the regulation of the articulation between a certain mode of production and a mode of consumption which comprises the focus of analysis. A historically achieved coherent articulation between a mode of production and a mode of consumption is conceptualised as a regime of accumulation. The distinction between different regimes of accumulation is defined by the historically dominant form of surplus value production (Aglietta 1979). For an introduction to the concepts of the RA see De Vroey (1984).

The proponents of the RA argue that a regime of accumulation presupposes a historical transformation of the relations of production and a corresponding development of value forms. The focus of analysis is thus the development of the wage relation, money forms (which include credit forms and inflationary pricing), international division of labour, international markets and the transformation of the articulation between the departments of production (which is regarded as the basis for a regime of accumulation's coherent structure (see Lipietz 1985)).

Although it is not discussed explicitly it would be misleading to assume that this analysis excludes the regulation of domination on a social level. The RA focuses on a unified social process within which social reproduction takes place. It thus intends to provide analysis of the accumulation process which is said to illuminate the colours of the social and political forms of capitalism (Marx 1973). As Aglietta (1979) claims, this restricted analysis of the development of capitalism provides a theoretically profound basis for an account of the determining historical transformation of state forms and state functions.

To summarise the argument: the aim of this approach is to provide an analysis of the historical development of capitalism within which all phenomena are illuminated by the dominant, historically changing, form of accumulation and thus by the dominant form of the social relations of production. According to the RA, the relative stability of a regime of accumulation has to be assured by corresponding modes of societal and hegemonic forms of integration and repression. This corresponding social and political mediation of accumulation is referred to as a mode of regulation. The concepts of integration/repression impinge, mainly, at the level of the state.

The term 'regime of accumulation' thus refers to a 'systematic mode of distribution and reallocation of the social product, which brought about a long-run correspondence between the changing conditions of production . . . and the changing conditions of final consumption' (Lipietz 1985b: xvi). The term 'mode of regulation' refers 'to the ensemblement of institutional forms, networks and explicit or implicit norms which assure compatibility of market behaviour within a regime of accumulation, in keeping with the actual pattern of social relations, and beyond (or even through) the contradictory, conflictual nature of relations among economic agents and social groups' (Lipietz 1985b, pp. xvi–xvii).

THE REFORMULATION OF STATE THEORY (REFORMULATION)

Assuming the methodological direction and field of analysis of the RA, the Reformulation theorises the historical development of corresponding state forms and functions as well as social forms of integration/repression and their historically changing form of interrelation. This process is seen as a process of development which is founded on a certain pattern of accumulation (see above). Thus, the crisis-ridden process of accumulation, which culminates in the law of the tendency of the rate of profit to fall and the mobilisation of countertendencies, is regarded as pivotal for an understanding of the development of the state (Hirsch 1974, 1983, 1985b, c).

The development of state forms and functions is conceptualised as corresponding to a regime of accumulation. The Reformulation strongly emphasises the importance of changes in production as the starting point for understanding the development of the state. It thus tries to unite complex economic, political and ideological phenomena into a unified structure the development of which is said to be determined by the laws of capitalist development and also class struggle (Hirsch 1983).

The coherent organisation of appropriate measures of labour disorganisation and capital organisation are said to include repressive, ideological and mass-integrative forms of regulation. Their corresponding and compatible operation (see 'mode of regulation') is said to ensure the historical reproduction of a specific social form of class relations. It is within the state that the regulative forms are condensed, homogenised, and their operation achieved (Aglietta; Hirsch). It is the state that carries through appropriate forms of disorganisation of the activity of labour which assure the channelling of class struggle into 'suitable' forms of capitalist reproduction. Within state theory, these regulative forms are conceptualised as parts of state apparatuses (Hirsch 1976, 1977) or, in more recent writings, as regulative transmission belts (Esser 1982; Esser and Hirsch 1984a). The condensing and homogenising of the fragmented structure of regulative forms is said to be achieved by the hegemonic fraction of capital within the power bloc. Assuming the relative stability of a certain pattern of social reproduction, these forms of regulation consolidated within the state provide a 'regulative ensemble' (Aglietta) which is said to correspond to a given regime of accumulation. Thus, the regulative forms are regarded as forms of mediation which assure a coherent process of social reproduction, which capital itself is structurally unable to organise.

The 'dialectic between structure and process' (see Jessop 1983), or in other words the interrelation of laws of capitalist development and class struggle, can hardly be understood except in complex economic, political and ideological terms (Hirsch 1983). It is precisely for this reason that, in contrast with the state derivation debate, an intermediate concept of the state — that is, a concept more specific than that of the 'capitalist state' in general — is introduced: the Fordist and post-Fordist states. These terms express historically distinct forms of labour subordination and capital organisation.

Considering the shared assumption of the RA and the Reformulation that the capitalist relation is a relation of struggle, the use of concepts like 'regulation' and 'correspondence' appears problematic. These concepts tend to emphasise the objective laws of capitalist development rather than class struggle. Accordingly, the notions of correspondence and regulation seem to be determined by their function within the context of capitalism as a structurally given entity comprised of different (that is, economic and political) levels. In this sense the historical constitution of those 'modes of regulation/correspondence' is a matter of the structural transformation of law-determined economic developmens at the level of the state. However, as far as, for example, Lipietz (1985) is concerned, the term regulation refers to the 'constellation of: relation-reproduction-contradiction and crisis'. This seems to refer more to social relations as relations of struggle. Nevertheless, within the Reformulation, regulation seems to be applied in such a way as to disarticulate class struggle from structure. Class struggle is reduced to, and conceptualised as, a 'but also position' (Hirsch 1983) within history and as such separated from objective laws of development (Hirsch 1985b, c).

Similar considerations apply to the term 'correspondence'. It refers to a relatively stable form of articulation between a distinct form of value production and a distinct form of regulation during a given period of time (that is, Fordism or post-Fordism). Thus, as far as this approach is concerned, 'correspondence' does not necessarily imply a functionalist configuration of compatible measures but a long-term relative stability of a peculiar class relation of equilibrium. On a practical level it grasps the relatively regular dynamic of the simultaneous operation of accumulation and structural forms, whereby the regularity of reproduction is generalised as a distinct form of correspondence. In this way, the dualism of structure and struggle is repeated, because the focus here is on the notion of regularity. In light of this, the conceptual meaning of the term 'correspondence' is far from clear, its meaning being descriptive rather than analytical.

Following Gramsci, the historical correspondence between a regime of accumulation and a mode of domination is characterised as an historical bloc (Esser; Hirsch; Roth). This term is regarded as a precise concept with which the unity of distinct accumulation strategy (Jessop 1983), a peculiar ensemble of class relations and social forms, together with a particular hegemonic structure or hegemonic project (Jessop 1983), could be grasped (Hirsch 1983). As such, the terms 'regulation' and 'correspondence' can be understood more precisely as the articulation between a mode of accumulation and a hegemonic structure. This articulation promotes a mode of regulation whose operation is a 'form of socialisation' (Hirsch) (that is, Fordism or post-Fordism) which implies the development of a recomposed mediation of capitalism.[4]

However, the question which remains open here is how an accumulation strategy, which is operational and relatively stable during a given period of time, is accompanied by a corresponding hegemonic project. Assuming the highly problematic presupposition of the relative autonomy of the hegemonic structure (that is, the notion of the political sphere having its own determination, development and crisis) this question leads to the theoretical problem, namely, how the mode of regulation is articulated and determined. Due to the disarticulation of structure and process, the answer given by Hirsch *et al.* is twofold. Firstly, they regard the historical imposition of a mode of regulation as a result of quite complex economic, political and ideological struggles. Secondly, contrary to this, they regard this imposition as a 'process without subject' (Hirsch 1985b, c; Hirsch and Roth 1986). Before examining this point at greater length, I want to concentrate on the historical and social process of accumulation and the accompanying forms of state development.

The process of capitalist development is conceptualised as an interrelated process of capital's penetration of society, of social disintegration and of the statification of society. The first of these processes refers to the structurally-given capacity of capitalism to establish its rule and thus the commodity-form as the universal governing form of society. This development tends to commodify the reproduction of labour power, to constitute a densely woven reproduction of both labour and capital, to lead to the universalisation of the wage relation as the primary source of reproduction, and to the tendential destruction of traditional support systems for young and old, sick and lonely, people. Hirsch (1980) conceptualises this far-reaching destruction of former patterns of reproduction as a 'process of social disintegration'.

The statification of society is regarded as a response to its penetration by capital (Aglietta; Hirsch). The term 'statification' implies that the state moves into society in order to recompose the social disintegration of society in the interests of capital reproduction. It thus suggests the erosion of the boundary between state and society. The state appears to assure the cohesion, condensation and regulation of society in all its ramifications. The equation of society and the state, however, is conceptualised as a gradual process of development rather than as a historical fact ('growing statification'). Commodification of social relations, the universalisation of the wage relation and the corresponding statification of society are thus regarded as united consequences of the transformation of the relations of production.

The Reformulation thus seems to suggest a politicisation of social reproduction by assuming the state's ability to recompose and to integrate society in accordance with the needs of expanded reproduction. The state is conceptualised as the primary force of reproduction. This politicist influence within the concept statification is reinforced by speaking about 'alternative hegemonic projects' (Jessop 1983; 1985) and 'alternative accumulation strategies' ('alternative capital logics' — Jessop 1985, p. 344). These terms indicate a degree of voluntarism which, however, is limited by the dualist conception of structure and struggle: that is, it is restricted by the existence of objective laws and thus by an objectively-given range of options. The term 'project' (as well as 'strategy'), adopted by Jessop, is based upon the recognition of structurally-given conditions (see Jessop 1983, 1985). Contrary to his previous critique of Jessop's emphasis on hegemonic projects and accumulation strategies (Hirsch 1983), Hirsch later picks up Jessop's concepts, albeit with a slight alteration:

the reference is now to hegemonic structures. Hirsch insists on the use of these concepts in order to grasp the subjective notion of decision-taking and the importance of subjective action within history. Nevertheless, 'projects' and 'strategies' are seen as structurally conditioned. The voluntarist impact is restricted to the recognition of the structurally-given hegemonic and valorisation options. Hegemonic projects and accumulation strategies operate within the structurally-given environment. Hence, the subordination of struggle is repeated and the disarticulation of structure and struggle reinforced. 'Voluntarism' is a product of this disarticulation which, in addition, prevents structures from being seen as mediations of struggle itself.

Theoretically, the term statification seems to contradict the notion of the structural particularisation of the state within the process of social reproduction accepted by these authors as a fundamental presupposition of the reproduction of capitalism. 'However, this should not be seen as an inadequacy of theory, but as an expression of contradictory social tendencies that manifest themselves in specific social conflicts, which in turn cannot be understood without this contradiction' (Hirsch 1983b, p. 80).

CRISIS

The Reformulation theorists argue that state theory has to be based on a theory of crisis. Hirsch (1983) insists that without such a theory state theory would remain a fleshless skeleton of general laws and structures.

Crisis is seen as the form taken by capital through which its contradictions are historically mediated and transformed. Crisis is a structurally-given form of the existence of the capital relation. The process and the objective conditions underlying it are expressed by the complex law of the tendency of the rate of profit to fall, which intrinsically includes the mobilisation of countertendencies. The crisis and transformation of a historically distinct form of accumulation is seen as due to the so-called 'long waves' of capitalist development (Hirsch), which are to be understood in terms of this law. Affirming this, the proponents of Reformulation theory simultaneously insist that the law of the tendency of the rate of profit to fall has to be understood in complex economic, political and ideological terms.

The Reformulation refers to the crisis of an historical bloc as a structural crisis, which affects the stability and consequently the functionality of structural forms simultaneously. The 'organic articulation of an accumulation strategy and a hegemonic project within an historical bloc' (Esser and Hirsch, 1984a, p. 58) is said to be in crisis if it fails to promote a sufficient mobilisation of countertendencies to the rate of profit to fall (see Hirsch 1985b). Despite the insistence of those involved in the Reformulation that the root of crisis is always the upsurge of class struggle in production, the dominant argument dwells on the notion of the dysfunctionality of a given mode of regulation so far as counteracting the fall in the rate of profit is concerned. The reorganisation of the mode of regulation is necessary because 'none of these forms [of regulation] can play its role in the mitigation of social contradictions without the simultaneous operations of all the others. The contradictions of accumulation affect them all, and the dysfunctioning of one tends to destabilise the others as well' (Aglietta 1979, p. 383). For the Reformulation, the restructuring of accumulation has to be accompanied by a corresponding reorganisation of the mode of domination. It is for this reason that the structural crisis consists of both an economic and a political crisis which are organically interwoven and whose differentiation is absurd (see Hirsch 1980b). The crisis-ridden restructuring of an historical bloc is said to lead to changes in the 'whole social formation' (Blackburn *et al.* 1982).

It is a shared assumption within the Reformulation that the current crisis, which has lasted since the late 1960s to early 1970s, is a structural crisis of a specific mode of regulation referred to as Fordism. The remaining problem, however, is to understand how the crisis-ridden process of transition is determined and how post-Fordism is promoted and pursued.

As indicated earlier the Reformulation theorists initially suggested a dualistic context of analysis, arguing that capitalist development is not determined simply by objective laws but, separately, also by class struggle (Hirsch 1983). In this view the scope of struggle is subordinated to the law-determined path of development which provides the 'environment' for struggle. Struggle is seen as either accelerating or retarding the definite course of the law-determined path of development but it is incapable of challenging it. Struggle thus decorates the environment provided by law-determined development. Thus, the proponents of Reformulation conceptualise the historical transition form Fordism to post-Fordism as a 'process without subject' (Hirsch

1985b, c; Hirsch and Roth, 1986). This term refers to the 'contradictory action of classes which is determined by structures' (Hirsch 1985b, p. 163; Hirsch and Roth 1986, p. 38). This notion seems to imply that the regulation of social reproduction is itself a 'process without subject' (see Jessop 1985). This understanding, however, contrasts with Hirsch's and Roth's insistence that it is the state which is the functional centre of social reproduction (Hirsch and Roth 1986, p. 66).

The disarticulation of structure and struggle is the basic conceptual pattern in this theory of capitalist development.

CRITIQUE

This disarticulation of objective laws and class struggle gives new life to the structuralist analysis of capitalist development to which the Reformulation was initially opposed. This reversal of the argument reduces class struggle once more to a subordinate factor. The 'dual perspective of structural determination and class position' (Jessop 1985, p. 344) fails to recognise 'objective laws' as tendencies implicit in the form of class relation (and thus struggle). The Reformulation reverses this relation: it is the development of capital accumulation which determines the environment for struggle, whereby the development itself is a 'process without subject'. The 'legitimation of chance' (Marx, 1973, p. 103) is thus reduced to the unpredictability of struggle as a merely accelerating or retarding influence without possessing the capacity to challenge the development. Thus, class struggle loses its Marxist significance as the motor of history.

Further, the Reformulation seems to imply a degree of teleologism of capitalist development: the objective laws of development imply the appearance of a specific form of regulation whose concepts are Fordism or post-Fordism. It thus promotes a normative analysis of capitalist development, constituted by the assumed functional need of the law-determined path of capitalist development. Despite Hirsch's claim that the development of capitalism is a non-linear, non-evolutionary and discontinuous process, the Reformulation does not succeed in developing this argument systematically. On the contrary, the Reformulation implies a particular mode of social coherence which is determined by its function within a system of law-determined illumination. Contrary to the Reformulation, the crisis-ridden process of social reproduction should be understood in terms of de- and recomposition of society rather than in terms of 'correspondence-regulation-regularity'. Thus, historical development should be conceptualised as a process of structure and struggle whereby structure is implicit in the form of class relation.

In the Reformulation, the statification of society is functionally determined because it is somehow 'required' in order to secure the reproduction of social relations. This leads to the subordination of the contradictions of class struggle and its replacement by the structural contradictions of different levels of the social formation. The interrelated process of capital penetration-social disintegration-statification is conceptualised as a law-determined process within which struggle is located. This can also be seen in the concept of 'hegemonic projects' (or 'hegemonic structures') and 'accumulation strategies'. These terms imply an incoherence of the social 'body'. Thus the segmented parts of this body have no unity until they are coordinated into a strategy or project by a somehow hidden agency of condensation. No answer is given to this question: which agency coordinates the strategy of accumulation and which one assembles the hegemonic project in order to achieve 'the state'? Further, Jessop (1983, 1985) refers to a number of constraining factors all of which reduce the implied range of alternative economic strategies and the scope of optional hegemonic projects immensely. Jessop's term 'project' implies a state within whose structure a wide range of alternative interventions are embedded, but in the event he fails to indicate that the emerged 'strategy', as well as the emerged 'project', is one out of a series of alternatives.

Seeing the state not only in terms of piecemeal tinkering but as a field of modes of domination which are in part consciously assembled and implemented, Jessop takes on board the Poulantzian regional approach by grasping the state as a structurally determined battleground for various capital fractional strategies. This move is reinforced by his separation of accumulation strategies and hegemonic projects, which rests on the idea that 'there are alternative capital logics, so there can be alternative hegemonic projects' (Jessop 1985, p. 344). Jessop seems to imply that a successful hegemonic project leads to results which correspond to the needs of a specific accumulation strategy. This appears to be a functionalist view of capitalist reproduction. The struggle for access to state power appears to be important for every capital fraction (for critique, see Clarke, 1978). Hence, the reinforcement of Poulantzas' voluntaristic, politicistic and regional approach. Altogether, the distinction between accumulation strategies and hegemonic projects seems artificial. Jessop seems to neglect the circumstance that both of these regions are forms of the same class relation, and that their operation is closely interwoven since hegemonic projects depend on accumulation (see above: Crisis).

The criticism of functionalism also applies to the assumption that the structural forms of capitalism correspond to the need of expanded reproduction. According to Lipietz (1985) these structural forms include implicit and explicit norms and, under Fordism, regulative forms like free collective bargaining (see Aglietta 1979). These forms are said to be located, operated and homogenised within the state, or, to put it more precisely, within different state apparatuses. The term 'apparatus' implies a degree of planned interference from 'above' which dominates the course of class struggle. It also presupposes the functionality of their operation. Further, it implies the domination of the state over social relations, which is enforced by the successful homogenisation of the apparatuses and thus their functionality. The concept of state apparatuses ignores the contradictions in social relations and their existence as forms of mediation of class antagonism.

In recent writings, however, Hirsch speaks of regulative transmission belts instead of apparatuses (see Esser's critique, 1982, of Hirsch). This term relates to the concept of 'regulation' more precisely inasmuch as it focuses on relations rather than on the centrality of the state. Hirsch thus conceptualises the state-induced incorporation of organisations like the unions (Esser 1982) without equating the unions with the state. Nevertheless, this incorporation is explained functionally rather than as a particular outcome of struggle. The Reformulation fails to analyse 'regulative forms' as forms of mediation of the presence of labour within capital. The analysis of the specific form of social relations is replaced by the structural–functionalist explanation of corresponding articulations between accumulation and the state.

As indicated by the term 'statification', the Reformulation analysis of the development of capitalism is politicist. The analysis of the triangular development of penetration-disintegration-statification tends to regard the state as the only form by which capitalist society can be integrated and the social reproduction of capital realised. The Reformulation follows Poulantzas by arguing that the state moves into society in order to take over all the functions of society — a penetration of society in all its ramifications functionally required for expanded reproduction of the capital relation. The crisis-ridden process of accumulation thus leads to the statification of society. This implied erosion of the boundary between the state and society is seen as a precondition for recomposing society, which is regarded as being deprived of its (traditional) capacity for regulation. This argument presupposes the functionality of the statification of society, which, tautologically, is seen as determined by its function. In this sense, it is the state that constitutes, regulates, integrates and secures capitalist reproduction. Hirsch *et al.* overemphasise the state as the primary force of 'recomposition' of society. The Reformulation exaggerates the power of the state by assuming the functionality of compatible state action toward presupposed needs of capital reproduction. Finally, Hirsch's and Roth's (1986, p. 66) claim that 'the state is the functional centre of social reproduction' fails to apply the proposed concept of 'regulation' which was initially seen as the mode of articulation between a regime of accumulation and hegemonic structures (for critique, see Huebner 1987). The centrality of the state accounts for the functionalism of this approach. Regulation, as well as the Reformulation's own term 'process without subject' are deprived of their (mainly structural) focus on relations, such as 'the complex unity of implicit and explicit norm, institutions, social forms, intentional pattern etc' (Hirsch and Roth 1986, p. 44; Jessop 1985). Thus, the initial meaning of these concepts is reduced to the structural development of the state, in a way reminiscent of Poulantzas.

The centrality of the state implies that capital by itself is incapable of any relatively coherent form of self-reproduction. Here too, the Reformulation fails to apply the concept of 'regulation' which initially conceptualised the development of 'new capital forms' (see Juergens 1980), of value forms, of modes of consumption and of forms of competition. The centrality of the state in social reproduction implies the subordination of the distribution of surplus value of the state. It is for this reason that the state, rather than the capital relation, is seen as the main generator of struggle and resistance (that is, social movements). The statification of society results in the Gorzian 'farewell to the working class' and the welcome to its successor: social movements (see Hirsch 1980; Hirsch and Roth 1980, 1986). The Reformulation fails to specify the state as object and result of class struggle.

This understanding of statification leads to formalistic classification of phenomena as, for example, either Fordist or post-Fordist modes of socialisation. The analysis is formalist because it remains unclear how we should adduce historical evidence for the supposed transition of a quantitative development, as implied by the term 'growing statification', into a qualitative difference between the hitherto Fordist and subsequent post-Fordist forms of regulation.

This inherent formalism of the Reformulation 'corresponds' to its functionalism, teleologism and structuralism. It opens the door to a historical generalisation of discrete phenomena and developments. In this sense, the Reformulation replaces the proposed *analysis* of the development of capitalism with a theoretically informed *description* of contemporary capitalism (that is, Hirsch and Roth 1986). The main problem of the Reformulation to which all criticism comes back is the disarticulation of structure and struggle, as seen, for example, in the concept of 'process without subject'. In consequence, the Reformulation mystifies and overestimates state policy and state power which results in an overpoliticisation of reproduction and a 'confusing' acknowledgement of class struggle.

Instead of being seen in terms of a pluralist struggle for shares in power in order to secure the viability of a certain fractional accumulation strategy, the state should be analysed as a mediation of the historical transformation of the direct production process (see Negri 1977). The analysis of the state has to go beyond the circulation of, and the socialisation of, capital in order to place it in the wider context of this process: the expanded reproduction of the antagonism of production, which is located in the direct process of production. The state has once more to be seen as at the centre of the dialectic of the organisational and repressive aspect of the presence of labour within capital.

FORDISM

The Fordist mode of socialisation is referred to as 'Americanisation'. Fordism is founded on an intensive regime of accumulation in which the labour process is transformed by Taylorist and Fordist forms of work organisation and technology (assembly line work). 'Fordist' commodities are standardised mass produced consumer durable goods. The Fordist regime of accumulation is seen as a densely woven relation between the departments of social reproduction. Within Fordism the reproduction of labour power constitutes a substantial part of the reproduction of capital (see Aglietta 1979; De Vroey 1984). The consequent 'commodification of the means of consumption' (Blackburn *et al.* 1982) involves a major replacement of traditional forms of the reproduction of labour. This process tendentially leads to the commodification of social relations (Hirsch 1983), the universalisation of the wage relation (Aglietta; Hirsch) and the individualisation/atomisation of society, which appears as 'mass society' (Hirsch 1980, 1985b, c).

The main problem confronting capital, apart from the regulation of exploitation within production, is the regulation of a socially coherent circuit of capital within which a balance of the rate of distribution is achieved, which serves both capital profitability and social demand (see Lipietz 1985). Keynes had the merit of acknowledging the existence of this problem within the Fordist pattern and of formulating general conditions for regulating the Fordist mode of distribution which as such constitutes the Fordist regime of accumulation (mass production and mass consumption). The difficulty, however, is to regulate the rate of distribution without jeopardising profitable accumulation by increasing wages above the increase of productivity. The Keynesian effort to channel class struggle into appropriate forms for expanded social reproduction operates in the dynamic of the social transformation of Fordist accumulation. Hence, as Aglietta (1979, pp. 382–3) argues, 'social security is designed to maintain workers deprived of their jobs in their position as consumers'. Welfare spending is thus regarded as a necessary reduction from revenue to maintain a mode of consumption which is functionally determined in order to stabilise the Fordist mode of production and expanded social reproduction (see Aglietta 1979). Keynesian policy aims to provide the regulation required to meet the needs of capital during Fordism.

Thus, the specifically Fordist form of the state is the Keynesian corporatist, statist, welfare state (Esser/Hirsch/Roth) which, in the long run, was transformed into the Fordist social security state (Hirsch 1980, 1983b). Its emergence is regarded as a development of the state aiming to secure expanded reproduction during the crisis of Fordist accumulation. It indicates and is part of the crisis of Fordist regulation. The Fordist state achieves a central position in the regulation of social reproduction by penetrating society in all its ramifications (Hirsch 1980, 1983, 1983b). It plays an important role in the regulation of distribution.

The Fordist interventionist state has the following functions: to regulate the existence of labour power (labour as consumer), and to assure the regulation of distribution and the inflexibility of a growing nominal wage rate. It attempts to integrate society on the basis of individual claimants by addressing the socially disintegrated society as a conglomerate of tenants, employed, unemployed, car drivers etc. (see London . . ., 1980). Its policies aim to channel class struggle into a struggle for distributive shares. The attempt to reduce class interest to distribution interest coincides with the substitution of civic for class consciousness. Regulative forms like mass consumption, collective bargaining, ideological discourses on progress and equality and the ideology of the competence of state planning are said to correspond to the Fordist regime of accumulation. The pacification of class politics into income and redistribution policy are said to be functionally required to ensure the dynamic regulation of distribution within the Fordist framework.

Thus, the incorporation and social transformation of the unions into 'mass-integrative apparatuses' is analysed as functionally essential to ensure the continuity of production by unionised policing and disciplining of the rank and file. This incorporation supports the institutionalisation of class struggle which is seen as a development essential to safeguard the regulation of the increase of nominal wages on the basis of corporatist agreements. The statification of the unions alienates them from their membership and transforms them into responsible social partners concerned with the transformation of class policy into redistribution policy and thus consumerism (see Hirsch 1980; Hirsch and Roth 1986).

According to the Reformulation, the statification of society leads further to the transformation of the parties into people's parties, which are seen as integrated components of the state and which are said to support an institutionalised strategy of socio–political conservation. The people's party is an important component of the Fordist bargain concerning consumption and productivity. It supports the predominantly consensual integration of society. This consensual project of integration is regarded as the typical Fordist mode of domination. This so-called 'one-nation strategy' is immanently and inextricably bound up with material concessions (Jessop 1982).

The Keynesian effort to satisfy capital by feeding the workers seemingly transforms the capitalist state into a peacemaker which addresses capital and labour alike as contributors to the national welfare. The state's corporatist piecemeal policy is regarded as a regulative form of institutionalised class struggle. This institutionalisation is recognised as a regulative form of Fordism (see Aglietta 1979). The pacifying impact of corporatist policy is said to enforce consensual–concessional channelling of struggle and to ensure the disciplining of society by transmitting socially responsible agreements to the various clients of the party and to the rank and file as far as the unions are concerned. The Fordist one-nation project is regarded as appropriate for capital accumulation as long as the gains in productivity increases are higher than the increase in (direct and indirect) wage costs (see Davis 1978).

The Fordist bargain — more wages for nasty work — constitutes a constantly rising consumption norm, which is promoted as both reward for and stimulus to production (see Holloway 1987). The densely woven articulation between capital and labour reproduction apparently opens a possibility for 'socialist' redistribution policies on the basis of capitalist accumulation. It is for this reason that the Reformulation regards social-democratic parties in government as the ideal appearance of Fordist regulation.

Nevertheless, these 'integration costs' (Agnoli 1968) of the Fordist mode of domination are hardly recognised by the Reformulation as concessions on the part of capital to a relatively strong labour movement after the Second World War. Instead, they are primarily conceptualised as a functional regulative form of the Fordist mode of regulation. The insistence that the 'Fordist deal' is a result of class struggle is reduced merely to an abstract point of reference.

The Fordist mode of domination is thus regarded as based on mass-integrative and ideological apparatuses, whose operations, nevertheless, are always founded on the operation of the repressive apparatuses (see Hirsch, 1976; 1977). The development of Fordist forms of regulation is seen as leading to the withering away of society into the state, especially by socially tied state apparatuses, which, however, operate 'from above'. The Fordist mode of domination leads to a shift within the repressive apparatus itself. The decline of parliament in favour of the administration (for example, corporatist-statist-state) is regarded as a major shift towards the dominance of the executive forces at the expense of democracy and thus, paradoxically, at the expense of evolutionist strategies on the left (Reformism). The Reformulationist thesis of the predominance of consensual–concessional policy at the expense of the repressive means of integration/disintegration is reminiscent of Gramsci's notion of 'state = civil society and political society that is hegemony armoured with coercion' (Gramsci, according to Buci-Glucksmann 1981, p. 61).

Inherent in Fordist regulation is said to be the surveillance of society by bureaucratic means, the supervision of marginalised groups who are regarded as operating outside the one-nation project, and welfare policy as a means of pre-emptive security (see Hirsch 1980;

1983b). Consequently, the Reformulation sees the Fordist state as both a welfare and a surveillance state (see Hirsch 1983b; Hirsch and Roth 1980).

This double character becomes increasingly apparent in the crisis of the Fordist regime of accumulation since it increases unemployment and thus reduces the financial resources for the typical Fordist hegemonic project. This leads inevitably to the tightening of the prospects of redistribution policy (see Hirsch 1978) and thus to the destabilisation of the operation of Fordist forms of regulation. This constellation intensifies during the crisis-ridden restructuring of production which increases the irregular workforce (see Esser and Fach 1981). The term 'irregular workforce' refers to the growth in structural unemployment. This irregular workforce is excluded from the wage-relation and depends entirely on welfare spending by the state. This spiral development of growing social dependence on welfare spending and fiscal crisis of the state is seen as a consequence of the crisis-ridden transformation of production during the 1970s. It results in the enhanced repressive impact of Fordist regulation. This shift includes advanced selective spending, a strengthening of the repressive state apparatus and the tightening of the one-nation project. Thus, the stigmatising division into core and parasites (see Esser and Fach 1981; Jessop *et al.* 1984), the development of a selective corporatist policy (Esser and Fach 1981) and the intensification of selective spending and repressive supervision (Hirsch 1980) lead to the development of a surveillance state. 'The "security state" has emerged as a new form in history. In a certain sense it is simultaneously a post-fascist and a post-democratic state, and therefore class struggle is now taking place within a very different arena' (Hirsch 1983b, p. 80). This post-fascist state is still regarded as operating within the Fordist pattern of regulation. Society is subject to its ubiquitous presence.

POST-FORDISM: ON METHOD

The period of crisis and transition is divided into two phases: the crisis of Fordism since the late 1960s to early 1970s and the phase of post-Fordist explorations and experiments which is said to be taking place since the conservative shift to power in the main Western capitalist countries. The latter is interpreted as a historical break which signifies a definite end to Fordist crisis regulation (see Hirsch 1982). This transitional period, however, consists of a confusing complexity of Fordist patterns of regulation and of new socio–political phenomena which latter are regarded as tending towards a new coherent form of regulation, referred to as post-Fordism.

The problem, however, is whether this account of the further development of capitalism takes into account class struggle.

As far as Hirsch is concerned, a definite prognosis of the transition towards post-Fordism is not possible precisely because of the unpredictability of class struggle. The 'contingent outcome of a dialectic of structure and strategy' (Jessop 1983, p. 98) makes it difficult to specify in advance a relation of a regime of accumulation and hegemonic forms. The problem thus remains, how a prospective theory of capitalist development can be generated and how emerging socio–political phenomena can be conceptualised as definite indications of a future transformed historical bloc.

According to Hirsch, a reasonable prognosis has to start from the analysis of the crisis of Fordism, has to consider already existing tendencies of restructuring and transformation and has to take into account party programmes and strategic proposals (Hirsch 1985c, p. 326). In this regard, the development of the economic–political–ideological structure of the United States plays a major role because of its military and economic hegemony (Hirsch 1985b, c). The notion of 'riding ahead' of the United States provides a pattern of classification for emerging national phenomena. Post-Fordist socialisation is seen as a new form of 'Americanisation' (see Hirsch 1985c).

POST-FORDISM

The post-Fordist mode of production and consumption will, it is argued, materialise a new form of intensive regime of accumulation, which will provide the basis for a new long wave of capitalism. Developments like the new information, computer-processing and telecommunication technologies as well as molecular- and biotechnology, whose effects cannot be evaluated yet, and the microelectronic transformation of Taylorism are seen as the technological means of a distinctive form of relative surplus value production (see Hirsch 1985b, c). The post-Fordist transformation of the mode of production provides flexible all-purpose machinery producing a variety of products. The output goes beyond standardised mass production towards mass production of different products by the same machinery. Post-Fordist production replaces economy of scale — a distinctive pattern of Fordism — by economy of scope (see Junne 1985; Aglietta 1979).

Beyond the production process, the spreading of post-Fordist technology into the sphere of capital circulation involves a major transformation of office work and social services (for example, computer processing or computer diagnosis). The post-Fordist transformation of production is said to require an increased flexibility of labour far beyond the traditional work-practices and demarcations. There is a separation of machinery and living labour in time and space. This relates to the flexibilisation of tasks and the possibly home-based isolated labour process of data-processing which is centralised and controlled by telecommunication technology (for critique, see Laufenberg and Spellerberg 1986). For Hirsch, these transformations indicate the possibility of the desocialisation of production and thus a further individualisation of living labour which tendentially leads to the abolition of the collective worker typical of Fordist production. Following the increase in flexibility, the workforce is said to be divided into a qualified core worker and a peripheral post-Fordist mass worker. The core worker is said to have a safe workplace and high income, and to enjoy the merits of job enrichment.[5] The Reformulation assumes the core worker to have an affirmative attitude towards management policy. The post-Fordist mass worker, on the other side, is characterised as an individualised, flexible, non-unionised worker with low income, short-term employment contracts and fewer safety provisions (see Hirsch 1985b, c). The debate seems to assume the Japanisation of industrial relations and of employment organisation. The peripheral worker exists both within the factory and outside regular employment as a casual, seasonal, part-time, informal labourer.

The post-Fordist mode of production seems to decrease the scope of living labour and to flexibilise wages, work practices and labour markets.

Socially, its enforcement has to be assured by a decrease in the social reproduction costs of labour in order to counterbalance the increase of the organic composition of capital. This dramatic reversal of the Fordist pattern of a constantly increasing social consumption norm has the consequence that wage labour is no longer sufficient to cover the material costs of reproduction. This relates entirely to the peripheral fraction of the workforce. The post-Fordist reproduction of labour power is seen as leading to a massive expansion of a new form of subsistence production in the informal sector (ranging from self-production and self-exploitation in cooperatives to community initiatives and moonlighting) and new enthusiasm for home work (ranging from do-it-yourself to romantic cottage life). Within the Reformulation, these developments are seen as a major differentiation and heterogenisation of society which crystallises society into the polarised strata of two nations. Hirsch regards the reduction of variable capital and the immense increase of cheap labour (peripheral workforce) as a reproduction of the imperialist north–south polarisation within metropolitan capitalism itself. Consequently he speaks about the 'southafricanisation' of metropolitan capitalism (Hirsch 1985c).

According to Aglietta (1979) and Hirsch (1985c, b), the post-Fordist mode of production involves the commodification and privatisation of a wide range of collective services previously organised by the Fordist state. Aglietta (1979) argues that automation, commodification and privatisation of the social services could play a role for the development and social consolidation of post-Fordism analogous to that which 'auto production played in the transition to Fordism' (Davis 1978, p. 246).

For the Reformulation, the increasing commodification, capital penetration and social disintegration ('southafricanisation') corresponds to a major 'de-statification' of society. In this respect the post-Fordist state is less responsible for, and less involved in, the securing of the means of collective consumption. The Reformulation sees the destruction of the welfare state as a transitional step towards a mainly subsidiary intervention of the state through which the post-Fordist articulation of production and consumption could be achieved. For Hirsch, the informal sector plays an important role in the post-Fordist project of domination. This part of society might cover the production of commodities which are somehow 'ignored' by the development of so-called 'post-Fordist hyperindustrialisation' (Hirsch 1985c). Hence, the functionally assumed self-regulation of the marginalised sector, which reduces concessional state intervention, might lead to a polarised consumption structure which ranges from cheap banal mass products to luxury consumption by the integrated core of society (Hirsch 1985c). The marginalised, self-exploiting sector of society appears to play a crucial role in establishing a mode of consumption appropriate for the post-Fordist regime of accumulation. The incorporation of this sector into the post-Fordist hegemonic project has to be induced and consolidated by the state.

As for the mass-integrative state apparatus of the unions, post-

Fordism will reshape their existence into something light years away from the Fordist type of unions. The post-Fordist mode of production and the corresponding effects on the composition of the working class are said to promote a non-unionised sector whose effects on trade union membership reinforce the massive losses of members in traditionally highly unionised industries through de-industrialisation — a development which is not likely to be compensated for by attracting new members in new industries. The Reformulation assumes that Fordist structural forms of collective bargaining and centralised negotiations over constantly rising nominal wages are undermined in favour of the promotion of flexible, decentralised and differentiated agreements on wages, safety and labour time (all of which were previously defended by the Fordist union).

The transformation of the unions is seen as promoted by the recomposition of the labour force which tends to concentrate trade union representation on the core of the remaining workforce. New unionism is said to adopt an increasingly selective policy of representation, which systematically excludes the interest of the post-Fordist peripheral worker. Post-Fordist unions are said to promote a co-operative attitude with management by representing the affirmative core worker. This transformation tends to reduce trade unions to service organisations like the AA (Automobile Association).[6] The delivery of certain services and a moderate policy of cooperation and responsible recognition of production targets do not deprive unions of their mass-integrative function. Instead of the 'militant' appearance of the Fordist unions (payment for change), post-Fordist unions are seen as stripped of their power to participate in corporatist regulations and to oppose management successfully (see Holloway 1987). New unionism plays the role of a decentralised factor of moderation and discipline without having the power of opposition. Post-Fordist unions are regarded as stripped of their socio–political influence and power ('Americanisation'). Further, the post-Fordist flexibilisation of production, and the differentiation and division of the workforce may lead to a replacement of central unions by company unions. The consequence of this could be a strengthening of workers' councils at the expense of the national union body. This development is referred to as Japanisation of the unions. Both Japanisation and Americanisation are regarded as complementary figures.

Thus, in Britain, the miners' strike is seen as an anachronistic attempt to preserve the old unionism which is inadequate in the world of populist new realism. This aspect of the Reformulation's argument concludes that, contrary to its intention, the miners' strike served to support the political and conceptual hegemony of the Conservatives. Thus, it shows the inability of the left to adjust their political strategy to the new face of capitalism (see Esser 1985) whose development cannot be withstood. The assumption is that the working class is gradually 'overtaken' by the new changes (see Hall 1985). 'Just as in bourgeois analysis, struggle is omitted, post-Fordism merely emerges/develops and the new realism of capitalism is given' (see Holloway 1987b, p. 58). All that remains is the recognition of, and respect for, the miners' 'courage of desperation' (Esser 1985) in a fight impossible to win.

The political parties are also said to be affected deeply (Haeusler and Hirsch 1987). The post-Fordist party is seen as the central political body for the development of a coherent mode of regulation and domination (see Esser and Hirsch 1984a). Its general characteristic is the party's attempt to reorganise the hegemonic bloc (Hirsch 1985a) towards the post-Fordist project of domination.

The debate considers the post-Fordist party as consisting of two contradictory forms. Firstly, there is a further increase of party bureaucracy, and centralisation of decision making and, secondly, there is a diversification and decentralisation of party apparatuses into segmented units capable of establishing links with 'southafricanised' society. The latter provides a flexible framework of operation by establishing direct connections with divergent social groups. This 'socialisation of the party' is considered to involve a sophisticated control over society, a flexible integration of social segments and a direct ideological attempt to homogenise society. This framework constitutes a segmented corporatist structure linking certain groups and the party. It establishes a less expensive, more flexible and repressive operation of social policy whose structure and strategy are referred to as segmented corporatism (Esser and Hirsch 1984a; Hirsch 1985b).

The post-Fordist party is seen as policing social interest into a decentralised mode. The post-Fordist party's operation reinforces the differentiation of society which is apparently appropriate for accumulation: flexible, cheap, mobile and less state-oriented. The party's operation seemingly reinforces the post-Fordist discourse of anti-statism and self-responsibility. The party is thus seen as imposing ideological homogenisation directly on social groups and as assuring at the same time a pre-emptive security policing. Along with the 'authoritarian discourse' (see Esser and Hirsch 1984a) of free market forces and destatification of regulation, the party is said to be capable of attracting various sections within the informal and peripheral sector of society. Hence, the party is considered capable of integrating them into the post-Fordist hegemonic project (see Esser and Hirsch 1984a).

The ideology of destatification is regarded as a 'statist' privatisation of the regulation of social reproduction. The 'socialisation of the party' reverses the statist promotion of the one-nation people's party. This 'growing into society' (Esser and Hirsch 1984b) contrasts with the increased bureaucratisation and centralisation with which the hegemonic project is to be achieved, homogenised and consolidated. Esser and Hirsch (1984a) argue that the centralised coordination of the operation of the segmented party apparatuses could perhaps be mediated by the use of communication technology, which then could give rise to the modification of the party into a 'political mega-machine' (Hirsch 1985c). The party 'headquarters' acquire the function of controlling the operation of diverse local party segments and of reacting to their notifications. This structure provides the organisational background to commercial marketing strategies which are said to transform the party into a public relations agency (Hirsch 1985b, c). It reinforces the attempt to depoliticise social problems and transfers politics into a problem of public relations without losing control over the restrictive means for integrating society. The implication of this aspect of the Reformulationists' argument is, therefore, that the party is constructed as a highly elaborated mega-machine to supervise society and as a supreme coordinator of the affairs of southafricanised society. The post-Fordist party thus appears to be a populist state party without mass support.

The post-Fordist restructuring of the state apparatuses (trade unions, political parties) is said to indicate a further development of the security state which is expressed by the predominance of repressive means of regulation, and by socio–political reinforcement of the polarised structure of society (two nations). Considering the post-Fordist state, the Reformulation claims a major deregulation of former interventionist efforts to maintain the existence of labour power on the part of the Fordist state. The privatisation, commodification and subsidiary control of social services, and the intensification of selective policy in education and caring systems as well as the repressive and disciplinary operation of social benefit schemes appear as a political 'radicalisation' which is said to correspond to changes in the labour process.

The policy of deregulation seems to indicate a trend towards the re-autonomisation of the state (Hirsch) which in the view of the Reformulation mystifies the state as a strong, neo-Keynesian administrative machine (Esser and Hirsch 1984a). The destruction of old patterns of consensus and compromise as well as the adoption of monetarist, free market ideology coincide with subsidy policy towards new developing industries and a further advanced security state (Hirsch 1985b, c). The operation of this state within society is regarded as distinctively enhanced and rationalised in comparison with the allegedly post-democratic and post-fascist security state of Fordism (Hirsch 1985c). This perfection of statist supervision within all ramifications of society is regarded and conceptualised as an independent process of development within the relatively autonomous level of the state. This development is seen as not being affected by political constellations of power, that is, by which party is in control (see Hirsch 1986). Considering the modifications of unions and parties, the Reformulation envisages the post-Fordist state as capable of segmented corporatist arrangements to carry through the flexibilisation, cheapening and differentiation of labour. This could reduce the problems of legitimacy for the state even though its intervention into, and regulation of, society are more advanced and differentiated.

The post-Fordist hegemonic project replaces Fordism's consensual–concessional mode of integration with the development of a socially divided consensual–concessional strategy for the core, and subsidiary support for privatised social self-regulation combined with enhanced supervision of society (two-nation strategy — see Jessop *et al.* 1984).[7] This selective redistribution of wealth is part of a predominantly repressive mode of regulation.

The Reformulation considers that, despite the ideological implications of the discourse of anti-statism, the post-Fordist state is a strong state whose intervention penetrates society deeply. The decentralisation and flexibilisation of state apparatuses and enhanced repressive regulation appear as a further move of the state into society in all its ramifications. Post-Fordism promotes a far more intensified statification of society. According to Aglietta (1979, p. 386), 'the overall organization of society within the state, by which modern capitalism attempts a solution at the political risk of universalizing its social conflicts, evidently gives rise to a strong totalitarian tendency under the ideological cover of liberalism'. Referring to Poulantzas, Hirsch conceptualises this development as 'authoritarian statism' (see Hirsch 1985c, p. 335).

CRITIQUE

It cannot be denied that the social phenomena discussed by Hirsch *et al.* are important current tendencies which are perhaps more striking in West Germany than in Great Britain (although the EETPU and the development of 'new unionism' are a striking British example of this same thing — see Bassett 1986; Lloyd 1986). The merit of this discussion is surely the attempt to conceptualise the current stage of capitalism as a transitional period which is founded on changes in the relations of production. The systematisation of newly developing social phenomena clarifies the confusing appearance of contemporary capitalism which is typical in periods of transition. The Reformulation helps us to understand, for example, Thatcherism as a period of political 'radicalisation' which follows the restructuring of the relations of production. Thus, the attempt of the approach to give a materialist account of changes in society and to reconsider politics as a form within the constellation of social antagonism is very much to be welcomed.

The weakness of the approach, however, is a consequence of the way it is pursued: structuralism. Its disarticulation of structure and struggle reverses its own initial attempt to analyse the development of capitalism through class struggle. The concrete application of the Reformulation reduces the importance of class struggle for the development of capitalism and construes class struggle merely as a component of structural development (see Esser's understanding of the miners' strike). Class struggle is thus seen merely as mediating (retarding and accelerating) the transformation of social structures. This merely structural conception of class struggle is basic for the classification of social phenomena as post-Fordist. The conception of a post-Fordist historical bloc abstracts social phenomena from the complex diversity and heterogeneity of a transitional period and integrates them into a model of development whose key factors of classification are founded on the development of the US. This method of analysing the future tends to ignore the reality of national patterns of capitalism by establishing a model or norm of capitalist modes of socialisation (for example, Fordism and post-Fordism). The Reformulation fails to recognise social phenomena as tendencies inherent in the form of struggle — instead it construes these phenomena as establishing a norm or model of capitalist development. The Reformulation sees the development towards this norm as a law-determined process-without-a-subject. Thereby the importance of struggle for this development is undermined. The Reformulation's law-determined structural norm envisages Americanised unions which were and are dominant in the States during so-called Fordism. Further, the transformation of the party is mainly concerned with the Americanised commodification of politics, a phenomenon of US politics during Fordism, whereas the social-democratic type of party — the heart of Fordist regulation — never existed in the States. In other words, aspects of the American Fordist period are incorporated into the post-Fordist norm. This illustrates the arbitrary and formalist character of the norm itself. The debate on Fordism and post-Fordism confuses the time of appearance, dismisses the persistence of national development patterns (the notion of 'riding ahead of America' — 'Americanisation'), and artificially synchronises disparate developments of social relations within and outwith the national framework. This historical generalisation involves a selective description of the past and an abstract norm for the development for the future. The structuralist understanding of social phenomena and capitalist development treats, for example, the incorporation of the unions during Fordism as a functionally required transformation of the unions. The analysis of Fordism presupposes the functional operation of the unions within the model of Fordist socialisation. This functional interpretation of social phenomena presupposes a definite logic of capitalist development. The notion of correspondence in the development of capitalism suggests that capitalist development is *linear*.

The gap between the model of post-Fordism and the politics of restructuring during the last ten years is, moreover, mystified by overestimating the changes that have taken place. Thus the 'post-democratic and post-fascist' security state of Fordism (see Hirsch 1983b) seems to be old-fashioned and undramatic compared with the post-Fordist perfection of social supervision by the state (Hirsch 1985b). This reinforces the criticism of such historical generalisation, structuralism and formalism.

The same argument applies to the core-and-parasite discourse (Esser and Fach 1981) during the crisis of Fordism and to the two nation discourse of post-Fordism. Thus, Esser *et al.* (1980) regard the development of 'authoritarian statism' (Poulantzas) and 'authoritarianism' (hegemonic project of 'social disintegration/polarisation') as a 'support-corset' of 'Modell Deutschland' which is referred to as a pattern of Fordist crisis regulation in the FRG. Later it is precisely this concept with which a novel form of domination is conceptualised: post-Fordism (Hirsch 1985c; Esser and Hirsch 1984a). No answer is given to this question: where is the specific difference between the 'two-nation strategy' of Fordist crisis regulation and the 'two nation strategy', of post-Fordism?

This inability to conceptualise the complexity of the socio–political mediation of class antagonism is the consequence of a 'phenomenology of phenomena' which Marx criticised as 'abstract materialism' (Marx 1976, p. 494n). As struggle, Fordism and post-Fordism are inevitably full of 'cracks, fissures, contradictions' (see Holloway 1987b) and never just a synchronisation of functionally required regulative forms. Instead of an analysis of the 'heresy' of reality (see Agnoli 1980; Bonefeld 1987), which challenges academic generalisation, and instead of an analysis of the inconsistencies of social reproduction, we are confronted with a norm of socialisation. The Reformulation's own claim that class struggle is unpredictable is reversed into the assumption of an imperative transformation of the capitalist system whose coherent form is called post-Fordism.

To construe Fordism and post-Fordism as models of capitalist socialisation, and to construe capitalist development from one to the other as a 'process without subject', is to impose arbitrary theoretical constructs and to downplay the struggle in which that development consists. History is unfolded from theory rather than theory from history, and disarticulation of structure from struggle is the result.

Hirsch (in contrast to Jessop 1986) assumes qualitative changes and a profound break in capitalist development since the Conservative shift to power. This shift is said to express a qualitatively new dimension of capital penetration, social disintegration and statification. Assuming the validity of the concept of Fordism, the sudden change in the mode of socialisation with the election of a Conservative government remains problematic. The development of the Fordist mode of socialisation is seen as lasting from the 1920s till after the period of reconstruction following the Second World War. Its 'emergence' was facilitated and mediated through social catastrophes such as the crisis in the 1930s and the Second World War. This period of development of Fordism can be described as a form of primitive accumulation. The crisis of Fordism is said to have been manifest internationally from the late 1960s to early 1970s. The appearance of 'real Fordism' is thus limited to a very short period of approximately 15 years. As regards the emergence of post-Fordism, the assumption of a historical break since the electoral victory of Conservative parties in Europe implies a relatively 'smooth' and short transition. This assumption presupposes that the crisis of Fordism which appears as a dysfunctionality of Fordism could successfully be recomposed by conservative policy. Here again there is confusion about the time of appearance. The inconsistencies of social reproduction are neglected, and the centrality of the state and the functionality of its operation are assumed.

The hypothesis of the Conservative shift to power as a historical break leads to the obscure formalism of a classification of complex social phenomena into Fordist and post-Fordist patterns. On this ground, for example, the unrealism of the miners' strike was condemned and the task for the left was to accommodate its strategies to the emerging new reality (see Esser 1985). The imposition of 'new realism' is not seen as struggle. Rather, it appears as the inevitable future of trade unionism. As struggle, 'new realism' does not just exist. It is always full of inconsistencies and cracks. Instead of an analysis of the inconsistencies of 'new realism' and its force within the trade union movement (see Bassett 1986), the debate assumes the universalisation of this type of skilled workers' union. The debate on post-Fordism thus treats the working class as merely an object of history. Hence the blindness to the heresy of reality and to the scope of possible solutions to crisis due to class struggle as the motor of history.

The Fordist/post-Fordist debate interprets historical tendency in terms of its more or less close approximation to a model, whose pure form is allegedly progressively disclosed. But this is to depart from the conception of historically-specific 'determination' (see Negri 1984) on which Marx's own method turns. Moreover, it is to read historical development teleologically, and to subordinate the process of struggle to a deterministic scheme. Such a subordination carries with it the danger that it is in the end tautological: first of all a model or norm is abstracted from disparate historical tendencies, and then it is in the light of this model that the significance of these same tendencies is assessed. The consequence of the gap between model and reality is an overestimation of the degree of change which capitalism has undergone (Fordist post-fascist security state and its post-Fordist counterpart). To be sure, the tendencies identified by the Reformulation are real ones, but only relative to struggle and, as such, object and result of struggle: they are thus 'in every sense open ended' as Negri (1984) insists. The reality of 'tendencies' is a tendential reality for its part. For example, whether or not the politics of the EETPU is indicative of the future of British trade unionism as a whole is a matter which struggle only can decide. For this reason, the future remains open, and not theoretically or politically closed. The 'heresy of reality' always challenges 'abstract materialism'.

The concrete application of the Reformulation thus reinforces the earlier criticism of it as a structuralist approach. This criticism relates to the functionalism, formalism and teleologism of the debate, which in turn arise from the debate's disarticulation of structure and struggle.

CONCLUSION

In my criticism I emphasised the basic presupposition of the debate in terms of its disarticulation of structure and struggle. Its methodological limitations as structuralist, formalist and therefore deterministic eliminate all dynamic of struggle. Its political implications are therefore the accommodation of working-class policy to a 'new face of capitalism'.

The analysis of post-Fordism is thus part of the imposition of post-Fordism itself. Within the Reformulation and its inherent political implications, the working class appears once again only as object, as victim. This victimisation of the working class is entailed in the presupposition of the debate: the dualism of structure and struggle.

NOTES

* This article was first published in *Capital & Class* 33, Winter 1987. I am grateful to Richard Gunn, without whose help my article would never have reached its present form.

1. On the state derivation debate see Holloway and Picciotto 1978 and Jessop 1982.
2. In the interest of a clear presentation, I do not discuss a possible criticism of the RA, namely, that it puts forward an ultimately non-class based conception of the relation of production.
3. My criticism leaves aside the problematic application of the concepts of the RA by the Reformulation theorists, i.e. the question of whether the meaning of the concepts is changed in their new use.

4. On mediation see Gunn 1987.
5. For Hirsch (1985b, c) job enrichment inverts the Taylorist division and deskilling of work. Referring to Aglietta, however, it doesn't include direct control over the means of production, nor the inversion of alienation. It rather expresses a further deskilling by the shift from empirical to scientific production knowledge. Thus, 'industrial job recomposition and enrichment seem to be, then, only an adaptation of labour processes . . . to new conditions of control over labour power' (Palloix 1976, p. 65).
6. See Bassett's (1986) account on the EETPU and 'new realism'.
7. In contrast to Jessop's (*et al.*, 1984) term of a 'two-nation strategy', Hirsch *et al.* refer to Hall's concept of 'authoritarian populism'. For this discussion see Hall 1980, 1985b and Jessop *et al.* 1984.

REFERENCES

Aglietta, M. (1979), *A Theory of Capitalist Regulation: The US Experience* (London: New Left Books).
Agnoli, J. (1968), 'Die Transformation der Demokratie', in Agnoli and Brueckner, *Die Transformation der Demokratie*, (Frankfurt/Main).
Agnoli, J. (1980), Mandel and Agnoli, *Offener Marxismus — Ein Gespraech ueber Dogmen, Orthodoxie und die Haeresie der Realitaet*, Frankfurt, New York).
Bassett, P. (1986), *Strike Free, New Industrial Relations in Britain* (London).
Blackburn *et al.* (1982), P. Blackburn, K. Green, S. Liff, 'Science and Technology in Restructuring', *Capital & Class* 18, p. 15.
Bonefeld, W. (1987), 'Open Marxism', in *Common Sense* 1, p. 34 (Edinburgh).
Buci-Glucksmann, C. (1981), *Gramsci und der Staat* (Koeln).
Carter, P. (1986), *Trade Unions, The New Reality, The Communist View* (London: Communist Party Publication).
Clarke, S. (1978), 'Capital, Fractions of Capital and the State: "neo-Marxist" Analyses of the South African State', *Capital & Class* 5, p. 32.
Davis, M. (1978), '"Fordism" in Crisis: A Review of Michel Aglietta's Regulation et crises: L'experience des Etats-Unis', *Review* 2, p. 207.
De Vroey, M. (1984), 'A Regulation Approach Interpretation of the Contemporary Crisis', *Capital & Class* 23, p. 45.
Esser, J. (1982), *Gewerkschaften in der Krise*, (Frankfurt/Main).
Esser, J. (1985), 'Britische Bergarbeiter ohne Perspektive', *Links* 3/85.
Esser, J. *et al.* (1980), J. Esser, W. Fach, C. Simonis 'Grenzprobleme des Modell Deutschland', *Prokla* 40, p. 40.
Esser, J. and W. Fach (1981), 'Korporative Krisenregulierung', in Alemann (ed.), *Neo-korporatismus* (Frankfurt, New York) p. 158.
Esser, J. and J. Hirsch (1984a), 'Der CDU-Staat: Ein politisches Regulierungsmodell fuer den "nachfordistischen" Kapitalismus', *Prokla* 56, p. 51.
Esser, J. and J. Hirsch (1984b), 'Das Gesellschaftsprojekt der CDU — Autoritaerer Populismus', *Links*, Jan/Feb.
Gunn, R. (1987), 'Marxism and Mediation', *Common Sense* 2 (Edinburgh).
Haeusler, J, and J. Hirsch (1987), 'Regulation und Parteien, Fordismus-

Krise und Transformationsprozesse im Parteiensystem', unpublished paper, Frankfurt, May.
Hall, S. (1980), 'Popular-democratic vs Authoritarian Populism: Two Ways of Taking Democracy Seriously', in Hunt (ed.), *Marxism and Democracy* (London), pp. 157–85.
Hall, S. (1985), 'Realignment for What?' *Marxism Today*, December.
Hall, S. (1985b), 'Authoritarian Populism: A Reply to Jessop *et al.*', *New Left Review* 151, May/June, pp. 115–24.
Hirsch, J. (1974), *Staatsapparat und die Reproduktion des Kapitals*, (Frankfurt/Main).
Hirsch, J. (1976), 'Bemerkungen zum theoretischen Ansatz einer Analyse des buergerlichen Staates', *Gesellschaft, Beitrage zur Marxschen Theorie* 8/9, (Frankfurt/Main).
Hirsch, J. (1977), 'Kapitalreproduktion, Klassenauseinanderesetzugen und Widersprueche im Staatsapparat', in Brandes *et al.* (ed.), *Handbuch V. Staat*, (Frankfurt/Main).
Hirsch, J. (1978), 'Was heisst eigentlich "Krise der Staatsfinanzen"?' in Grauhan/Hickel (eds), *Krise des Steuerstaates*, Leviathan Sonderheft 1/78.
Hirsch, J. (1980), *Der Sicherheitsstaat, Das 'Modell Deutschland', seine Krise und die neuen sozialen Bewegungen*, (Frankfurt/Main).
Hirsch, J. (1980b), 'On Political Development in West Germany since 1945', in R. Scase, *The State in Western Europe* (London).
Hirsch, J. (1982), 'Das Ende des keynesianischen Zeitalters', *Links* 153.
Hirsch, J. (1983), 'Nach der Staatsableitung', *Argument Sonderband* 100.
Hirsch, J. (1983b), 'The Fordist Security State and new Social Movements', *Kapitalistate* 10/11.
Hirsch, J. (1985a), 'Weder links nach rechts, sondern vorn: die FDP', *Links* 183.
Hirsch, J. (1985b), see Chapter 2 of this volume, 'Fordism and Post-Fordism'.
Hirsch, J. (1985c), 'Auf dem Weg zum Postfordismus', *Argument* 151.
Hirsch, J. (1986), 'Die Abstraktheit der Macht, Soziale Bewengungen ohne Zukunft?', *Links* 6/86.
Hirsch, J. and R. Roth (1980), 'Modell Deutschland und neue soziale Bewegungen', *Prokla* 40, p. 14.
Hirsch, J. and R. Roth (1986), *Das neue Gesicht des Kapitalismus, Vom Fordismus zum Post-Fordismus* (Hamburg).
Holloway, J. (1987), 'The Red Rose of Nissan', *Capital & Class* 32.
Holloway, J. (1987b), 'A Note on Fordism and Neo-Fordism', *Common Sense* 1 (Edinburgh), p. 52.
Holloway, J. and S. Picciotto (1978), *State and Capital. A Marxist Debate* (London).
Huebner, K. (1987), 'Neue Gesichtszuege?, "Das neue Gesicht des Kapitalismus" Debatte des neuen Theorieentwurfs von Joachim Hirsch und Roland Roth', *Sozialismus* 4/87, p. 39.
Jessop, B. (1982), *The Capitalist State* (Oxford).
Jessop, B. (1983), 'State Forms, Social Basis and Hegemonic Projects', *Kapitalstate* 10/11, p. 89.
Jessop, B. (1985), *Nicos Poulantzas, Marxist Theory and Political Strategy* (London).

Jessop, B. (1986), 'Warum es keinen Kohlismus gibt', *Links* 1/86.
Jessop, B. *et al.* (1984), K. Bonnet, S. Bromely, B. Jessop, T. Ling, 'Authoritarian Populism, Two Nations and Thatcherism', *New Left Review* 147.
Juergens, U. (1980), 'Selbstregulierung des Kapitals. Erfahrungen aus der Kartellbewegung in Deutschland um die Jahrhundertwende. Zum Verhaeltnis von Politik und Oekonomie', Campus Forschung Band 132 (Frankfurt, New York).
Junne, G. (1985), 'Neue Technologien bedrohen die Exporte der Entwicklungslaender', *Prokla* 60, p. 142.
Laufenberg, M. and A. Spellerberg (1986), 'Tele-Homework — The Great Temptation for Women', in European Conference on Women, Natural Science and Technology, Women Challenge Technology, Elsinore, Denmark.
Lipietz, A. (1985), 'Akkumulation, Krisen und Auswege aus der Krise, Einige methodische Ueberlegungen zum Begriff der "Regulation"', *Prokla* 58.
Lipietz, A. (1985b), *The Enchanted World, Credit and the World Crises* (London: Verso Books).
Lloyd, J. (1986), 'The Sparks are Flying', *Marxism Today* 3/86.
London . . . (1980), London Edinburgh Weekend Return Group, *In and Against the State* (London: Pluto Press).
Marx, K. (1971), *Capital*, Vol. III (London: Lawrence & Wishart).
Marx, K. (1973), *Grundrisse, Introduction to the Critique of Political Economy* (Harmondsworth: Penguin).
Marx, K. (1976), *Capital*, Vol. I (Penguin).
Negri, T. (1977), *Staat in der Krise* (Muenchen: Merve-Verlag).
Negri, T. (1984), 'Marx beyond Marx: Lessons on the *Grundrisse*' (Massachusetts: Bergin and Garvy).
Palloix, C. (1976), 'From Fordism to Neofordism', in Conference of Socialist Economists Pamphlet 1: *The Labour Process and Class Struggle* (London: Stage I), p. 46.

4 Regulation Theory, Post-Fordism and the State: More than a Reply to Werner Bonefeld*

Bob Jessop

Werner Bonefeld has performed a valuable service in presenting and criticising some recent work of West German state theorists on the capitalist state and the current crisis-ridden transformation of capitalist societies. But there are several problems with his account of this work and its links with French regulation theory as well as with his critique of both theories; and there are also problems with his own alternative approach to political analysis and the transition to post-Fordism.[1]

BONEFELD'S MAIN ARGUMENTS

Bonefeld claims that the 'reformulation' has reversed the slow-down in the West German state debate and has attempted to regenerate state theory by combining it wih the assumptions, concepts and explanatory principles of the French regulation school. Thus it has gone beyond abstract, formal analyses of the capitalist state in general (for example, as in 'ideal collective capitalist') to develop a more concrete, institutionalist theory of the state under different accumulation regimes. This can be seen, according to Bonefeld, in the attempts of the reformulation to describe two different types of state system, corresponding to the Fordist and post-Fordist accumulation regimes. Bonefeld also notes that these interrelated changes in both accumulation and political regimes have implications for socialist strategy. Thus Hirsch and Roth (1986) argue that the old working-class movement can no longer play a revolutionary role and that new sources (rooted in civil society and the state) and new forces (new social movements) of resistance have emerged.

Bonefeld's critique consists in three interwoven sets of comments concerning the methodological assumptions, substantive arguments, and political–strategic conclusions of the reformulation. The principal methodological criticism is that, even though the reformulators initially intended to re-introduce class struggle into state theory and to give it the central role, their work still analyses structure and struggle separately and regards struggle as secondary. According to Bonefeld, the reformulation first describes the structures of capitalist society together with the pre-given, objective laws of capitalist development that are inscribed within these structures; and it then suggests that class struggle serves merely to accelerate and/or retard the realisation of these laws and thus has no truly independent role in capitalist development. Against such arguments Bonefeld insists that class struggle is the primary motor force of historical development. Thus class struggle is somehow always already present within all the various moments of the capital relation rather than being external and secondary to the structures of capitalist society. In turn this implies that 'the crisis-ridden process of social reproduction should be understood in terms of de- and recomposition of society rather than in terms of 'correspondence-regulation-regularity' (Bonefeld above, p. 46). He develops this alternative approach in several directions to provide a general methodological critique of the reformulation.

Bonefeld also offers several substantive criticisms of the reformulators' analysis of West Germany and post-war Britain. He does not provide an alternative analysis beyond that implicit in his criticisms but does cite John Holloway's paper in *Capital & Class* 32 which gives some clues as to his preferred approach (Holloway 1987). Related to this critique is the political–strategic claim that reformulation analyses tend to legitimate the current changes in capitalism by treating them as inevitable and, in so doing, undermine the working-class movement and its capacities for resistance.

My chief disagreements with Bonefeld concern his methodological remarks; there is much that I agree with in his more substantive criticisms. Thus my own remarks will concentrate on questions of methodology in both state and regulation theory. Specifically I will examine: (a) his account of the regulation approach and some of its key concepts; (b) his functionalist reading of the reformulation and its relation to the regulation school; (c) his understanding of the dialectic between structure and strategy; and (d) his comments on Fordism and post-Fordism as analytical categories. My paper concludes with some general remarks on the most appropriate research agenda for regulation and state theory.

THE CRITIQUE OF FRENCH REGULATION THEORY

Bonefeld's account of the regulation school is largely intended to establish some affinities and shared assumptions with the reformulation and does not develop a detailed critique. He gives only a short summary of its analysis of capitalism and therefore glosses over some important differences within the overall approach. His main point is that, although the regulationists and the reformulators recognise that capitalism is a relation of class struggle, they deploy analytical categories which uncouple struggles from structure and then subordinate them to a structural logic. This can be seen, according to Bonefeld, in such central concepts as correspondence and regulation: for correspondence, defined as a 'relatively stable form of regulation', has structuralist connotations and regulation itself appears functionalist. Before commenting on this critique, I will present more fully the regulation approach.

Genesis and Concepts of the Regulation School

The French regulation school[2] developed in the 1970s. Emerging in part out of Althusserian structuralism (Aglietta 1979, 1982a; Lipietz, 1987), but intending to overcome the latter's assumption that structures somehow maintain themselves quasi-automatically without effective social agency and without significant transformations, regulation theorists replaced the notion of 'reproduction' with that of 'regulation'. They asked how capitalism could survive even though the capital relation itself inevitably generated antagonisms and crises which made continuing accumulation improbable. They found an answer in specific institutional forms, societal norms, and patterns of strategic conduct which both expressed and regulated these conflicts until the inevitable tensions and divergencies among these various regulatory forms reached crisis point (Lipietz 1987, pp. 3–4).

The key concepts offered by the French regulationists were 'regime of accumulation' and 'mode of regulation' (for example, Aglietta 1979; Lipietz 1985a). An accumulation regime is a particular combination of production and consumption which can be reproduced over time despite conflictual tendencies; and a mode of regulation refers to an institutional ensemble and complex of norms which can secure capitalist reproduction *pro tempore* despite the conflictual and antagonistic character of capitalist social relations (Lipietz 1985a; Boyer 1986a). After the initial studies of Aglietta (1979) and CEPREMAP/CORDES (1977), regulationist analyses have multiplied with two contrasting effects. Further concepts have been added to produce a richer and more complex conceptual matrix: for example, mode of growth, international strategic space, regional armatures, and hegemonic blocs. But the school has also divided into several currents. These differ not so much in terms of their substantive focus (which still remains wide) as in the relative weight given to Marxian, Keynesian, Kaldorian and Kaleckian concepts in the overall institutionalist perspective (see de Vroey 1984; Mjoset 1985; Noël 1987; for further nuances, see appendix below).

It is worth emphasising here that regulation theorists have not confined their analyses to economic matters. Indeed they emphasise that the improbable discovery of effective modes of regulation is an outcome of social and political struggles which stabilise to form a *hegemonic system* — class alliances, based on consensus armoured by coercion, which shape the interests both of the ruling and dominated classes into conformity with the accumulation regime (Lipietz 1986a, p. 20; see Aglietta 1979).

On Class Struggle and Crisis Tendencies

These comments suggest that regulationists are well aware of class struggle and crisis and their interrelations; indeed, they take all this for granted. For them, the problem is not to explain the generic origins of class struggle and/or crisis tendencies but the specific forms that these actually assume in different conjunctures. In turn this should help to explain the capacities of capitalism to survive despite both class struggle and crisis tendencies. Regimes of accumulation are stable to the extent that they provide specific means of mobilising counter-tendencies to the generic and specific crisis tendencies of a given stage of capitalism. Likewise modes of regulation provide means of institutionalising class struggle and confining it within certain parameters compatible with continuing accumulation.

Bonefeld claims that class struggle only enters as an 'and also' or 'but also' factor, separated from objective laws and, at most, affecting how they are realised. This argument is directed mainly against the reformulation but is also relevant to the regulationist approach. In both cases it is based on misunderstanding. Regulation and reformulation theorists alike deny that there is a single objective logic of capitalist development which transcends all particularities: the development of capitalism is always mediated through historically specific institutional forms, regulatory institutions, and norms of conduct. Included here are the wage relations; forms of competition; monetary emission; the state; international commercial and financial system; and the norms of conduct and modes of calculation which correspond to these institutional forms and regulatory institutions.

Far from regulationists assuming that accumulation regimes or modes of regulation somehow precede struggle, they argue that these are always the product of past struggles and are always penetrated with present struggles. The legacy of past struggles is a structurally inscribed, strategic selectivity which favours some class forces over others. Thus, once accumulation regimes and mode of regulation have become relatively stable, they comprise a specific strategic terrain on and through which particular forms of struggle take place. Since there are no institutional guarantees that struggles will always be contained within these forms and/or resolved in ways that reproduce these forms, the stability of an accumulation regime or mode of regulation is always relative, always partial, and always provisional. Thus regulation involves a set of temporary institutional solutions which contain and limit the basic conflicts of capitalism but cannot do so for ever (Aglietta 1982; Lipietz 1986a). Sometimes crises can be confined within the dominant accumulation regime or mode of regulation through marginal adjustments or incremental change; but sometimes this is not the case. When the accumulation of contradictions and struggles is no longer manageable, regulationists speak of a crisis *of* (rather than *in*) an accumulation regime or mode of regulation (see Boyer 1986a; Lipietz 1986a). They stress that the transition to a new phase of accumulation depends on class struggle, trial-and-error experimentation, chance discoveries, and so forth. There is no objective developmental logic of capital that inevitably and painlessly ensures passage from one regime to another (Lipietz 1986b).

Three Specific Misreadings

As well as this general problem of interpretation, Bonefeld makes three specific misreadings. Firstly, he suggests that regulation theory is concerned with value-theoretical issues and ignores forms of domination. But not all regulation theory adopts value-theoretical categories even indirectly (let alone directly) to analyse the historical transformation of capitalist production and its regulatory forms: thus Boyer, one of the three leading regulation theorists, examines the wage relation rather than value production as such. Likewise Lipietz (1986a), André and Delorme (1982), Ominami (1986) and Mjoset (1987) have examined forms of domination, hegemony and political organisation.

Secondly, Bonefeld conflates the concepts of 'reglementation' and 'regulation'. Whereas reglementation refers to detailed regulation by an institution located outside and superordinate to a system of social relations (such as the market), regulation refers to complex processes of mutual adjustment and accommodation within and among different institutions. Thus Aglietta, the first French regulation theorist, rejects the notion of general equilibrium and market-mediated regulation; and also denies that the state can act as a subject intervening from outside in the name of a global regulation of the whole economy to compensate for any or all market failures (Aglietta 1982). Regulation assumes no sovereign power of command or privileged point of coordination and does not imply that there is a unique hierarchy of institutions. Instead it is a complex, multilateral, and provisional process mediated through institutions and conducted by social forces. In this sense it refers to specific forms of institutionalisation of the class struggle and not to the suspension or abnegation of class struggle.[3]

Thirdly, in arguing that 'correspondence' is a structuralist notion referring purely to relations among structures, Bonefeld ignores its links to the Gramscian concept of 'historic bloc'. For Gramsci (and the reformulation theorists) an 'historic bloc' is a configuration of economic base and political and ideological superstructures that are mutually supportive and co-evolving and whose coherence depends on specific practices rather than deriving from the objective laws of capitalist development (Gramsci 1971, pp. 137, 366, 377). In so far as such a correspondence among structures exists, it is not an automatic effect of structures or objective developmental laws (a view Bonefeld incorrectly ascribes to regulation and reformulation theorists). Instead it is the product of a long-term equilibrium among class forces institutionalised on a specific field of class conflict and organised under the hegemony and/or domination of the capitalist class.

Concluding Remarks on Regulation Theory

This brief account of regulation theory shows that Bonefeld has not fully grasped its implications for crisis and class struggle. This suggests that his account of how regulation theory could be taken up in developing state theory might also be weak. However, since his critique is primarily aimed against the reformulation, it is more important to see how reformulation theorists have used regulation concepts than to see whether Bonefeld himself correctly understood them in their original form. This is the task of the next section.

THE REFORMULATION OF STATE THEORY

The reformulation, according to Bonefeld, founds state development on accumulation. It supposedly argues that the forms and functions of the state correspond to a regime of accumulation and thereby constitute a unity determined by objective laws of capitalist development *and also* class struggle. The key to this emergent unity is the mode of regulation and this operates in turn through state apparatuses (ideological, repressive and mass integrative). Thus it is in and through the state that regulatory processes are condensed, homogenised, and achieved. The pivot around which these processes occur is, however, the tendency of the rate of profit to fall. In this sense one could perhaps argue that the economy plays a determining role but the political has the dominant role.

Bonefeld's principal criticisms of this analysis (as understood and presented in his account) concern its structuralism, functionalism, teleologism and politicism. He claims that the reformulation is too concerned with structures and their relations (neglecting the primary role of class struggle); treats the state's role as one of functional compensation for the social disintegration continuously generated through capitalist relations of production; analyses the transition from one accumulation regime to another as a linear, quasi-automatic process determined by objective laws of capitalist development; and reduces the complex ensemble of regulatory mechanisms to the functions and activities of the state. I will respond to each of these criticisms below but in reverse order.

Politicism

The charge of politicism is partly justified. The West German state theorists have focused primarily on politically-mediated counter-tendencies to the rate of profit to fall and/or on the role of the state in consolidating modes of regulation. In turn this has sometimes led them to suggest that the 'state constitutes, regulates, integrates and secures capitalist reproduction' (Bonefeld above, p. 48); and it does mean that 'Hirsch's and Roth's claim that "the state is the functional center of social reproduction" fails to apply the proposed concept of "regulation" which was initially seen as the mode of articulation between a regime of accumulation and hegemonic structures' (ibid.). But there is more to be said on these issues.

These politicist tendencies occur partly because the West German contributors to the reformulation are first and foremost state theorists; thus they tend to ignore issues such as forms of competition, the nature of monetary emission, patterns of collective bargaining, and so forth and/or to focus primarily on their political implications. Their politicism can also be explained by the fact that the main outlines of their analysis of the West German state were developed before they turned to regulationist concepts to deepen their analysis of the crisis tendencies of post-war capitalism. This belated discovery of the regulation approach means that the correspondence between new regulation concepts and more established concepts in the reformulation approach is sometimes weak (see Jessop 1988a). This does not seem to me too destructive a criticism because it can be remedied within the overall methodological framework adopted by the reformulation theorists. For the method of articulation means that the conceptual and empirical links between economic and political factors in accumulation regimes and modes of regulation can be redefined without serious difficulties.

Teleologism

This charge is more difficult to sustain: the basic thrust of the reformulation is anti-teleological. It is systematically stressed that there is no single objective logic of capitalist development: indeed, it is for this reason that Jessop (1983) has written about the alternative logics of capitalist development corresponding to different regimes of accumulation, modes of growth, and regulatory patterns and has developed the concept of accumulation strategies to emphasise the alternative paths of accumulation which could be pursued within the basic framework of the capital relation. Where the charge might be justified is in the empirical rather than the theoretical analyses. For it is true that reformulation theorists have tended to use formal categories such as Fordism and post-Fordism not only as heuristic ideal types but also as descriptive categories imposed directly on complex and contradictory conjunctures. This is particularly serious when it is actually agreed by the reformulation theorists that we are still living through a transitional period whose eventual outcome cannot be forecast or guaranteed. But even then it is clearly recognised that there are different national Fordisms, different national roads to post-Fordism, and different possible post-Fordist futures; and that these national specificities are the result of the balance of class forces in specific national conjunctures (see especially Hirsch and Roth 1986; and Jessop 1988b).

Functionalism

This charge is also hard to sustain. The West German contributors to the reformulation developed the anti-functionalist approach in the state derivation debate. Two main approaches can be discerned in the inordinately complex and convoluted state derivation debate (for general accounts, see Jessop 1982; Rudel 1981). Starting from the inherent capitalist tendencies to market failure, economic crisis, and class struggle, one approach tried to derive the necessary form of the capitalist state from the functions it must perform to correct these deficits and thereby secure capitalist reproduction. But the other approach *first* derived the form of the capitalist state from the nature of generalised commodity production in the capitalist economy and *then* showed how this form problematised the state's functionality for capitalist reproduction. The former approach soon re-entered the theoretical cul-de-sac of economic reductionism because it adopted a capital logic analysis in which politics was reduced to the global dynamic of class struggle and/or policies to the needs of capital (see Hirsch 1980, pp. 54–6). But the latter approach remained fruitful because it opened a space for a *sui generis* dynamic of political struggles and a specific institutional logic in policy-making. This has provided the theoretical means to avoid functionalism in so far as the activities of the state are determined in the first instance by political considerations and need not coincide (even in the last instance) with the 'needs' of the economy. A further consequence of this approach is to deconstruct the concept of the 'needs' of the economy: if the economy is not self-sufficient, self-reproducing, and self-steering and, if the political is formally rather than functionally determined by the economy, there can be no unambiguous economic needs. The needs of capital must be assessed strategically in relation to complex conjunctures rather than formally in terms of an abstract, purely economic, circuit of capital (see Jessop 1984). Moreover, in opening up a space for politics in this way, the second approach has permitted more detailed and conjunctural analyses of politics and political struggles. This may reinforce the politicist tendencies within the reformulation but it tends to undermine any functionalist bias.

Structuralism

This is the most difficult of the four charges to uphold. Indeed, in making it, Bonefeld is guilty of misreading the reformulation on several points. These concern: the concepts of correspondence, regulation, and apparatus; the meaning of 'process without a subject'; and the nature of the dialectic between structure and strategy. Since I have already addressed the first misunderstanding in my comments on regulation theory, I deal here only with the last two problems.

Bonefeld interprets the claim that capitalist development is 'a process without a subject' as meaning that it is a process without subjects: this is wrong. All that this phrase means is that there is no transcendent, global subject which alone determines the logic of capitalist development: this is beyond the scope of the productive forces, the economy in the last instance, the state, a given class, or any other putative 'cause without cause'. It does not mean that there are no subjects: indeed both regulationists and reformulators recognise many different subjects, modes of calculation, patterns of strategic conduct, and forms of struggle. In turn this means that the course of development is the result of interactions on many different terrains and among many different forces. Accordingly there is no inconsistency between the Hirsch/Roth claim that the imposition of a mode of regulation flows from quite complex economic, political and ideological struggles and their claim that this occurs as a process without a subject.

Bonefeld's comments on the structure–strategy dialectic are complex. He refers to a duality of structure and strategy (or structure and struggle); claims that the reformulation subordinates struggle to structure; and then sometimes charges the reformulation with structuralism and sometimes with voluntarism. There is some evidence for such a duality but not where Bonefeld claims to find it. Elsewhere I have noted that there is a doubling of concepts in Hirsch's work so that key concepts appear twice: accumulation regime and accumulation strategy, mode of regulation and *Regulationsweisen*, hegemonial structures and hegemonic projects. My own work also refers to accumulation regimes and accumulation strategies and to two aspects of hegemony: structural determination and class leadership. The relations between these two sets of concepts may not always be clear but I believe they can be established theoretically and empirically. Accordingly, to reply to Bonefeld's twin charges of structuralism and voluntarism, I will now summarise briefly the nature of structure/strategy dialectic (see Jessop 1983, 1988a).

The Dialectic Between Structure and Strategy

We can best begin this summary by looking at the possible relations between structural and strategic categories in the regulation and reformulation theories. What purpose is served by talking about accumulation regime and accumulation strategies, modes of regulation and regulatory strategies, hegemonial structures and hegemonic projects? If one or other concept in each pair is not to become redundant, two theoretical fallacies must be avoided.

The first fallacy would be to reduce the structural category to, and/or derive it from, a strategic category; the second would be to derive a single strategy from a given structure. But neither an accumulation regime nor a mode of growth can be understood as the product of a single accumulation or a single national growth strategy. Except when analysed at high levels of abstraction, accumulation regimes and modes of growth have only a *relative* unity: they are better described as structural *ensembles* than as simple structures. Among the elements which could be articulated into an accumulation regime or mode of growth on a given territorial space, there will be many irrelevant, residual, marginal, secondary, and even potentially contradictory elements and the unity of the more central elements will always be marred by gaps, redundancies, interstices and contradictions.

Likewise, given the complex and overdetermined structure of an accumulation regime (or mode of growth), one could not calculate an effective general strategy to maintain it: the relative success or failure of a strategy typically depends on unacknowledged structural conditions of action which may alter as well as on the changing balance of forces (including changing organisational capacities and strategies) relevant to its successful realisation. In addition, of course, there are always competing strategies. Thus the actual course of accumulation (over a given economic space from global to local levels) always results from their interaction in particular circumstances on a given terrain constituted not only by the existing regime or industrial profile but also by existing modes of regulation.

This means that there can never be a one-to-one correspondence between structures and strategies. To argue otherwise is to run the risk of re-introducing a transhistorical subject whose global strategy is realised and/or of re-introducing the concept of reproduction and reducing concrete subjects to the necessary *Traeger* (supports) of the dominant structure. And Hirsch and the regulationists alike reject both these theoretical fallacies.

The dialectic between structure and strategy does not involve a simple oscillation between two formally homologous poles (structural and strategic) which dove-tail neatly together. Instead it involves a complex process of mutual historical conditioning and reciprocal recursive transformation. Both the structural and the strategic moments are complex and changeable: the boundaries and articulation of structural ensembles are unstable, the world of strategies is pluralistic and conjunctural. Their dialectic is nothing more (and nothing less) than the structural conditioning of strategies (both as explicit reference points for strategic calculation and as a partly and partially unacknowledged set of structural constraints and conjunctural opportunities) and the strategic transformation of structural ensembles (both through deliberate, if often unsuccessful, attempts to modify them and through the unanticipated consequences of interaction among patterns of strategic conduct with other objectives).

Even if one allows for competing strategies and thus for a certain contingency in their interaction, another risk still remains: that the emergence and subsequent dynamic of structures might be endowed with greater intentionality than is actually justified. This is an issue difficult to resolve in the abstract beyond the comments already made. But it is worth noting that Aglietta (1982) has described the emergence of modes of regulation as improbable and Lipietz speaks of them as *Fundsachen* (chance discoveries) (1985a). In both cases this is meant to stress the contingent, non-intentional emergence of accumulation regimes and modes of regulation; strategic conduct might be involved but with no guarantee of success and, perhaps, more concerned to impose some coherence and direction on an already emergent structure than to bring it into existence. Hirsch's position on this point is less clear. On occasion he treats the emergence of new structures as the result of successful strategies but sometimes they are simply treated as emergent historical ensembles.

Finally, given that strategies have unacknowledged conditions for success and are always realised in specific structural contexts, what sense can be attached to the notion of alternative strategies? This question must be answered on several levels. In general terms structure should be seen as the ensemble of structural constraints *and conjunctural opportunities* which exist over a specific time horizon and within given spatial boundaries for different social forces: what is a constraint for some forces could be an opportunity for others. In this sense alternative strategies could exist to the extent that: (a) calculating subjects are differentially located in relation to the structure (so that the same structure presents them with a different ensemble of constraints and opportunities); (b) calculate their strategies over different time horizons and/or spatial boundaries; (c) engage in strategic conduct over a more or less extensive social terrain — embracing various fields of action (such as economic, political, juridical, moral, educational); and (d) enter into different types of alliance with other social forces. If we now shift attention from what makes alternative strategies possible to what makes their more or less successful realisation possible, we must consider the relations among different strategies. The success of the '*n*th' strategy depends on its complementarities to all other relevant strategies within the overall structural ensemble. Moreover, since the success of all other strategies depends on the nature of the '*n*th' strategy, there is clearly a complex web of contingencies. It is for this reason that some of the French regulationists insist that accumulation regimes, modes of growth, and modes of regulation are 'discovered' rather than planned. There is no global subject to plan accumulation strategies, regulatory mechanisms, or hegemonic projects and to guarantee their successful implementation. Instead we find only different subjects whose activities are more or less co-ordinated, whose activities meet more or less resistance from other forces, and whose strategies are pursued within a structural context which is both constraining and facilitating.

Thus, whilst there is real scope for class struggle in the structure–strategy dialectic, class strategies can never be purely voluntarist. To understand how capitalism is reproduced despite these complex contingencies, we must examine both the institutional inertia and strategic selectivity inscribed in specific accumulation regimes, modes of growth, and modes of regulation. The multiplication of institutional forms and regulatory mechanisms (as well as the self-substituting character of many of them such that, for example, black markets emerge when normal markets are suspended) actually create significant barriers to a general attack on the capital relation by fragmenting and disorganising opposition and resistance and/or channelling it along particular paths where it threatens less harm to the core institutions of capitalism. Thus the structure/strategy dialectic does not separate struggle from structures but shows their complex forms of interaction. Structures are only prior to struggle in the sense that struggles always occur in specific conjunctures: but these conjunctures (with their complex and differential sets of constraints and opportunities) are themselves the product of past struggles.

FORDISM AND POST-FORDISM

Although he notes, correctly, that the description holds better for West Germany than Britain, Bonefeld agrees with much of the analysis of Fordism and post-Fordism in the reformulation. His objections concern less the description of certain *tendencies* discernible in the current transition than to their subsequent treatment as the process of realisation of objectively pre-given features of *the* coming post-Fordist system. Thus he argues that the reformulation sees class struggle merely as an accelerating or retarding factor in the transition rather than as its primary motor force. He also criticises the strategic conclusions and resulting political passivity which supposedly follow from this approach.

I have already addressed the methodological criticism in general terms but some specific comments are appropriate. Bonefeld is quite right to criticise the formalism of general models of Fordism and post-Fordism: these must remain abstract until specified in terms of specific national growth models and their corresponding modes of regulation. Such models are particularly misleading when they are simply generalised from one specific rational model. Thus Hirsch fails to distinguish between the Fordist accumulation regime in formal, abstract terms and the national modes of growth compatible with Fordism on a global scale and then compounds this failure by failing to note the specific features of the West German mode of growth. Further problems arise when certain tendencies in the current transition are reified to become *the* post-Fordist model. This will prove difficult because post-Fordism differs from Fordism in a key particular: whereas Fordism could plausibly be interpreted in terms of the diffusion of the American model to other national economies, there is currently no single hegemonic growth model (Japanese, American and West German models are in competition) and ever more extensive financial and industrial internationalisation makes it even more important for most national economies to find distinctive niches in the worldwide division of labour. But recognising these problems does not as such invalidate regulation or reformulation theories — it merely cautions against over-hasty generalisations within their overall theoretical framework.

Bonefeld is also right in criticising the reformulation for overestimating the extent of changes which have already occurred. This stems from the contraposition of abstract, formal models and the corresponding neglect of the 'impurities' of national modes of growth and regulation as well as of the incomplete character of any transition. In this sense the danger of imposing normative models on complex changes is very real and care must be taken to avoid it. It is for this reason that my own recent work has focused on national modes of growth and their insertion into the international hierarchy constituted through the global division of labour and international modes of regulation (for example, Jessop 1988b); has considered different strategies (neo-liberal, neo-statist, neo-corporatist) which could be adopted in the transition from Fordism to post-Fordism (Jessop 1986, 1988b); and discussed different forms of the welfare state which would be consistent with a transition to a post-Fordist accumulation regime (Jessop 1986). Likewise recent work by French regulation theorists has been concerned to sketch different trajectories and types of post-Fordism and their different economic and political preconditions (for example, Lipietz 1987; Boyer 1987). Here too, then, the solution is to be found within the regulation approach; not in rejecting this approach.

Further elaboration on these lines would also provide the basis for avoiding the final criticism which Bonefeld offers. For, the more clearly it can be shown that there are different types of post-Fordism and different national roads, the more self-evident it becomes that there is nothing inevitable about the transition. Not only is a transition to this or that type of post-Fordism an open question but so too is the issue of whether any sort of transition to post-Fordism will occur. If national roads and the eventual form of national post-Fordism depend on the course of class struggle within the structural conditions established by an initial starting point, then there may be nothing inevitable about the transition at all. In this respect it is worth noting that Bonefeld's criticism about political passivity is directed mainly against left theorists in Britain (notably contributors to *Marxism Today*) and not to the regulation or reformulation theorists themselves. At most one could criticise Hirsch and Roth for their relative neglect of the working-class movement compared to the attention they give to new social movements. But their discussion of the integration of the old working class into the Fordist model does not mean that it was inevitable when it occurred (as opposed to being a problem to be overcome now); and it does not mean that new social movements will inevitably be absorbed into the structures of post-Fordism — indeed they might even be criticised for their excessive 'faith in the democratic miracles' to be worked through these movements.

CONCLUDING REMARKS

In the final analysis Bonefeld's criticisms are mainly directed at the method which he attributes to regulation and reformulation theories. But, as I have tried to show, the method is not really that of either theory. The separation which Bonefeld discerns in them between structure and strategy is at most analytical and it certainly does not involve the subordination of class struggle to pre-given structures which exist beyond struggle. On the contrary, as this paper tries to establish, regulation theory introduced the concept of 'regulation' precisely to overcome the structuralist bias of studies of 'reproduction'. Likewise the type of West German state theory with which Hirsch, Esser and their colleagues are associated has long argued that the form of the capitalist state problematises its functionality for capital and therefore places a premium on the political class struggle in securing the conditions for continued capital accumulation and political class domination.

In this sense I believe that Bonefeld's principal criticisms are misdirected. But this does not mean that we should accept all the substantive arguments put forward by regulation and reformulation theorists: indeed, since they are often ambiguous, contradictory, or plain wrong, this would be foolish. What is more important is to decide whether the basic research agenda implied in regulation and reformulation theory offers more chance for theoretical and political advance than available alternatives. And here I take my stand with the regulation and reformulation theorists. Their research programme shows a clear commitment to concrete analysis of concrete conjunctures through a rich and complex range of economic and political concepts directly related to the nature of the capitalist exploitation and domination. That some of the analyses so far offered have short-circuited the analytical method implied in the overall research agenda does not as such condemn the approach but merely points to the dangers of applying it too hastily and/or unthinkingly. I would also argue that it is only through the detailed conjunctural analyses which this method facilitates (but whose accuracy it cannot guarantee) that one can develop alternative strategies which have some chance of success. Indeed, as Hirsch himself remarked, in drawing on (and extending) regulation theory and combining it with West German state theory, he can 'proceed from general (and therefore abstract) political theory to a concept useful for the analysis of actual changes in the political apparatus, essential for the political usefulness and relevance of theory' (Hirsch 1983, p. 75).

In terms of a research agenda, a synthesis of regulationist and reformulation concepts is needed. Both the state derivation debate and the regulation school have produced concepts at a middle range, institutional level; both are concerned with stages and phases of capitalist development rather than with the abstract laws of motion and tendencies operating at the level of capital in general; both are sensitive to the relative autonomy of the economic and political spheres — seeking to avoid economic reductionism and to explore state intervention; both are committed to conjunctural analysis; and both emphasise the role of strategic conduct and struggle in the transition from one phase to another of capitalism. But there is still much work to be done.

So far the regulation approach has been extensively applied only to the French and Nordic economies (Mjoset 1987) and, to a lesser extent, to the American, West German and British economies. Some other comparative econometric studies of European economies exist (for example, Mazier *et al.* 1984) and Lipietz (1986) and Ominami (1986) have written general studies on accumulation regimes in less advanced economies (a short bibliographical guide can be found in Boyer (1986a). Clearly, until more detailed local, national, regional, and international studies have been completed, the dangers of analytical short-circuiting will remain. Particularly important for such research are intermediate concepts such as modes of growth and international regimes for economic analysis, forms of state for political analysis, and modes of regulation and historic blocs for societal analysis. It is in this intermediate area that the regulation and reformulation approaches are most promising.

What is needed above all are accounts of national modes of growth, their insertion into the international economy, the specific national modes of regulation with which they are associated, the dynamic of specific forms of state, and the specific 'historic blocs' to which these have given rise. Only through such detailed studies will it be possible to formulate general strategies oriented to current changes in capitalism rather than to engage in specific forms of resistance or struggle and/or to fight old battles in radically changed conditions. The success of Thatcherism has much to do with its ability to discern some order in the myriad confusing changes currently under way in Britain and to give a particular coherence and political direction to them. This does not mean that the strategies pursued by Thatcherism are the only feasible strategies nor that the emerging neo-liberal Thatcherite strategy is guaranteed success. The appropriate lesson to draw is that a socialist alternative must also take account of current changes and adapt its strategy to them. But the coherence it discerns and the direction it will seek to give these changes will be entirely different. In this sense an alternative socialist project must start out from the current changes — but not through passively acquiescing in them but through developing a coherent alternative to them and mobilising broad popular support for this alternative.

Appendix: Four Types of Regulation Analysis

We can distinguish four main regulationist approaches in terms of their substantive focus (national or international) and theoretical complexity (concern with economic mechanisms alone or also with societalisation mechanisms). Together with some examples these are portrayed in Table 4.1 (see below); and they can be briefly described as follows:

One approach focuses on national accumulation regimes and modes of growth understood mainly in terms of their economic determinations. This was the approach adopted by Aglietta in the first regulationist analysis: a study of Fordism in the United States from a value-theoretical viewpoint (1974–79). Subsequent studies have extended this approach to other national economic formations: either in terms of the diffusion of the American model of Fordism to other countries and/or in terms of the development of *sui generis* national modes of growth analysed without regard to their insertion into the international economic order. Some of these studies have remained within a value-theoretical framework but others have considered the economic mechanisms in different, but still primarily economic, terms (for example, the *rapport salarial* or 'wage relation').

A second approach focuses on the international economic dimensions of regulation. It studies the distinctive modes of *inter*national regulation and/or the form and extent of complementarities among different national modes of growth. Rather than treating the global economy as the mechanical sum of different national modes of growth and regulation, it argues that the international economy has its own *sui generis* properties, modes of regulation and problems. Thus it examines the international accumulation regime as a hierarchy of national modes of growth, with its own specific modes of regulation, its own crisis forms; and it examines national modes of growth in terms of their possibilities of adhesion or exclusion from the international order and the interaction between nationalisation, transnationalisation, and internationalisation tendencies. Aglietta, who pioneered the regulation approach for the USA, has also presented an important account of the complementarities among national modes of growth in his analysis of France and West Germany (1982). Likewise we find approaches to the peripheral Fordism and bloody Taylorisation in Lipietz (1986b) and Ominami (1986).

A third approach examines the complex patterns of societalisation (*Vergesellschaftung*) or 'social structures of accumulation' (in the American equivalent to regulation theory) on the national level. The concept of 'societalisation' refers to the dynamic process of structuration and regulation at a societal level; it implies that the emergence and maintenance of societies is problematic. The reproduction of societies depends on a complex ensemble of institutionally mediated practices which secure at least a minimal correspondence among different structures (the 'system integration' aspect of

TABLE 4.1 *Four foci of regulation approaches: some examples*

	Economic focus	*Societalisation focus*
National level focus	A.1 Aglietta (1979) on American Fordism A.2 Mjoset (1987) on Nordic models A.3 Boyer (1979) on wage relation A.4 Mazier (1982) on growth and crisis	B.1 Hirsch and Roth (1986) on 'Model Germany' B.2 Gordon (1980) on social structures of accumulation B.3 Davis (1985) on Reaganism B.4 Jessop (1986) on welfare state
International focus	C.1 Aglietta (1982) on complimentarities C.2 Lipietz (1982) on peripheral Fordism C.3 Mistral (1986) on 'international space' C.4 Ominami (1986) on crisis in Third World	D.1 (Beaud (1987) on global hierarchies) D.2 (international regimes)

the 'social formation') as well as an 'unstable equilibrium of compromise' among social forces (the 'social integration' or 'social cohesion' aspect of the 'social order'). Thus the concept of societalisation adopted in the state reformulation adopts similar assumptions and explanatory principles to that of 'regulation' in the regulation school. This approach is concerned with the development and dynamic of modes of regulation extending beyond the economic sphere as well as with the 'historic blocs' (that is, the contingent societal formations based on structured complementarities between the economic base and political and ideological superstructures) which arise on the basis of relatively stable modes of growth and regulation and help to consolidate them. This approach gives particular attention to the state and hegemony as central elements in societal regulation but also examines other social forms and institutions.

A fourth approach would study international 'societalisation', that is, the complementarities among emergent international structures and strategies and/or attempts to establish a global order through international regimes of one kind or another. As yet this approach is relatively underdeveloped within the regulationist school and should therefore figure centrally in any future regulationist research agenda. An interesting approach close to regulation theory can be found in Michel Beaud's recent study on interrelations among national societies within the framework of evolving global hierarchies (Beaud 1987). This is all the more urgent because of the growing hold in anglophone literature of the so-called 'international regimes' approach with its mixture of idealist and realist arguments (for recent critical surveys of international regimes studies, see: Krasner 1983; Haggard and Simmons 1987; Wolf and Zuern 1986).

NOTES

* This article was first published in *Capital & Class* 34, Spring 1988.
1. In writing this paper I have benefited from discussions with Werner Bonefeld, Robert Boyer, Josef Esser, Joachim Hirsch, Hans Kastendiek, and Hugh Ward. Naturally I alone am responsible for the final arguments.
2. Strictly speaking this should be termed the 'Parisian regulation school': a second, *grenoblois* school is associated with G. Destanne de Bernis (1977) and a third 'regulation' approach with the PCF's state monopoly capitalism analyses of overaccumulation and devalorisation most consistently presented by Boccara (1976).
3. Likewise Bonefeld errs in arguing that the notion of 'apparatus' implies 'a degree of planned interference from "above" which dominates the course of struggle' (above, p. 47); and also implies 'the domination of the state over social relations, which is enforced by the successful homogenisation of the apparatuses and thus their functionality' (above, p. 47). Although the Second International usage of apparatus does treat the state apparatus as an autonomous origin of power, subsequent use of the term (especially in the Gramscian tradition) denies the autonomy of state power and treats the state apparatus as the material condensation and centralisation of power relations. For further discussion, see Balibar (1982).

REFERENCES

Aglietta, M. (1979), *A Theory of Capitalist Regulation: the US Experience* (London: New Left Books).

Aglietta, M. (1982a), 'Avant-propos à la deuxième édition', *Régulation et crises du capitalisme: l'expérience des Etats Unis* (Paris: Calmann-Levy).

Aglietta, M. (1982b), 'Capitalism in the Eighties', *New Left Review*, 136, pp. 25–35.

Andre, C. and R. Delorme (1982), *L'Etat et l'économie* (Paris: Seuil).

Balibar, E. (1982), 'Appareil', in G. Labica (ed.), *Dictionnaire critique du marxisme* (Paris: Presses universitaires de France).

Beaud, M. (1987), *Le système national mondial hiérarchisé* (Paris: La Découverte).

de Bernis, G. Destanne (1977), 'Régulation ou équilibre dans l'analyse économique', in Lichnerowicz *et al.* (eds), *L'Idée de régulation dans les sciences* (Paris: Maloine-Douin).

Boccara, P. (1976), *Traité d'économie politique: le capitalisme monopoliste d'état* (Paris: Editions sociales).

Bonefeld, W. (1987), see Chapter 3 in this volume, 'Reformulation of State Theory'.

Boyer, R. (1979), 'Wage Formation in Historical Perspective: the French Experience', *Cambridge Journal of Economics*, Vol. 3.

Boyer, R. (1986a), *La Théorie de la Régulation: une analyse critique* (Paris: La Découverte).

Boyer, R. (ed.) (1986b), *Capitalismes fin de siècle* (Paris: Presses Universitaires de France) pp. 167–202.

Boyer, R. (1987), 'The Eighties: the Search for Alternatives to Fordism', paper for the panel on 'Neo-Fordist Accumulation Regimes and the Regulation Model?' (Washington DC).

CEPREMAP/CORDES (1977), *Approches de l'inflation: L'Example français, rapport au CORDES* (J.P. Benassy *et al.*), CEPREMAP (Paris), Mimeo.

Davis, M. (1986), *Prisoners of the American Dream* (London: Verso).

Gordon, D. (1980), 'Stages of Accumulation and Long Economic Cycles', in T.K. Hopkins and I. Wallerstein (eds), *Processes of the World System* (London: Sage) pp. 9–45.

Gramsci, A. (1971), *Selections from the Prison Notebooks* (London: Lawrence & Wishart).

Haggard, S. and B.A. Simmons (1987), 'Theories of International Regimes', *International Organization*, Vol. 41 (1987), pp. 491–517.

Hirsch, J. (1980), *Der Sicherheitsstaat* (Hamburg: EVA).

Hirsch, J. (1983), 'Fordist Security State and New Social Movements', *Kapitalistate* 10/11, pp. 75–88.

Hirsch, J. (1984), 'Notes towards a Reformulation of State Theory', in S. Haenninen and L. Paldan (eds), *Rethinking Marx* (Berlin: Argument Verlag) pp. 155–60.

Hirsch, J. and R. Roth (1986), *Das neue Gesicht des Kapitalismus* (Hamburg: VSA Verlag).

Holloway, J. (1987), 'The Red Rose of Nissan', *Capital & Class* 32, pp. 142–65.

Jessop, B. (1982), *The Capitalist State* (Oxford: Martin Robertson).

Jessop, B. (1983), 'Accumulation Strategies, State Forms, and Hegemonic Projects', *Kapitalistate* 10/11, pp. 89–112.

Jessop, B. (1984), 'Business Organizations and the Rule of Capital', *West European Politics*, Vol. 10, pp. 139–62.

Jessop, B. (1986), 'Der Wohlfahrsstaat im Uebergang vom Fordismus zum Postfordismus', *Prokla* 65, pp. 4–33.

Jessop, B. (1988a), 'Post-Fordismus, Massenintegration, und der Staat: eine Kritik zum Joachim Hirsch', *Das Argument* (forthcoming).

Jessop, B. (1988b), 'Neo-Conservative Regimes and the Transition to Post-Fordism: the cases of Great Britain and West Germany', in M. Gottdiener (ed.), *Modern Capitalism and Spatial Development: Accumulation, Regulation and Crisis Theory* (New York: St Martin's).

Krasner, S.D. (ed.) (1983), *International Regimes* (Ithaca: Cornell University Press).

Leborgne, D. and A. Lipietz (1987), 'New Technologies, New Modes of Regulation: Some Spatial Implications', *Couverture Orange: CEPREMAP* (Paris), no. 8726.

Lipietz, A. (1982), 'Imperialism or the Beast of the Apocalypse', *Capital & Class* 22, pp. 81–110.

Lipietz, A. (1985a), 'Akkumulation, Krisen und Auswege aus der Krise: Einige methodische Ueberlegungen zum Begriff "Regulation"', *Prokla* 58, pp. 109–37.

Lipietz, A. (1985b), 'Le national et le régional: quelle autonomie face à la crise capitaliste mondiale?' *Couverture Orange CEPREMAP*, no. 8521.

Lipietz, A. (1986a), 'Behind the Crisis: the Exhaustion of a Regime of

Accumulation. A "Regulation School" Perspective on some French Empirical Works', *Review of Radical Political Economy*.
Lipietz, A. (1986b), *Mirages and Miracles* (London: New Left Books).
Lipietz, A. (1987), 'La Régulation: les mots et les choses. A propos de *La Théorie de la régulation: une analyse critique* de Robert Boyer', mimeo.
Marx, K. (1857), 'Introduction to the Critique of Political Economy', in idem, *Grundrisse: Foundations of the Critique of Political Economy*, trans. M. Nicolaus (Harmondsworth: Penguin, 1973).
Mazier, J. (1982), 'Growth and Crisis — A Marxist Interpretation', in A. Boltho (ed.), *The European Economy: Growth and Crisis* (Oxford University Press) pp. 38–71.
Mazier, J., M. Basle and J.-F. Vidal (1984), *Quand Les Crises Durent . . .* (Paris: Economica).
Mistral, J. (1986), 'Régime international et trajectoires nationales', in R. Boyer (ed.), *Capitalismes fin de siècle* (Paris: Presses universitaires de France) pp. 167–202.
Mjoset, L. (1985), 'Regulation and the Institutionalist Tradition', in L. Mjoset and J. Bohlin, *Introduksjon til Reguleringskolen: tre arbeidsnotater* (Aalborg: Nordisk Sommeruniversitet) pp. 1–101.
Mjoset, L. (1987), 'Nordic Economic Policies in the 1970s and 1980s', *International Organization*, 41, pp. 403–57.
Noël, A. (1987), 'Accumulation, regulation, and social change: an essay on French political economy', *International Organization*, Vol. 41, pp. 303–33.
Ominami, C. (1986), *Le tiers monde dans la crise* (Paris: La Découverte).
Rudel, W. (1981), *Die Entwickelung der Marxistischen Staatstheorie in der Bundesrepublik* (Frankfurt Campos).
de Vroey, M. (1984), 'A Regulation Approach Interpretation of the Contemporary Crisis', *Capital & Class* 23, pp. 45–66.
Wolf, K.D. and M. Zuern (1986), '"International Regimes" und Theorien der Internationalen Politik', *Politische Vierteljahresschrift*, Vol. 27, pp. 201–220.

5 The Great Bear: Post-Fordism and Class Struggle. A Comment on Bonefeld and Jessop*

John Holloway

Werner Bonefeld's article on the 'Reformulation of State Theory' (Chapter 3 in this volume) is important in at least two respects. It gives a comprehensive introduction to, and critique of, the 'Reformulation' theories on the 'Fordist' and 'neo-Fordist' state, and, in doing so, it implicitly develops elements of a theoretical framework for understanding current changes in capitalism and the capitalist state.

Bonefeld's central argument is that in the Reformulation theory, of which Hirsch is the main exponent, 'class struggle is reduced to a "but also position" within history and as such separated from objective laws of development' (above, p. 40), that the role of class struggle, although mentioned, is subordinated to the 'objective laws' of capitalist development. Consequently, by treating the working class 'as merely object of history' (above, p. 64), the theory ultimately promotes the accommodation of working-class struggle to the new face of capitalism.

The relation between class struggle and the 'objective laws of capitalist development' has always been the central issue of Marxist theory. This is especially so at the moment, when it often seems that the objective laws are having it all their own way and that class struggle has been suppressed. In particular, the issue is central to any discussion of regulation theory or any of the other theories of Fordism and post-Fordism which have gained such influence in the last few years.

It is not only the work of Hirsch that can be criticised for subordinating class struggle to the objective laws of capitalist development. On the contrary: the tension between structure and struggle is at least a constant and conscious preoccupation in Hirsch's work: in many other contributions to the discussion on the current changes in capitalism, struggle is totally absent.

This suppression of struggle from the analysis of current changes has very important political and theoretical implications. The capitalist resolution of the crisis involves a rewriting of history: the inevitability of capitalism must be established, the instabilities and struggles of the past and present hidden from sight (see Holloway 1987). Those who claim to be Marxists, it would seem, can play an important part in this purging of the memory. By a strange twist of theory, the 'objective laws of capitalist development', which were previously used to point to the inevitability of capitalist crisis, are now used to support the inevitability of capitalist recovery.

The question of the relation between structure and struggle thus goes far beyond a specific critique of the Reformulation debate: it is the central question in any attempt to understand the current development of capitalism and the perspectives for class struggle. Jessop's reply to Bonefeld in *Capital & Class* 34 (Chapter 4 in this volume) failed to deal with this central point adequately, making, as it did, an extraordinary equation between class struggle and capital strategies. The aim of this paper is not to solve the problem, but to carry forward the discussion opened by Bonefeld by examining some of the theoretical bases of the reformulation debate and their political implications.

STRUCTURE AND STRUGGLE IN THE STATE DERIVATION DEBATE

The central problem of Hirsch's work has always been an unresolved tension between the 'objective laws of capitalist development' and class struggle. This tension is present in all his work, from his contribution to the state derivation debate onwards.

The state derivation debate, which sought to provide a rigorous framework for the analysis of the capitalist state by deriving the form of the state from the nature of capital, has often been accused of adopting a capital-logic or functionalist approach. While it may fairly be said that some contributions to the debate assumed that the development of the state could be deduced from the 'logic of capitalist development', the great merit of Hirsch's article, 'The State Apparatus and Social Reproduction: Elements of a Theory of the Bourgeois State' (1974/1978), was that it sought to break away from the capital-logic approach, while continuing to emphasise the importance of grounding the analysis of the state in the nature of capital. A major theme in Hirsch's article was its argument against functionalism, *against* the functionalism of which Bonefeld accuses him in his discussion of Hirsch's latest work. To this extent, Jessop is correct when he says that 'the West German contributors to the reformulation developed the anti-functionalist approach to the state derivation debate' (above, p. 77).

On closer inspection, however, it can be seen that Hirsch's article was contradictory. This contradiction can be traced in the history of the article. The article was in fact published twice: in a first version published in Braunmühl *et al.* (1973), and a second, revised version published the following year as part of a book by Hirsch (1974) — the version translated into English in Holloway and Picciotto (1978).

In the first version of the article, Hirsch derives the existence of the state from the lack of social cohesion in a commodity-producing society. In a society based on the division of labour and private property, social cohesion is established primarily through the law of value, behind the backs of the producers. As the spread of commodity production destroys the social cohesion of feudalism, it is necessary for value to be complemented by the state as the alien embodiment of the social totality:

> As the individuals 'are neither subsumed under a natural community, nor do they, as conscious members of the community, subordinate the community to themselves, it must confront them, as autonomous subjects, as an equally autonomous, external, fortuitous objective thing. That is precisely the condition for their being able, as autonomous private persons, to exist at the same time in a social connection (Grundrisse, German ed., 909). Just as the connection between their labours presents itself as something alien to the individuals, as a thing (money), so it is necessary that the social generality should take on a particular form. Just as exchange value — embodied in money — produces the social unity of production independently of the will of the individuals, so the state is necessary to guarantee the general conditions of production and reproduction, which lie outside the individual producers.
>
> [Hirsch 1973, pp. 201–02]

After deriving the necessary existence of the state under capitalism in this manner, Hirsch goes on, in an important section of the article, to argue that the development of the state can only be understood in the context of the analysis of capitalist crisis and particularly the mobilisation of the counter-tendencies to the tendency of the rate of profit to fall. This is followed by a discussion of state functions and of the contradictions in the relation between state and capital accumulation. As always with Hirsch, the article is rich in insights, but these need not be discussed here.

In the 1974 article, the derivation of the state is sharply revised. The earlier derivation is implicitly rejected as being functionalist. After again underlining the importance of value as the means by which social cohesion is established in a commodity-producing society, Hirsch now points out that the 'establishment of capitalist social relations is the condition for the full development and generalisation of commodity production' (1974/1978, p. 59), and then he goes on to derive the state form not from commodity production and exchange, but from the nature of capitalist social relations:

> Because the process of social reproduction and the appropriation of the surplus product by the ruling class is mediated through the unimpeded circulation of commodities based on the principle of equal exchange and through the free disposal by the wage labourer of his own labour power and by the capitalist of the surplus value which he has appropriated and accumulated, the abolition of all barriers which stand in the way (i.e. of the direct relations of force between the owners of the means of production and of private relations of dependence and restraints ('feudalism') in the sphere of commodity circulation) is an essential element in the establishment of the capitalist form of society. The manner in which the social bond is established, in which social labour is distributed and the surplus product appropriated necessarily requires the direct producers to be deprived of control over the physical means of force and that the latter be localised in a social instance raised above the economic reproduction process: the creation of formal bourgeois freedom and equality and the establishment of a state monopoly of force.
>
> [1974/1978, p. 61]

The importance of this derivation of the state lay in the fact that it grounded the form of the state not in the necessity of establishing some sort of general interest in an anarchic society (as implied in the 1973 article and in many of the other contributions to the state derivation debate), but in the nature of the social relations of domination in capitalist society. This implies a change in the concept of capital. Capital is understood as a social relation, as a relation of domination between capital and labour, as a class relation. Capital is not the economic which determines the political, but the economic and the political are (superficial) forms of a historically specific form of class domination (see Holloway and Picciotto 1978; Clarke 1988). Capital is not external to class struggle, but is the historical form assumed by class struggle. This derivation of the state opened the way to an understanding of the state as a particular form of the capital relation, understood as a relation of class struggle. From this view of capital, it followed that the analysis of the development of the state could not simply be 'a question of the logical deduction of abstract laws but of the conceptually informed understanding of an historical process' (Hirsch 1974/1978, p. 82): the new derivation provided the basis for a historical non-functionalist analysis of the state (see Holloway and Picciotto 1978 for a fuller discussion).[1]

The problem is that Hirsch never fully followed through the implications of this derivation of the state. The 1974 version of his article revised the most functionalist parts of his earlier argument, and emphasised at several points the importance of historical analysis, but most of the analysis of the relation between state and crisis and much of the analysis of state functions remained unchanged. The result was a highly contradictory article, in which the importance of understanding the state in the context of the concrete development of class struggle is stressed at several points, while class struggle actually plays little or no part in Hirsch's more detailed account of the development of state functions. This contradiction led Sol Picciotto and myself to suggest, in our introduction to the English translation of the state derivation debate, that there was a shift in Hirsch's article 'from arguing that accumulation must be seen as a form-determined and crisis-ridden process of class struggle . . . to suggesting that the relation between accumulation and state activity must be seen as being mediated through class struggle' (Holloway and Picciotto 1978, p. 28). The unresolved tension between structure and struggle, so fully analysed by Bonefeld in relation to the Reformulation literature, was present already in Hirsch's contribution to the state derivation debate.

The tension between structure and struggle can be seen crucially in the analysis of crisis. One of the most important contributions of Hirsch's article was to establish the centrality of crisis as the key to an understanding of the development of the state. A large part of both versions of the article is taken up with the analysis of the tendency of the rate of profit to fall and of crisis as the mobilisation of the counteracting tendencies. Crisis is presented, not as an economic phenomenon but as a total reorganisation of the social conditions of production, a reorganisation which is achieved, if at all, through a process of social struggle in which the state plays an important part, and through which the state develops. Nevertheless, even at the heart of this analysis of crisis as a process of social struggle, the tension between objective laws and subjective struggles reappears:

> the course of capitalist development is not determined mechanically or by some kind of law of nature. *Within the framework* of its general laws, capitalist development is determined rather by the actions of the acting subjects and classes, the resulting concrete conditions of crisis and their political consequences.
>
> [1974/78, 74–75; my emphasis]

The tension is expressed by the phrase 'in the framework', which implies an external relation between the objectivity of the general laws of capitalist development and the subjectivity of class struggle, a relation in which class struggle is clearly subordinate.

CRISIS AND CLASS STRUGGLE

The purpose of analysing the dualism of Hirsch's contribution to the state derivation debate is not to stir up old debates. The point is that the same dualism is at the heart of his fatalistic analysis of the current development. Social struggles are important, but 'it is always capital itself and the structures which it imposes "objectively", behind the backs of the actors, which set the decisive conditions for class struggles and crisis processes' (Hirsch and Roth 1986, p. 37).

Historical development has given a new meaning to the theoretical frameworks of the 1970s. What could previously be seen as productive ambiguities have now become contradictions with reactionary implications. To emphasise the objective laws of capitalist development in the early 1970s was to emphasise the inherently unstable nature of capitalism. In the late 1980s, the appeal to 'the inescapable lines of tendency and direction established by the real world' (Hall 1985, p. 15), has become a reformist argument for adaptation to the inevitable restructuring of capitalism. In a world in which it seems that the objective laws of capitalist development have crushed the subjective struggles of the working class, it seems that the only option open to Marxists is to choose between lamenting the growth of capitalist violence and repression (Hirsch) or to argue for accommodation to the new 'realities' (Hall, Jessop). Though very different in their origins and inspiration, both of these variations on the theme of post-Fordism have the same implications: struggle against laws of capitalist development is hopeless. The world is closed, the future is determined.

To speak of an external relation between the 'objective laws of capitalist development' and class struggle does not make sense. The 'laws of capitalist development' are nothing other than the movement of class struggle. The categories of *Capital* are categories of struggle.

Conflict is at the core of the analysis of *Capital*. It is the form in which one part of the population exploits the other which is the key to the understanding of society (vol. III, p. 791), an antagonistic relation of exploitation and resistance. Marx's materialism is not the lifeless determinism suggested by the unfortunate base-superstructure metaphor in the 1859 Preface: it is conflict, conflict focused on production, which is the core of the patterns of development in any class society. It is not the laws of capitalist development but the forms taken by this conflict under capitalism which are the focus of the analysis in *Capital*.

The categories of *Capital* are categories of antagonism from the very beginning. That is clear from the very first paragraph of *Capital*. In capitalist society, wealth presents itself to us as a vast collection of commodities, and the commodity is in the first place 'a thing outside us'. Right at the outset, we are presented with the most violent antagonism of all: capitalism is the rule of death, of untruth, the denial of our identity. The wealth of society is of course not something outside us: it is the fruit of our work, the only source of its value. In the discussion of value, the violent antagonism of capitalism is developed. Capitalism is the rule of things, things produced by us, but which we neither control nor recognise as ours, things which stand against us: the rule of dead labour over living labour.

The theory of value can be seen as a theory of the struggle between life and death. The form of value converts the expression of our living labour into dead things, into fetishised commodities which confront us as alien, powerful things.

The theme of life and death is central to the whole analysis in *Capital*. Capital is the unstable and transitory domination of death over life, the domination of the commodity which is the dead form of our labour over the living labour which makes us human and distinguishes us from nature. This theme is constantly reflected in Marx's analysis, in the fundamental contrast between variable and constant capital, in the discussion of the labour process and in the discussion of accumulation.

The fundamental critique of bourgeois theory is that it does not see the distinction between life and death,[2] between variable and constant capital. For bourgeois theory, there is no life. For that reason, it cannot understand surplus-value, because the distinction between profit and surplus-value makes sense only in terms of the antagonism between living labour and dead labour. For bourgeois theory, profit is external to us, a thing outside us. The category of surplus-value prises open the appearance of profit, showing that the source of profit is exploitation, that it is the result of a constant struggle against the working class, the struggle of the alarm clock, of the details of the organisation of the workplace, the struggle of time, of the minutes and the seconds. Profit is not something outside us: on the contrary, it exists because we are inside it. Bourgeois theory presents profit as a thing outside us: *Capital* shows us that it is one moment of a relation of domination-and-struggle of which we are part, whether we like it or not.

Working-class struggle is not the explicit object of the analysis in *Capital*, but it is implicit in every category. *Capital* is an analysis of bourgeois society from the perspective of working-class struggle, looking at the world through the eyes of the working class. Precisely for that reason, the working class is not the focus of analysis, but all the time it is present as the implicit subject of the analysis, as constant counterpoint, as threat. The growing power of the working class is a constant sub-theme throughout the pages of *Capital*. The worker begins as a poor individual forced to sell his (the worker is generally assumed in *Capital* to be male) labour power on the market. Once the sale is completed and the poor man follows Moneybags into the factory at the end of Chapter 6, his physiognomy changes and he is transformed from poor man into a worker, from passive victim of misfortune into active producer and protagonist in a relation of exploitation and struggle. In Chapter 10, the worker joins forces with other workers to fight for the reduction of the working day. Later, through the developing forms of cooperation, a qualitatively different relation develops between the workers, as parts of the collective worker. Through the analysis of circulation, the working class spreads outwards from the factory to the whole of society. Never the explicit focus of the analysis, the development of the working class and of working-class struggle is an inherent part of the development of the analysis of capital. The analysis of capital cannot be separated from the analysis of class struggle, for the simple reason that capital *is* class struggle, a class struggle in which we inescapably participate.

It is the presence of the working class as an antagonistic force inside capital which is the key to understanding the development and the instability of capitalism. All modes of exploitation are unstable, simply because they are based on the domination of the majority of the population by the minority and because the ruling minority is always dependent on the work of the ruled majority, but capitalism possesses a particular instability because of its historically unprecedented greed, its werewolf hunger for the labour of the workers. This greed is expressed in the contradiction of relative surplus-value: to increase surplus-value, capital is obliged to expel living labour from the process of production. But without living labour, without us, capital cannot survive: that is the central contradiction of modern capitalism. It is expressed in economic form in the tendency for the rate of profit to fall, but that is simply an economic manifestation of the basic contradiction: the presence of living labour in capital.

To make a contrast between the laws of capitalist development and class struggle is to fall into precisely the fetishism which is the object of Marx's critique in *Capital*. The laws (or tendencies) of capitalist development are not the framework within which class struggle takes place (as Hirsch says): they simply describe the typical rhythms of struggle which result from the specific historical form of domination and resistance. These rhythms are very important, but they are not external to class struggle, they are rhythms which are expressed through class struggle, rhythms which can be broken or changed. Like the rhythms of the body, they affect the pace of our activity, but they are not external to it.

Crisis, then, is not an external framework imposed on class struggle: it is the crisis of the class relation, the crisis of the rule of capital over labour. Crisis shows the limits of capitalist domination: the established patterns of class relations can no longer contain labour, can no longer suppress life. In crisis, the patterns of rule are torn at the seams: outbursts of future, of possibility, of the Not-Yet appear all over the place. Crisis is the breakdown of domination.

To survive, capital must reimpose its authority and restructure its domination. The world must be sewn up again, the future closed off. But that is far from being an automatic process. There is a tendency in much of the literature on Fordism and post-Fordism to elide crisis-as-breakdown and crisis-as-restructuring, and to assume that the transition from one to another is unproblematic, or can be taken for granted. But this is to forget much of the excitement of recent history. Fear of the future and urgent awareness of the need to reimpose discipline, morality and the right to manage is expressed in all forms of bourgeois culture from the early 1970s. To the extent that capital has managed to reimpose a greater measure of stability, it has been through a hard, and bloody, process of struggle, a struggle that is far from over, as Simon Clarke's article (Chapter 6 in this volume) makes clear. To assume that post-Fordism simply emerges, to consolidate present tendencies into a new pattern of domination, as many of the analyses of Fordism and post-Fordism do, is to take part in the sewing up of the world, the closing of the future which is the essential prerequisite for capitalist rule.

To emphasise the openness of capitalist development, to agree with Bonefeld on the importance of respecting the 'heresy of reality', does not simply mean an empty optimism through thick and thin. The black picture painted by Hirsch of current developments is correct in very many respects. The current changes in capitalist domination are radical and generally very negative: there has been a very severe decomposition of the working class internationally. Criticising the fetishisation of current theoretical tendencies should not lead us to deny the importance of the changes taking place. The problem with Hirsch's analysis, and with many other analyses of Fordism and post-Fordism, is not that the picture they paint is inaccurate, but that it is a still-life picture, a dead picture, a picture which seals the appearance of bourgeois society rather than prising it open. The present development is far more contradictory, far more alive than these analyses allow.

NOTES

* This article was published originally in *Capital & Class* 36, Winter 1988.

1. Jessop is quite wrong to suggest that the significance of Hirsch's article lay in opening up space for autonomous political analysis (Above, p. 77). People working in Politics departments (like Jessop, like Hirsch, like myself) have never had the slightest difficulty in finding space for autonomous political analysis. If we feel we're on the left and still want to be 'political scientists', we can always look to Poulantzas to salve our consciences. That, thank goodness, was never Hirsch's contribution. The whole point of the state derivation debate, including Hirsch's article, and the reason why it was

revolutionary in its implications, was precisely the opposite: to say that the development of the state cannot be analysed in autonomy from the analysis of capital. This point is stressed repeatedly in Hirsch's article. It is precisely for this reason that much of Hirsch's article is taken up with a discussion of crisis.

2. There is no continuity between Marxism and bourgeois theory. Bourgeois theory, by definition, assumes the continued existence of bourgeois society: it can conceive of no other future. Its categories are categories of predetermination, categories of death. Marxism, on the other hand, is based on the transitory nature of capitalist society. Its categories have no meaning at all unless the future is seen as being open, unless the transition to a different form of society is assumed to be the central problem. Too often, the aim of Marxist state theory has been to provide an alternative political science, alternative answers to the questions posed by bourgeois theory. But that cannot be: the result is a confusing and reactionary mish-mash of categories. If this sort of state theory is supposed to be Marxist, then all one can do is quote Negri: 'It's obvious that with such people we are talking about different things — it is as if we were both talking of the Great Bear, but for them it means some distant constellation of stars, while for us it means the present reality of a ferocious animal' (Negri 1978/79, p. 116).

REFERENCES

Bonefeld, W. (1987), see Chapter 3 in this volume, 'Reformulation of State Theory'.

Braunmühl, C., *et al.* (1973), *Probleme einer materialistischen Staatstheorie* (Frankfurt/Main: Suhrkamp).

Clarke, S. (1988), *Keynesianism, Monetarism and the Crisis of the State* (Aldershot: Edward Elger).

Hall, S. (1985), 'Realignment for What?', *Marxism Today*, December.

Hirsch, J. (1973), 'Elemente einer materialistischen Staatstheorie', in Braunmühl *et al.*

Hirsch, J. (1974/78), 'The State Apparatus and Social Reproduction: Elements of a Theory of the Bourgeois State', in Holloway and Picciotto (1978).

Hirsch, J. and R. Roth (1986), *Das neue Gesicht des Kapitalismus* (Hamburg: VSA).

Holloway, J. (1987), 'The Red Rose of Nissan', *Capital & Class* 32.

Holloway, J. and S. Picciotto (eds) (1978), *State and Capital* (London: Edward Arnold).

Jessop, B. (1988), see Chapter 4 in this volume, 'Regulation Theory, Post-Fordism and the State'.

Marx, K. (1974), *Grundrisse der Kritik der politischen Ökonomie* (Berlin (E): Dietz Verlag).

Marx, K. (1965/71), *Capital* (Moscow: Progress Publishers).

Negri, T. (1978/79), 'Capitalist Domination and Working Class Sabotage', in CSE/Red Notes, *Working Class Autonomy and the Crisis* (London).

6 Overaccumulation, Class Struggle and the Regulation Approach*

Simon Clarke

THE LIMITS OF KEYNESIANISM

The crash of 1987, with its ominous parallels with that of 1929, led commentators to dust off their history books. Nevertheless comparisons were made only to insist that there were no parallels to be drawn. Bourgeois commentators reassured us that the crash was merely an adjustment of overheated stockmarkets. The Left similarly dissociated the crash from conditions in the real economy, the crash indicating the parasitic and speculative character of financial markets. But can the parallels be dismissed so easily?[1]

For Marxists a speculative boom is not simply the result of the 'animal spirits' of investors, but is rather a symptom of the overaccumulation and uneven development of capital, as the associated expansion of credit increasingly spills over into unproductive and speculative channels. The consequent crash is correspondingly a symptom of a deeper crisis of overaccumulation. Nevertheless, although the crash of 1987 bears comparison with earlier crashes, it does not necessarily follow that the outcome of this crisis will match that of previous crises. Although there are some striking parallels between 1987 and 1929, there are also very considerable differences.[2] The crucial question that any diagnosis of the current crisis must confront is whether these differences are of a fundamental significance. Can the modes of regulation of contemporary capitalism succeed in overcoming the contradictions inherent in the accumulation of capital, to secure a renewal of accumulation without the collapse into depression, and, more ominous, the formation of blocks, and even inter-imperialist war?

The idea that capitalism has developed the means of resolving crises of overaccumulation without plunging the world economy into deep depression is, of course, the mark of Keynesian analyses. For Keynesians fiscal and monetary expansion provides the growing demand that will absorb the products of surplus capital. However, Keynesianism was discredited by the experience of the late 1960s and early 1970s, in which expansionary policies stimulated escalating inflation alongside a squeeze on profits, the collapse of investment, and rising unemployment. This experience led to the distinction between 'Keynesian unemployment', which was the result of a generalised deficiency of demand, and which could be remedied by expansionary macroeconomic policies, and 'classical unemployment', which was the result of a structural imbalance between the various branches of production, caused by price and wage rigidities imposed by monopolies, state intervention and trades unions. For the monetarists of the New Right, Keynesian policies exaggerated such structural imbalances as credit expansion sustained unprofitable producers while inflation increased uncertainty and discouraged productive investment. Price stability, a restrictive monetary policy, and the removal of barriers to competition in labour, product and financial markets would restore the conditions under which the market could do its work in rectifying such structural imbalances, as capital and labour-power were reallocated among the various branches of production in accordance with the equalisation of the rate of profit and of wage rates. The recessions of 1974–75 and 1979–82 were the result of the shake-out required to achieve such a rectification, as surplus capacity, which had been sustained by inflationary credit expansion and government subsidies, was liquidated to prepare the way for the renewed accumulation that drove forward the boom of the 1980s.

The crash of 1987 revealed the limits of the analysis of the New Right. Far from eliminating the tendencies of the overaccumulation and uneven development of capital by reimposing the rule of money and the market, liberalisation stimulated such tendencies to an unprecedented degree, accumulation only being sustained by an explosion of domestic and international credit which was extended not to fund productive investment, but to fund private consumption, unproductive expenditure and financial speculation. The crash of 1987 therefore brought the question of state intervention to the fore once more. However, the question was not raised in the Keynesian context, of a deficiency of demand, but in the context of rectification of the structural imbalances of global accumulation. These structural imbalances were generally explained not by the failure of the market, but primarily by the failure of the United States authorities to curb their budget and balance of payments deficits by pursuing appropriately restrictive fiscal policies.

The growing crisis of Keynesianism provoked a crisis on the Left which had associated itself closely, if critically, with social democratic Keynesianism. The dominant diagnosis of the crisis during the 1970s saw the crisis in rather mechanical terms, focusing on the crisis of profitability, which was seen variously as the result of working class militancy, labour shortages, or the tendency of the rate of profit to fall. However, mass unemployment, and the sustained offensive of employers and the state, permitted an intensification of labour and the restoration of profitability, without overcoming the crisis-ridden tendencies of accumulation. It was clear that a more sophisticated analysis of the overaccumulation and uneven development of capital was required. This analysis has been provided over the past decade by the French Regulation School, building on the work of Michel Aglietta.

Aglietta's pioneering book, *A Theory of Capitalist Regulation*, was very much a product of the crisis of Keynesianism in the 1970s. Keynesian macroeconomic policies presumed that the microeconomic problem of the allocation of resources between branches of production would be resolved by the smooth operation of the market. Aglietta abandoned this naive assumption, drawing on various strands of criticism of the market process, from Marxist critiques of the anarchy of the market, through the Durkheimian account of the market as a system of moral regulation, and the American institutionalists, to deny the adequacy of the market as the means of securing the integration of accumulation. Thus sustained accumulation depends on the development of institutional forms which can maintain the proportionality of the 'macrostructure of production and the distribution of total income' (Aglietta, p. 355). The system constituted by such 'modes of regulation' defines a particular 'regime of accumulation'.

Aglietta's central argument was that post-war capitalism has been marked by a very different 'regime of accumulation' from that which had characterised capitalism before 1929, the transition being marked by a shift from a regime of extensive to a regime of intensive accumulation, associated with the development of Fordist methods of production. The different regimes of accumulation define very different modes of integration of capital accumulation, and in particular imply very different forms of overaccumulation and crisis. The crisis of 1929 was essentially a structural crisis of the regime of extensive accumulation, which led to the development of new modes of regulation which laid the foundations for the post-war boom. However, the stability of the regime of intensive accumulation was only provisional, depending primarily on the ability of capital to stave off the tendency for the rate of profit to fall. As this tendency reasserted itself from the late 1960s the modes of regulation of the regime of intensive accumulation began to break down. Thus the crisis of the 1970s marked the structural crisis of the Fordist regime of accumulation, from which may emerge a neo-Fordist or post-Fordist regime. The immediate implication of such an analysis is that the crashes of 1873 and 1929 have no relevance to the understanding of the crash of 1987.

REGIMES OF ACCUMULATION

Aglietta's book is empirically and theoretically very rich, and his analysis complex, at times almost to the point of obscurity and inconsistency. Nevertheless it remains theoretically the most sophisticated formulation of the regulation approach. Subsequent regulationist analyses have tended to use a more or less vulgarised version of Aglietta's model, which was developed primarily in relation to the United States, as an 'ideal type' against which to measure the incomplete development of Fordism in particular countries, against which to measure the depth of the 'crisis of Fordism', and in relation to which to elaborate a variety of comparative and historical typologies of regimes of accumulation and modes of regulation. Despite the fact that such analyses find it difficult to discover any examples of 'Fordism' in its pure form, even in the United States, the regulationists take it for granted that the crisis of the 1920s was a crisis in the regime of extensive accumulation, and that the crisis which has been unfolding since the late 1960s is a 'crisis of Fordism'. Meanwhile, although Aglietta's original analysis remains the foundation of the regulation approach, there has been very little discussion of the coherence and historical relevance of his model. In this article I want to develop a critique of that model.[3]

The starting point of Aglietta's analysis is a critique of the neoclassical conception of the market, a conception shared by many Marxists. For Aglietta the market is not the anonymous mechanism of the hidden hand, but a social institution, whose regulatory function cannot be presupposed. Thus the operation of the market has to be conceived within the framework of a theory of regulation, which establishes the possibility and limits of social and economic reproduction through an analysis of the complex web of historically specific and socially determined modes of regulation which constitute a regime of accumulation.

Within equilibrium theories, both neo-classical and Marxist, the market ensures the proportionality of the various branches of production, and of production and consumption. However, this idealist conception of the market is inadequate primarily because it abstracts from the historical dynamics of accumulation, through which proportionality is constantly disrupted, as capitalists respond to opportunities for surplus profit. Within a particular branch of production new methods of production offer such opportunities. Competition is the social process through which new 'production norms' are then generalised within that branch of production. However, competition cannot so smoothly regulate the relations between branches and departments of production. In particular, opportunities for surplus profit stimulate new investment and so the more rapid accumulation of capital in the branches of production which produce the means of production (Department I). The more rapid growth of Department I leads to a subsequent increase in productive capacity in Department II, which produces means of consumption. Accumulation can only be sustained if a harmonious relationship can be maintained between Departments I and II. However, this relationship is subject to two constraints. On the one hand, consumption has to grow sufficiently rapidly to absorb the growing product of Department II. On the other hand, rising consumption is the result of rising wages, which can only be reconciled with stable profits if productivity rises sufficiently to absorb rising costs. Thus the problem of proportionality focuses on the regulation of the wage relation in its dual aspect, as a cost to capital and as the source of purchasing power. There is no a priori reason why the competitive determination of wages and prices should reconcile these two aspects and so permit sustained accumulation. The pivot of a regime of accumulation is accordingly the modes of regulation of the norms of production and consumption.

For Aglietta the regime of extensive accumulation was based on competitive regulation, and the barrier to sustained accumulation was primarily the limited consumption power of the mass of the population, which was the result of competitive wage regulation and of the limited commodification of the wage. Nevertheless accumulation was possible on an extensive basis, because there was only a slow growth of productivity. The competitive mode of regulation underlay the typical investment cycle of the regime of extensive accumulation. The discovery of new products or of new methods of production led to a rapid growth in the production of the requisite means of production, without an immediate increase in the production of means of consumption, stimulating a boom. However, the boom did not lead to a significant rise in real wages, so the market was unable to absorb the increased mass of means of consumption as the new capacity came into production. The barrier of the limited market appeared to individual capitals in the form of increased competitive pressure and the accumulation of unsold stocks, resulting in competitive wage and price cutting and widespread bankruptcy, driving the economy into a cumulative downward spiral. The resulting crises put considerable strain on the financial system, leading to waves of bank failures, the crisis being resolved only by falling prices, the devaluation of capital, and the destruction of productive capacity until eventually the proportionality of Departments I and II was restored. In the face of such a crisis the limited commodification of working class consumption severely limited the possibility of Keynesian remedies, and the dominance of commodity money limited the possibility of relieving the pressure by credit expansion. The cyclical form of accumulation was further exaggerated by the tendency for real wages to move contracyclically, the lag of money wages behind prices as the boom gathered momentum stimulating the more rapid accumulation of capital, but weakening the conditions for its realisation.

The extensive regime of accumulation reached its limits with the transition from the production of absolute to relative surplus value, associated with the development of Taylorist and then Fordist methods of production. This led to a more rapid growth in Department I, associated with the increasing organic composition of capital, but was accompanied by the even more rapid growth of productivity in Department II. The cyclical dislocation of the relations between the two Departments, which marked the regime of extensive accumulation, now became a structural feature of the new form of accumulation. This dislocation underlay the crisis of 1929, which marked the breakdown of the regime of extensive accumulation.

The regime of intensive accumulation emerged in the wake of the crisis of 1929 through the development of new modes of regulation appropriate to the new forms of mass production and accumulation based on the production of relative surplus value. At the heart of the regime of intensive accumulation lay a new mode of regulation of the wage relation which integrated the wage relation into the regulation of accumulation. This was achieved by the development of 'Fordist' modes of regulation through which rising wages and social expenditure both reconciled workers to the intensification of labour associated with Fordist methods of production and provided the rising mass consumption which absorbed the growing product of Department II. The intensive regime of accumulation does not overcome the tendency to the uneven development of the major branches of production. Indeed the tendency is now internalised, deriving not from the anarchy of the market but from the revolutionising of methods of production which underlies the production of relative surplus value, resulting in the overaccumulation of capital in Department I. However, monopolisation makes it possible for capitals to anticipate the ensuing devaluation of capital and destruction of productive capacity in the form of accelerated depreciation, which is absorbed in their selling prices and accommodated by the inflationary expansion of credit, so that overaccumulation leads to creeping inflation rather than to the investment cycle of the extensive regime of accumulation.

For Aglietta the intensive regime of accumulation defines new modes of regulation and new forms of crisis. Inflation provides the mechanism through which proportionality is maintained, socialising the impact of the devaluation of capital, so protecting individual capitals from the risk of bankruptcy which precipitated crises in the extensive regime of accumulation, but at the cost of depressing the overall rate of profit. However, the depressive impact on the rate of profit is compensated on the one hand by rising productivity and, on the other hand, by the erosion of real wages by rising prices.

The limits of the regime of intensive accumulation are defined by the tendency for the rate of profit to fall. This tendency does not lead to a smooth decline in the rate of profit because it disrupts the proportionality of accumulation embodied in the existing modes of regulation. The failure of productivity to rise sufficiently rapidly to compensate for the rising organic composition of capital leads to an intensification of competition and the more rapid adoption of new methods of production, which intensifies the overaccumulation of capital in Department I, and so the rate of devaluation of fixed capital, which in turn stimulates more rapid inflation. For a while the rate of profit may be maintained as inflation erodes the growth of real wages, but at the cost of provoking a class struggle which undermines the Fordist regulation of the wage relation. As workers manage to secure money wage increases to compensate for inflation and to achieve the rising consumption norm, the rate of profit falls and accumulation slows down. However, despite rising unemployment, accumulation is sustained as demand is maintained by rising welfare benefits. Meanwhile inflation escalates, disrupting economic calculation, and leading to an increasingly unbalanced credit structure which is ever more vulnerable to financial crises, in which credit is subjected to the 'monetary constraint'. In the face of such crises governments cannot stand by, and permit the cumulative decline into depression, but have to act as lenders of last resort, limiting the rise in unemployment by providing credit to stabilise the financial system, so that crises lead not to depression but to stagnation, which is the typical form of crisis of the regime of intensive accumulation.

The limits of Fordist accumulation are set by the limited ability of capital to continue to raise productivity sufficiently rapidly to absorb the costs of the rising consumption norms and of depreciation charges. The expansion of credit may continue to relieve the pressure on profits for a time, but only at the expense of accelerating inflation, a fall in investment, a slowing down in the growth of real wages and rising unemployment. Although the source of the crisis appears at first sight to lie in the growing pressure of wages and taxation on profits, attempts to resolve the crisis of profitability through cuts in wages and public expenditure can at best provide temporary relief, at the cost of further exaggerating the disproportionality of Departments I and II by reducing demand for the means of consumption. The crisis can only be overcome, and accumulation sustained, if capital can find ways of increasing the production of relative surplus value to reconcile the requirements for the production and realisation of surplus value, particularly through the development of neo-Fordist production methods in the public sector, or, as others have suggested, such panaceas as 'flexible specialisation', the Japanisation of industrial relations, the microelectronics revolution, or the segmentation of the working class and the globalisation of production.

Although Aglietta was sceptical of the possibility of a neo-Fordist regime of accumulation, the concept has gained popularity as a theoretical prop to one or another version of the New Realism.[4] According to such interpretations the development of neo-Fordist production methods has changed the form and focus of the class struggle. Traditional forms of working-class organisation and of industrial and political struggle developed in the Fordist age are no longer appropriate to the neo-Fordist era. Correspondingly new forms of organisation and struggle have to be developed which can build on the progressive aspects of neo-Fordism to secure the economic and social advance of the working class. However, while it is important to respond to changes in the forms of capitalist exploitation, and to broaden and deepen the organisation and struggles of the working class, the underlying belief that neo-Fordism, whatever that may mean, provides the basis of a new regime of accumulation, and so of an accommodation with capital, is altogether more doubtful.

STRUCTURAL-FUNCTIONALISM AND THE CLASS STRUGGLE

Aglietta did not see the regime of accumulation as a means of overcoming the crisis-ridden tendencies of accumulation, but rather as a set of institutional forms which structured the tendency to overaccumulation and crisis. Thus the stabilisation of capitalism secured by the regime of accumulation was only limited and provisional, the regime defining new forms of class struggle and new mechanisms by which crises would restore the conditions for sustained accumulation by restoring proportionality. Moreover Aglietta emphasised the 'ideal-typical' status of the concept, which is one 'required for the development of a theory of social regulation, and not for a periodisation of concrete history' (Aglietta, p. 71), so that every particular social formation has to be analysed as a combination of the typical forms of the extensive and intensive regimes, although he never addressed the theoretical and methodological problems raised by such an approach (problems which are only too familiar to those who suffered the structuralist debates around the notion of the 'articulation of modes of production').

Although Aglietta's original analysis gave an important role to the class struggle in determining the course of wages, the growth of productivity, and the inflationary expansion of credit, the regulation approach has tended to adopt a structural-functionalist model of successive phases of structural integration and structural disintegration, which has been used as the basis of a periodisation of the long waves of capitalist accumulation. In a phase of structural integration sustained accumulation is possible within the framework of appropriate modes of regulation. As accumulation comes up against the limits of profitability within the existing regime of accumulation capital seeks to develop new forms of production to increase the rate of exploitation. However, these new forms of production undermine the structural integration of the regime of accumulation, leading to a phase of disintegration in which the foundations are gradually laid for a new regime of accumulation.

The proponents of this model, and Lipietz in particular, vehemently deny that it is either voluntarist or functionalist.[5] There is neither a subjective will nor an inevitable logic underlying the emergence of a new regime of accumulation. Thus the phase of disintegration is a phase of class and political struggles which may be long drawn out, involving a lot of trial and error, before, by luck rather than judgement, a stable regime of accumulation emerges.

The charge of structural-functionalism is not so easily dismissed. A structural-functionalist theory defines the conditions for social stability, but it does not necessarily presuppose that stability will be achieved or sustained indefinitely, if the structural conditions are not met or break down. While the institutionalisation of a regime of accumulation may be the purely contingent outcome of the class struggle, it is nevertheless the objective condition for the stabilisation of capitalist class relations, and it is this stability which regulation theory aims to explain. In the relation between structure and struggle it is the class struggle which takes the subordinate role, its significance constrained by the structural imperatives of the regime of accumulation (see Bonefeld, 1987).

This theoretical weakness is already inherent in the regulationist critique of neo-classical conceptions of the market. The regulationists are correct, but hardly original, in noting that the quantitative relations between things are the fetishised forms of social relations between people, so that the market has to be seen as a form of social regulation. The fundamental weakness of the regulation approach is that it does not take this insight far enough.

The crucial question is that of the relationship between these two aspects of commodity relations. For the regulationists it remains the quantitative relations between things which are primary. They criticise the neo-classical answers, but they still ask the same question: how is capitalist reproduction possible? They recognise that economic relationships are socially regulated, but the regulation of social relationships is still subordinate to the functional requirements of the expanded reproduction of capital. Thus the regulation approach stops short at a sociological critique of economics, and fails to develop the Marxist critique of political economy.[6]

The institutional forms identified by the regulationists are of fundamental importance to an understanding of the historical development of the capitalist mode of production. However, these forms are best understood as institutional forms of class relationships, through which the quantitative determination of relations of production and exchange is subordinate to the struggle over the reproduction of capitalist class relations. 'Modes of regulation' are better understood as institutional forms of class struggle, which certainly define the historical character of accumulation, but which do not define qualitatively different 'regimes of accumulation'. A crisis of these modes of regulation is correspondingly to be understood not as a crisis of disproportionality, but as a crisis in the forms of capitalist domination. In order to develop this argument it is necessary to examine more closely both the historical applicability and the theoretical coherence of the theory of regimes of accumulation.

THE CRISIS OF THE REGIME OF EXTENSIVE ACCUMULATION

Aglietta's characterisation of the contradictions inherent in the regime of extensive accumulation is based essentially on the US boom and crash of the 1920s. For Aglietta the crash was the expression of an underconsumption crisis, deriving from a sudden upsurge in the rate of productivity growth in relation to the limited consumption power of the mass of the population, while the severity of the crash and the failure of the authorities to relieve the crisis derived from the dependence of the financial system on gold as the money commodity. Thus the crash expressed a crisis in the regime of intensive accumulation. However, there is little quantitative or qualitative evidence that 1929 marked the transition of one regime to another.[7] In particular the crucial features of the regime of intensive accumulation (the production of relative surplus value, the growth of mass consumption, and the dominance of credit money) were well-established features of accumulation throughout the nineteenth century.

Working-Class Consumption and Extensive Accumulation

The idea that accumulation before the First World War was based on the production of absolute surplus value appears very strange to anyone familiar with the rudiments of the economic history of capitalism. Although the transformation of methods of production in

Department I was very limited before the late nineteenth century, this was certainly not the case in the dominant branches of production, such as agriculture, textiles, metal manufacture, brewing, food processing and the means of transport, which were precisely the branches whose products entered directly or indirectly into working-class consumption. It was the penetration of capital into these branches of production which provided the driving force of the agricultural and industrial revolutions of the eighteenth and nineteenth centuries, and which was inseparably associated with the proletarianisation of the direct producers and the commodification of the wage.[8] Moreover, there is no evidence that the low level of wages was a fundamental barrier to the sustained accumulation of capital on the basis of the production of relative surplus value.

There is no doubt that the basis of working-class consumption in the nineteenth century was more limited than it is today. Real wage rates probably did not increase significantly before the last quarter of the nineteenth century. In the nineteenth century many labourers supplemented their meagre wages with their own subsistence production, and a proportion of the commodities they purchased were the products not of capital, but of petty commodity producers. However, the crucial point at issue is not the general level of wages or of working class consumption, but of the dynamic relationship between production and consumption.

The limited base of working-class consumption corresponded to a limited development of the productive forces. Moreover, the relative stagnation of wage rates by no means implied a slow growth in the market for capitalists producing the means of subsistence. Although wage rates did not rise significantly, the massive sectoral shifts towards higher paid employment provided a rapidly growing market for the means of subsistence. Moreover, the extent of petty commodity production, far from constituting a drag on capitalist accumulation, presented advanced capitals with opportunities to expand the market not at the expense of their fellow capitalists, and so the rate of profit, but at the expense of petty producers, the only barrier to such expansion being the limited development of the means of transport. Thus the penetration of capital into the production of the means of subsistence, at the expense of petty commodity producers, provided both a growing supply of cheap labour-power and a growing market for the products of capital. Although the expansion of the market was indeed predominantly 'extensive' rather than 'intensive', it was by no means the case that the barrier to accumulation was low wages or the limited commodification of working-class consumption, or that periodic crises were crises of underconsumption. Nor was it the case that the dominance of commodity money limited the ability of monetary authorities to stimulate the growth of the market to sustain accumulation and stave off crisis by the expansion of credit.

Gold, Credit Money and Extensive Accumulation

The existence of the gold standard in the 1920s by no means implied the existence of commodity money. Although gold was a commodity which served as world money, it was not a form of commodity money. The money character of gold derived not from its direct convertibility into commodities, on the basis of its own value as a commodity, but from its immediate convertibility into national currencies at fixed exchange rates, a convertibility which was guaranteed politically by the *state*. Thus gold stood in relation to a particular national currency not as commodity money, but as the representative of all other currencies. It was correspondingly not gold which guaranteed the money character of the national currency, but the generalised commitment of national governments to the convertibility of their currencies into gold which guaranteed gold's money character. The gold standard was, from its very beginning, a gold-exchange standard, and gold was correspondingly no less a form of credit money than the national currencies through which alone it could serve as means of international payment.

The gold standard certainly limited the ability of national monetary authorities to expand credit. However, this was not an indication of the primitive development of the credit system, but was imposed politically on bankers and the state as the only guarantee against the temptation of politicians and bankers to stimulate the inflationary overexpansion of credit. The issue of gold convertibility was a deeply political issue, and essentially a class issue, which played a central role in the struggles between capital and the emerging working class over the form of the state. Currency reform was a central plank of the popular radical platform in Britain in the early nineteenth century, and currency reform meant freeing the currency from the gold fetish in order to relieve unemployment and distress by public works and the expansion of credit. The idea of labour money lay at the heart of the programme of the Owenite socialists in Britain, and of the Saint-Simonians and Proudhonists in France (and it was with the critique of such programmes that Marx returned to his economic studies in the *Grundrisse* in 1857). The demand for free banking, and later for bi-metallism, was the clarion call of populism in the United States.

The capitalist class fought hard to resist all these proposals to free the issue of the currency from the constraint of gold convertibility. The universal fear of capitalists was that the unrestricted issue of the currency would stimulate inflationary 'overtrading', which could only be corrected by a financial crisis and a depression. The gold standard, far from representing the persistence of antediluvian forms of money, marked the defeat of British popular radicalism in the first half of the nineteenth century, was only generalised in the wake of the world crisis of 1873, and only finally consolidated with the defeat of populism in the US election of 1896. Similarly the reconstruction of the gold standard after the First World War was again a class issue, as the capitalist class drew the lessons of the revolutionary impact of wartime inflation. The gold standard, far from representing a barrier to accumulation, was a device adopted to embody the political dominance of the money power of capital in the face of popular inflationism.

The gold standard by no means prevented the monetary authorities from pursuing more or less active stabilisation policies, nor from acting as lender of last resort. In the last analysis they could, and regularly did, suspend convertibility to sustain expansionary policies, particularly in wartime and in the peripheral regions. The question of whether the authorities should sustain the overaccumulation of capital by the inflationary expansion of credit, or should contain it by pursuing contractionary policies, even at the cost of a financial crisis and depression, has always been a political issue, the resolution of which expresses not the form of money, or the structure of a regime of accumulation, but the balance of class forces.

The pursuit of restrictive policies in the face of the 1929 crash was correspondingly not dictated by the dominance of commodity money, but was a political decision. The suspension of gold covertibility would certainly have allowed the authorities to pursue expansionary credit policies to alleviate the impact of the crisis. However, continued adherence to the gold standard was by no means irrational from the viewpoint of the state or of the capitalist class, however much damage deflationary policies caused. On the one hand, as happened in the 1930s, there was a real fear that the collapse of the gold standard would lead to competitive devaluation, protectionism and the formation of blocks. On the other hand, the ruling class feared the political consequences of inflationism even more than it feared those of depression, and for good reason. The class struggles unleashed by wartime and post-war inflation had been a major factor in precipitating the rise of revolutionary movements. The attempt of the German government to stave off the crisis of 1921 by inflationary means had led to the demonetisation of credit and the devaluation of capital by inflation even more surely than did the deflationary policies pursued on a world scale after 1929.[9]

FORDISM AND THE REGIME OF INTENSIVE ACCUMULATION

There is no evidence that the crisis of 1929 was a crisis of a regime of extensive accumulation, marking the transition to a new regime of intensive accumulation, because the elements of the intensive regime were in place long before 1929. The production of relative surplus value, rising mass consumption, and credit money all dated back to the eighteenth century. Even the specific institutional forms of 'Fordism' (monopolisation, the rise of mass production, industrial relations, and social reform) had been growing up alongside one another since the 1870s. However, this is not sufficient to discount the regulationist theory. Even if the theory of the extensive regime of accumulation is rejected, the regulationists might reinterpret the entire history of capitalism to 1945 as the prehistory of Fordism. Thus we must turn to the model of Fordism and the regime of intensive accumulation. We might start by asking the simple question, how long was the 'longish period' of Fordism (Lipietz 1984, p. 85)?

How Long did 'Fordism' Last?

The institutionalisation of the 'Fordist regime of accumulation' was associated with the monopolisation of industrial capital; the generalisation of Fordist methods of production; the institutionalisation of a generalised expectation of rising wages in the annual pay round; the institutionalisation of regular increases in welfare expenditure; and the liberalisation of monetary and financial markets, culminating in the adoption of Keynesian macroeconomic policies which set the seal on the regime of accumulation by maintaining full employment which could absorb overaccumulation through inflation.

The post-war boom was not initiated by Fordist modes of regulation. The immediate postwar period of reconstruction was marked not by Fordism, but by austerity, by sharp industrial and political class struggles, and by direct state intervention to establish both a high rate of profit and the proportionality of the various branches of production at the national and international levels. The looming postwar recession was staved off not by rising wages but by the Marshall Plan, rearmament and the Korean War.

It was not until the early 1950s that the elements of Fordism began to be put into place, and not until the early 1960s that the institutionalisation of Fordist modes of regulation could be considered anywhere near complete. On a global scale the key dates might be identified by the 'Americanisation' of European industry under the Marshall Aid programme and the subsequent flood of US direct investment, which generalised Fordist production methods and Americanised industrial relations; the 'Keynesian' impetus of rearmament and the Korean war boom, which established the inflationary environment which institutionalised monopoly pricing and the annual pay round; the restoration of European currency convertibility in 1958, which was the culmination of the dismantling of wartime controls; the endorsement of 'incomes policies' by a majority of OECD countries in 1961, which marked the rejection of deflationary responses to inflation and identified the wage relation as the focus of regulation; and the move to social democratic policies in the mid-1960s, dominated by Johnson's 'Great Society' programme, which institutionalised both expectations of rising social expenditure and inflationism on a global scale. We can perhaps say that the elements of the Fordist regime of accumulation were in place by the early 1960s, although in any particular country they were only imperfectly institutionalised.

If Fordism were more or less institutionalised by the early 1960s, its crisis developed as soon as it was in place. In Britain the failure of Keynesian policies to secure stable full employment growth led to the rise of Keynesian interventionism from 1961. The dash for growth in 1963 soon came up against the balance of payments constraint. Harold Wilson's Fordist hope that Keynesianism plus 'rationalisation' would provide the key to prosperity was soon thwarted by the same constraint. The devaluation of 1967 marked the crisis of Fordism not only in Britain, but also on a global scale, as it precipitated a rush into gold and brought the dollar into the speculative front line. The crisis was similarly expressed in the rapid intensification of the class struggle between 1967 and 1971. In the face of the growing pressure of working class demands accumulation was only sustained by the increasingly inflationary expansion of credit on a global scale, which was maintained as the postwar boom moved into the speculative phase that culminated in the crisis of 1974. The emerging crisis of Keynesianism led to the progressive abandonment of full employment, in favour of price stability, as the primary target of macroeconomic policy, and the corresponding reimposition of the 'monetary constraint' on public expenditure, credit expansion, and wage bargaining from the late 1960s, culminating in the rise of 'monetarism' through the 1970s. If such a thing as the 'Fordist regime of accumulation' ever existed, it was singularly ineffective at securing the 'stabilisation in the allocation of the product between production and consumption over a longish period'.

Fordism and the Postwar Boom

The regulation approach not only overestimates the stability and duration of 'Fordist' modes of regulation, it also overestimates the contribution of Fordism to the postwar boom even in its heyday, and so the extent to which Fordism can be considered a systematic 'regime of accumulation'. The emphases of its interpretation of the postwar period are, to say the least, very selective.

While there is no doubt that rising wages helped to sustain accumulation in the postwar period by providing a growing market for the products of capital, it is important not to overestimate the impact of mass consumption. The bulk of wages continued to be spent on food, clothing, fuel and housing. The consumption of the rapidly growing middle class, and increasingly sophisticated military expenditure, were more significant for the ultimate absorption of the product of the most dynamic branches of production than the consumption of the direct producers. While unproductive social expenditure and rapid depreciation absorbed surplus capital, there is no doubt that military expenditure, consumer credit, and unproductive capitalist expenditure were at least as significant in this respect.[10] While rapid productivity increases maintained profitability in the face of the growing overaccumulation of capital, rising wages and escalating unproductive expenditure, productivity increases in manufacturing were no more spectacular than in other branches of production, and only a part of manufacturing can be characterised as Fordist.[11] Indeed productivity rose more rapidly in agriculture and parts of transport and distribution than in manufacturing. Moreover, the improving terms of trade of the metropolitan centres of accumulation, based on the massive overaccumulation of capital in primary production between 1951 and the late 1960s, and then during the 1980s, gave profits an added boost.

When it comes to the modes of regulation of the postwar regime of accumulation the regulationists are on even shakier ground. It is simply not the case that wages were regulated in the postwar period according to the regulationist model. Although rising productivity, and the improving terms of trade, certainly made it possible for rising real wages to be reconciled with a relatively stable rate of profit, the postwar settlement was based on a generalised expectation of rising living standards, without regard to constraints of profits or productivity, an expectation that was institutionalised in the annual pay round and the 'going rate', a rate which was demanded by productive and unproductive workers, by private and public sector workers, by workers in manufacturing, services and agriculture. Thus the structure of pay differentials remained remarkably stable, despite the very different rates of growth of productivity (and employment) in different branches of production. Moreover, the evidence for the stability of the rate of growth in money wages, in the face of varying rates of price inflation, which for Aglietta stabilised the macroeconomic relationship between wages and profits, is tenuous to say the least (although stronger for the US, with its tradition of long-term pay bargains, than elsewhere). It was precisely because the system of wage bargaining did not provide any link between wage increases and the rate of growth of productivity or profits, either at the micro or the macro level, that governments turned to 'incomes policies' as profits came under pressure. However, far from confining the rate of growth of wages within the limits of profitability, such policies served only to politicise the wage struggle and intensify class conflict, which in turn played a central role in precipitating the crisis of the Keynesian welfare state.

Collective bargaining, monopolistic pricing policies, and easy credit certainly gave accumulation an inflationary bias and helped to prevent overproduction from leading to price wars, mass bankruptcies and depression. However, it was the inflationary environments of postwar reconstruction and military Keynesianism which permitted the institutionalisation of inflationary pricing policies, rather than the other way round. There is no doubt that rapid depreciation enabled capital more easily to absorb the costs imposed by overaccumulation of capital. However, the condition for such an absorption was not the expansion of credit, but the very high rate of profit, against which depreciation charges were set. Finally, there is no doubt that the overaccumulation of capital was accommodated by the inflationary expansion of credit on a global scale. However, Aglietta's identification of inflationary pressures with the financing of depreciation is questionable, since depreciation charges are only one element of the pressure of profitability, and investment finance only a small component of the demand for credit. Thus the inflationary expansion of credit was not inherent in the forms of investment financing and monopoly pricing of the Fordist regime of accumulation, but was rather the result of the adoption of Keynesian expansionary policies on a global scale.

These observations should be sufficient to cast doubt on Aglietta's characterisation of the postwar regime of accumulation. The driving force of accumulation was not mass consumption, but profits. The dynamism of the boom derived from the very high profits of the immediate postwar era. The massive increase in the product of manufacturing industry was absorbed more by unproductive expenditure and the growing middle class, associated with monopolisation, bureaucratisation and militarisation, than by rising mass consumption. The uneven development of the branches of production was countered by direct state intervention and accommodated by the rapid growth of international credit. The growing overaccumulation of capital was absorbed initially by the very high rate of profit, and by the intensified exploitation of the mass of the population in the peripheral regions, and subsequently by inflation and a rising savings ratio which sustained a massive expansion of credit. Far from adjusting the rate of growth of wages to the rate of growth of 'productivity', the system of industrial relations enabled workers to maintain their real wages without regard to productivity growth, and so only intensified the pressure on profits. The postwar boom was certainly different from previous booms, but the qualitative difference lay not in the structure of the regime of accumulation, nor in the extent or the forms of overaccumulation, but in the fact that the national and international authorities were willing and able to sustain accumulation, in the face of the growing pressure of overaccumulation, by means of an expansion of credit on a historically unprecedented scale.

When Aglietta published his book in 1976 it was not unreasonable to see the Fordist regime of accumulation as a coherent mode of integration of accumulation, and to see the inflationary crisis as a crisis which would have to be resolved within the confines of the

Fordist regime. However, the crisis of Keynesianism and the rise of monetarism cast doubt on the functionality of inflationism for the sustained accumulation of capital, and correspondingly on the ability of the state-regulated credit system to accommodate the tendency to overaccumulation and crisis. Far from containing the class struggle, expansionary policies intensified the struggle, stimulated the emergence of new forms of struggle, and precipitated a crisis of the state. In retrospect it is clear that Keynesian inflationism was dictated not by the structure of the regime of accumulation, but by the balance of class forces, institutionalised in the systems of industrial relations, electoral politics and the welfare state. The strength of Fordism lay not in its ability to contain the tendency to overaccumulation and crisis, but in its provision of an ideology which held out such a promise, a promise which, however, it was never able to fulfil.

OVERACCUMULATION AND THE REGIME OF ACCUMULATION

The weaknesses of the regulationist model are not simply a matter of detail, but point to fundamental theoretical errors at the heart of the regulationist approach. The source of these errors is the theory of overaccumulation underlying regulation theory.

Although the regulationists have been accused of the heresy of underconsumption (Weeks 1988), this is a misleading characterisation of Aglietta's work. The focus of Aglietta's theory is the tendency to the overaccumulation of capital in Department I. In the extensive regime of accumulation this tendency gives rise to underconsumption crises for the orthodox Keynesian reason that falling prices precipitate a deflationary wage–price spiral. However, in the intensive regime collective bargaining, monopolistic pricing and expansionary credit policies mean that overaccumulation in Department I leads to the devaluation of capital through inflation. The crisis in the intensive regime of accumulation is precipitated not by underconsumption, but by the tendency for the rate of profit to fall. This crisis cannot be resolved by cutting wages, since this would merely precipitate a Keynesian deflationary spiral, so the crisis leads to escalating inflation, which can only be resolved by increasing productivity. Thus the source of crises is the tendency to overaccumulation in Department I, while the barrier to their resolution is provided by a Keynesian analysis of the dynamic relationship betwen production and realisation. Thus Aglietta's theory is essentially a theory of disproportionality. Nevertheless, underlying this theory is the Keynesian belief, shared by underconsumptionism, that the driving force of, and limit to, accumulation is the growth of the market. It is this belief that underpins Aglietta's analysis of the possibility and limits of the stabilisation of the regime of accumulation.

Although the tendency to the overaccumulation of capital in Department I lies at the heart of Aglietta's theory, his analysis of this tendency is surprisingly undeveloped. He introduces the tendency with the vague assertion that 'the motive impulses in the transformation of the forces of production, in effect, derive from Department I', adding that 'the increase in the organic composition of capital inscribes this tendency into the structure of social capital' (p. 56). Although he does not explicitly develop the analysis further, it seems that the underlying idea is that overaccumulation is the result of the surplus profits in Department I which are available as a result either of the invention of new machines or as a result of increased demand resulting from the rising organic composition of capital. These surplus profits fuel the animal spirits of capitalists in Department I, their 'euphoria' (p. 358) sustaining their overinvestment even when overproduction appears, as they dispose of their machines on credit. Thus the source of overaccumulation is the prospect of surplus profits provided by the exploitation of temporary market opportunities, and the explanation is Keynesian, overaccumulation deriving from the subjective irrationality of entrepreneurial expectations. Accordingly the tendency to overaccumulation can be eliminated in the regime of intensive accumulation in which the regulation of production and consumption norms maintains the structural relations of proportionality between the main departments, while cyclical disproportionalities are accommodated through credit expansion.

Although this sort of theory of overaccumulation is common within Marxism, and the anarchy of the market certainly provides a possible source of overaccumulation and crisis, a Marxist theory must seek to locate the contradictions of capitalism not in the subjective irrationality of capitalists, but in the objective features of the capitalist mode of production. Aglietta fails to do this because he does not take his critique of neo-classical conceptions of the market far enough, exploring only the relations between the major departments of production, without questioning the efficacy of the market in regulating relations within branches of production. Thus Aglietta, like many Marxists, presumes that the market smoothly regulates the generalisation of 'production norms' within a particular branch of production, abstracting from the uneven development of the forces of production within branches of production which is the driving force of accumulation, and the source of overaccumulation and crisis. It is not the surplus profits offered by a growing market but competitive pressure, based on the uneven development of the forces of production, which forces individual capitalists to seek constantly to revolutionise the forces of production. However, this competitive pressure only makes itself effective through the overaccumulation of capital and the overproduction of commodities. Thus overaccumulation is not a pathological condition, but is the normal form of capitalist accumulation, and both the origin and the result of the dynamism of the capitalist mode of production.

The introduction of a new method of production offers the innovating capitalist the opportunity of appropriating a surplus profit. In introducing the new method of production the innovating capitalist will seek to expand productive capacity without regard to the limits of the market, in the perfectly rational anticipation of expanding his market at the expense of his competitors. The resulting overproduction of commodities leads to growing pressure on the profitability of the less advanced capitals, which can respond by introducing the new method of production in their turn, which only intensifies the overaccumulation of capital and the overproduction of commodities; by intensifying labour, extending the working day and forcing down wages, which intensifies both the overproduction of commodities and the class struggle; by seeking protection from the state, which politicises capitalist competition; or by going into liquidation, which threatens to precipitate a deflationary spiral.

The tendency to the overaccumulation of capital is not determined by the anarchy of the market, but by the contradictory form of capitalist accumulation, as the pressure of competition leads individual capitals to seek constantly to revolutionise and expand the forces of production without regard to the limits of the market, so that new methods of production are only generalised through the devaluation of capital, the liquidation of productive capacity, the intensification of labour and the 'redundancy' of workers. This is the essential form of accumulation in all branches of production, however large or small, however fast or slowly growing may be the market. However, the tendency to the overaccumulation of capital is likely to be more pronounced in those branches of production in which new methods of production promise substantial surplus profits, in which new productive capacity takes some time to yield an increase in output, and in which the stimulus to overaccumulation is sustained by the rapid growth of the market.[12] Thus the tendency to the overaccumulation of capital appears at the level of the accumulation process as a whole in the form of the uneven development of the various branches of production, being most pronounced in the most dynamic branches.

The fundamental error of Keynesianism, which is carried over into the regulation analysis, is the belief that overaccumulation and underconsumption are two sides of the same coin, so that the expansion of the market will resolve a crisis of overaccumulation. Once the source of overaccumulation is located in the social form of capitalist production, it becomes clear that the expansion of the market relieves the immediate pressure on profits only by reinforcing the stimulus of overaccumulation by sustaining the surplus profits of the more advanced producers and protecting the less advanced from liquidation.

The expansion of credit is no more able to resolve an overaccumulation crisis than is the growth of the market which it stimulates. As the overaccumulation of capital comes up against the barrier of the limited market, the rule of the market is imposed on individual capitals in the form of the 'monetary constraint'. Credit frees capital from this limit, not simply by augmenting the supply of money, but by monetising capital which would otherwise be immobilised in the form of commodity or productive capital. Moreover, credit does not simply redistribute the money available to serve as capital among the capitalist class. The credit-creating powers of the banks enable them to create additional capital, to free accumulation as a whole from the barrier of the market. For Aglietta the possibility of credit expansion makes it possible to stave off an overaccumulation crisis. However, Aglietta's otherwise exemplary analysis of credit, like that of the market, rests on a one-sided analysis of the relationship between credit and overaccumulation.

In the boom credit appears to have the magical power of suspending altogether the barriers to the accumulation of capital, providing finance for new ventures, sustaining unprofitable capitalists and impoverished petty producers through periods of difficulty. The only limit to accumulation appears to be the availability of credit. The growth of credit sustains profits and ameliorates the class struggle, facilitating the smooth liquidation of backward capitals and the generalisation of more advanced methods of production and so providing a favourable environment within which to mobilise the counter-tendencies to the overaccumulation of capital embodied in the tendency to the equalisation of the rate of profit. However, the expansion of credit simultaneously relieves the pressure to achieve such a restructuring by inflating the profits of the more advanced producers, while relieving the less advanced from the pressure of the market, so stimulating the even greater overaccumulation of capital. Thus the expansion of credit, far from accommodating the overaccumulation of capital, tends to intensify it, as it relieves capital from the monetary constraint through which the rule of the market is imposed on individual capitals. While credit expansion may sustain accumulation, and reduce the immediate danger of a deflationary crisis by 'socialising' the costs of the devaluation of capital, it does so only by stimulating the increasingly inflationary overaccumulation of capital with the attendant risks of an even more devastating crisis in the future.

The rapid growth of the market, a high rate of growth of productivity, and the expansion of credit certainly absorb the expanded product, accommodate the devaluation of capital, and sustain the uneven development of accumulation. However, this does not define a virtuous circle of 'balanced growth' described by the regulation theorists because exactly the same factors also stimulate the increased overaccumulation of capital. The regulation of credit accordingly cannot overcome the contradictory form of accumulation, it can merely reinforce one or the other pole of the contradiction. It cannot overcome the tendency to overaccumulation and crisis, it can at best modify the amplitude of the cycle and the form of the crisis.

OVERACCUMULATION CRISES, CLASS STRUGGLE AND THE STATE

While the tendency for accumulation to take the form of overaccumulation and crisis is inherent in the capitalist mode of production, the historical development of this tendency is certainly mediated by the institutional forms of the social relations of capitalist production. However, these institutional forms are not the 'modes of regulation' of a 'regime of accumulation', they are the institutional forms of the class struggle.

The overaccumulation of capital appears to individual capitalists in the form of growing pressure on profitability. The ability of the capitalist to restore profitability is constrained by the competitive pressure from other capitalists for markets and for credit, on the one hand, and by the resistance of the workers to the introduction of new methods of production, the intensification of labour, the lengthening of the working day and the reduction of wages, on the other. Thus the overaccumulation of capital appears in the form of an intensification of the competitive struggle between capitalists and of the industrial struggle between capitalists and the working class. The outcome of these struggles is conditioned by the historically developed institutional forms of competition, of credit, and of industrial relations, behind which stands the institutional form of the state. However, the struggle is not confined within these forms, but is at the same time a struggle to reproduce or transform them, as capitalists and workers confront the existing forms as barriers to their own reproduction. Thus the emergence of a crisis of overaccumulation does not simply lead to the dislocation of the structural integration of the regime of accumulation, more fundamentally it leads to an intensification of the competitive and class struggles which develop in and against the existing institutional forms of capitalist class domination, struggles which necessarily take on a political form and so impose themselves on the state.

The state does not stand above these struggles, as the guarantor of the functional integration of the 'regime of accumulation', for the state is an aspect of the institutional forms of capitalist class relations, and so is itself the object of struggle. Thus the state does not, and cannot, resolve the contradictions of capital, but reproduces them in a political form.[13] Nor can the state be reduced to a superstructural expression of the 'structural forms' of the monetary relation and the wage relation which are constituted in civil society (Aglietta, p. 27), for the state plays a fundamental role in attempting to confine social reproduction within the alienated forms of the wage relation and the monetary relation, by enforcing the laws of capitalist property and contract, by regulating the reproduction of the working class through the system of social administration, and by maintaining the rule of money and the integrity of the currency. This is why the class struggle necessarily takes on a political form, as the struggle over the forms of capitalist domination necessarily becomes a struggle over the form of the state. This is also the ultimate reason why the institutional forms of capitalist social relations are not 'modes of regulation', which institutionalise some kind of social democratic class compromise according to the structural imperatives of a regime of accumulation, but institutional forms of class domination, which express a particular configuration of class struggle. The development of these institutional forms is correspondingly not determined by the functional imperatives of the 'regime of accumulation', but by the development of the social and political struggles unleashed by the contradictory tendencies of capital accumulation.

CLASS STRUGGLE AND THE POSTWAR BOOM

In retrospect it is increasingly clear that rising mass consumption, growing social expenditure, and the inflationary expansion of credit are best seen not as aspects of the regulation of a regime of accumulation, but as related aspects of the institutionalisation of a particular balance of class forces in the postwar period, in which rising wages and rising levels of social expenditure were the price capital paid for the industrial and political integration of the working class in the immediate postwar period. While the rising consumption norm indeed played its part in sustaining the postwar boom, it soon became a barrier to accumulation as the overaccumulation of capital increased the pressure on profits. The inflationary expansion of credit sustained accumulation in the face of such pressure, but inflationism was not an expression of the functional integration of the 'regime of accumulation', but rather a result of the inability of capital to overcome the barrier of rising working-class aspirations institutionalised in the Keynesian welfare state. Nevertheless inflationism unleashed new political forces, which underlay the crisis of Keynesianism and the rise of monetarism, and enabled capital and the state to move on to the offensive and to restruture the relationship between capital, the state and the working class.

The 1970s were indeed marked by 'stagflation'. However, the balance between stagnation and inflation was not determined by the structure of the 'regime of accumulation', but primarily by the balance of class forces, domestically and on the world scale. Meanwhile rising unemployment, and the increasingly aggressive stance of employers and the state as profits and public finances came under pressure, eroded the strength of the working class, and escalating inflation mobilised new political forces which endorsed restrictive anti-inflationary policies and the growing offensive against the organised working class.

The past decade has not so much seen a restructuring of the regime of accumulation, based on the development of neo-Fordist forms of production, as a sustained offensive against the working class, aimed primarily at the destruction of the institutional forms of the Keynesian welfare state which underlay the ability of the organised working class to realise a consumption norm based on a generalised expectation of rising living standards. However, the assault on the working class has not taken the form of a generalised offensive against the working class as a whole so much as a restructuring of the institutional forms of the state and the system of industrial relations on the basis of a fragmentation of the working class, in the attempt to confine the aspirations of the working class within the limits of capital by confining wages and social expenditure within the limits of profitability. While Keynesianism was the ideological expression of the attempt of capital and the state to respond to the generalised aspirations of the working class in the postwar boom, neo-liberalism is the ideological expression of the subordination of working-class aspirations to the valorisation of capital.

The political stability of monetarism, no less than that of Keynesianism, has depended on the sustained, if uneven, accumulation of capital on a world scale which have enabled the state to isolate and fragment working-class resistance, while capital has been able to concede a steady rise in wages to sections of the working class. However, the relative industrial peace and political stability of the mid-1980s does not indicate the stability of a 'neo-Fordist' regime of accumulation. The boom of the 1980s has not been based on the development of new forms of production, still less on restrictive credit policies, but primarily on the intensification of labour, fiscal expansionism and a credit explosion. The devaluation of capital and destruction of productive capacity in the recession of the early 1980s, and the associated offensive against the organised working class, restored profitability, while the massive redistribution of income in favour of the rich, domestically and on a global scale, and the enormous rise in military expenditure, suspended the barrier of the limited market for the more dynamic branches of production.[14] High interest rates accelerated the devaluation of capital and the liquidation of productive capacity in the face of overaccumulation, and have enabled the banks to absorb heavy losses without defaulting, while high unemployment and aggressive management have enabled capital to restore profitability and contain inflationary pressures. However, while restrictive monetary policies have helped to contain inflation, they have by no means contained the tendency to the overaccumulation and uneven development of capital, but have rather served to sustain and intensify overaccumulation by diverting surplus capital into financing the growing mountain of public and consumer debt.

The crash of 1987 has dramatically brought home how precarious are the foundations of the apparent success of monetarism, and how illusory the foundations of the New Realism. Although it is impossible to anticipate the future course of accumulation, it is clear that we are moving back into the crisis phase. The crisis may be acute, as between 1929 and 1932, with a financial crash precipitating a deep depression, or it may be long drawn out, as in the period leading from 1873 to the First World War, with alternating phases of recession, stagflation, and even renewed bursts of accumulation. However, there is no doubt that we are entering a period in which the overaccumulation of capital will lead to an intensification of class struggle and increased domestic and international political tensions. It is primarily the outcome of the resulting struggles, rather than the structure of a particular regime of accumulation, which will determine the forms in which the crisis unfolds.

The possibilities which confront capital in the face of the looming crisis are severely circumscribed. Attempts to resolve the crisis through either inflationary or deflationary means carry enormous risks, either course threatening to destabilise the precarious international financial system and trigger a financial collapse, which would in turn threaten to intensify the class struggle and precipitate a political polarisation. For this reason it is likely that capital will continue to make every effort to sustain the boom by reconciling the expansion of debt with the stability of the financial system through international cooperation, just as it did through the late 1920s. Nevertheless, such cooperation presupposes the willingness of governments to sacrifice immediate national interests in order to sustain accumulation on a global scale, so is constantly threatened by domestic political pressures which make such sacrifices politically unacceptable.

The historical parallels are by no means encouraging, previous phases of global overaccumulation having culminated in the formation of blocks and inter-imperialist war. While such developments are not on the immediate horizon, they could rapidly emerge in the face of a renewed crisis.[15] Moreover, there is a real danger that social democracy, far from resisting such tendencies might play the leading role in developing them. Social imperialism remains an attractive way of salvaging the social democratic project, which has always been premised on sustained domestic accumulation, and so the prosperity of domestic productive capital, to maintain full employment and provide rising wages and social expenditure. While capital has sought to overcome the growing barriers to accumulation through global liberalisation, it has been the Left which has prepared the ground for a social imperialist response to the crisis, confronting the international freemasonry of capital not with a socialist internationalism, but with schemes for the regeneration of the 'national economy', in the naive expectation that a nationalistic confrontation with the global aspirations of capital will acquire a socialist momentum, rather than degenerating into an offensive against the working class as the attempt to regenerate the national economy by fostering the accumulation of domestic productive capital confronts the barrier of working-class aspirations. The anti-imperialism of the Left has similarly had a national rather than a class character, taking the predominant form of anti-Americanism rather than a socialist internationalism.

The incipient tendencies to economic nationalism and inter-imperialist rivalry make it more imperative than ever that socialists should resist the temptations of social imperialism in the name of a socialist internationalism. However, this is easier said than done. If social imperialism is as deeply entrenched as ever, socialist internationalism seems even more utopian today than it did before the First and Second World Wars, when the Second and Third Internationals had some political significance, and maintained a nominal internationalism. Nevertheless, although a call for world revolution is empty utopianism, there are internationalist tendencies in the labour movement, and there are strong internationalist sentiments in the women's movement, the peace movement, the environmental movement, solidarity movements, and the world development movement, which provide a political basis on which to build an internationalist alternative to social imperialism. Even if such an internationalism is not wrapped in the rhetoric of socialism, its political content is far more radical than that of social imperialism, in being based on the subordination of capital not to the illusory community of the nation embodied in the national form of the capitalist state, but to the expression of human needs and aspirations, which alone point the way forward to socialism.

NOTES

* This article was published originally in *Capital & Class* 36, Winter 1988.
1. This article is a substantially revised version of a paper presented to an

International Conference on Regulation Theory in Barcelona in June 1988. It draws heavily on the analysis in my recently published book, *Keynesianism, Monetarism and the Crisis of the State*, in which I develop an analysis of the politics and ideology of money and the state through a historical account of the development of the capitalist state form in relation to the changing forms of class struggle associated with the tendency to overaccumulation and crisis. I began writing the book with a view to providing a historically more adequate typology of regimes of accumulation. However it soon became clear that the concept of the regime of accumulation was inadequate in stressing the systematic, as against the contradictory, integration of accumulation, and in stressing the discontinuities, as against the underlying continuity, of the various phases in the accumulation of capital.

2. In many ways the parallels between the unfolding of the crisis since 1974 and the period following the crash of 1873 are closer than those of the inter-war period.

3. Some commentators have so extended the concept of regulation as to embrace just about anything in the regulation school (see Jessop 1988). The focus of this critique is the theories of intensive and extensive regimes of accumulation, and of Fordism and post-Fordism, which are distinctive of the 'Paris School'. The obscurity and inconsistency of Aglietta's work makes it difficult for the critic to pin down the object of criticism. For alternative critical expositions see especially Driver (1981) and Dumènil and Levy (1988). The leading vulgariser of Aglietta is Lipietz.

4. The concept of neo-Fordism is nebulous, to say the least. It is not clear whether the concept refers to a variant of Fordism, in which case its novelty is dubious, or to a new 'yuppie' regime of accumulation, in which case its empirical relevance is suspect. The elements of neo-Fordism, like those of Fordism, are hardly new. Indeed in a different context it has been argued that production to order, product differentiation, flexible specialisation and fragmented labour markets, which are the mark of neo-Fordism, were precisely the characteristics of British manufacturing, established in the second half of the nineteenth century, and only finally liquidated in the crisis of the early 1980s, which explain the failure of British capital to adopt Fordist methods (Elbaum and Lazonick 1986).

5. Lipietz's aversion to voluntarism is strange. Although the idea of a super-capitalist conspiracy may be far-fetched, the foundations of the postwar boom were laid by very deliberate strategies of postwar reconstruction, which drew heavily on the lessons learned by the failure of the 1920s.

6. Aglietta has gone furthest in moving from Marxism to sociology (Aglietta and Orlean 1982), but the French sociologist Bourdieu is a favourite authority of Lipietz. See also Cartelier and de Vroey (1988).

7. I do not want to go into the quantitative issues here. Data on wages and productivity show marked cyclical variations, so that secular trends are difficult to identify, but there is no evidence that the crisis of the 1920s marks a fundamental break in the trend of these parameters (Brenner 1988; Dumènil and Levy 1988). Nor do I want to get into the question of a supposed transition from competitive to monopoly pricing in this article because it raises so many side issues (see Dumènil and Levy 1988). Monopolisation in its modern form dates back to the 1870s. However it is not so much the

degree of monopoly as the prevalence of cost-plus pricing which is important for Aglietta, in sustaining inflation and limiting competitive price and wage cutting. It is by no means clear that the post-war period has been marked by a fundamental shift from competition to monopoly, nor that the degree of monopoly is a significant factor in the inflationary process, nor that relative prices have become more inflexible.

Similarly I do not intend to explore the issue of the relation between domestic and global accumulation. The regulationists insist on taking the national economy as their focus, and see the international economic and political system as an aggregation of national states and national economies, rather than locating the national economy within the framework of global accumulation and the nation state within the framework of the international state system. While I think that this approach is patently absurd, particularly when trying to understand the global cycles of the 1920s and of the post-war period, there is no inherent reason why the regulationist approach could not be reformulated within a global framework.

8. Indeed the concept of the capitalist mode of production presupposes the constant transformation of methods of production and the production of relative surplus value to provide the driving force of accumulation, see Brenner 1988.

9. Keynes's famous opposition to the restoration of gold convertibility in his *Tract on Monetary Reform* was based not on an opposition to the deflationary bias of the gold standard, but to his fear that the return to gold would give free rein to US inflationism. Similarly European resistance to US inflationism in the late 1960s was a primary factor behind the collapse of the gold-exchange standard which had been resurrected at Bretton Woods.

10. Rapid depreciation was more the result of tax legislation and high profits than a new-found means of absorbing the devaluation of capital consequent on overaccumulation.

11. How large or small a part depends on the precise definition of Fordism. Some definitions which identify Fordism with a very specific form of the labour process would apply only to a few assembly plants. Definitions which identify it simply with the production of relative surplus value would embrace not only large parts of manufacturing, but also agriculture.

12. Although the long gestation period of fixed investment makes branches of production in Department I particularly prone to overaccumulation, this is only one factor in determining the tendency to overaccumulation (and one shared by agriculture). Thus there is no *a priori* reason to single out over-accumulation in Department I.

13. Aglietta would no doubt not disagree with all this — after all he strongly rejects structural-functionalist analyses of the state, insisting that the state is an institutional form of capitalist social relations, and stressing the role of the class struggle in the development of those relations (pp. 26–9). Nevertheless, as noted above, Aglietta's protestations are merely rhetorical, for the fact of the matter is that for the regulationists the outcome of the class struggle, however contingent that outcome might be, is the installation of a regime of accumulation which neutralises the tendency to overaccumulation and crisis for a relatively long period. These two aspects of regulationism can only be reconciled if the stabilisation of accumulation by the 'regime of accumulation' is

seen as the objective foundation of collaborative class relations.
14. This strategy, pursued on a global scale, closely parallels that which underlay the short-lived Brazilian economic miracle from the mid-1960s. The image of the future is not provided by Japan, but by Brazil.
15. The 'internationalisation of capital' need not be a barrier to the formation of blocks in the 1980s, any more than it was at the turn of the century or in the 1930s, for the formation of blocks is not a matter of the ownership of capital, but of relatively closed regional networks of trade and payments, which present barriers to the mobility of the capital, but which are not inconsistent with its internationalisation.

REFERENCES

Aglietta, M. (1979), *A Theory of Capitalist Regulation* (London: New Left Books).

Aglietta, M. and A. Orlean (1982), *La Violence de la Monnaie* (Paris: PUF).

Bonefeld, W. (1987), see Chapter 3 in this volume, 'Reformulation of State Theory'.

Brenner, R. (1988), 'The Regulation Approach to the History of Capitalism', International Conference on Regulation Theory, Barcelona, June 1988.

Cartelier, J. and M. de Vroey (1988), 'L'Approche de la regulation: un nouveau paradigm?', International Conference on Regulation Theory, Barcelona, June 1988.

Clarke, S. (1988), *Keynesianism. Monetarism and the Crisis of the State* (Aldershot: Edward Elgar).

Driver, C. (1981), Review of Aglietta, 1979, *Capital & Class* 15.

Dumènil, G. and D. Levy (1988), 'Theory and Facts', International Conference on Regulation Theory, Barcelona, June 1988.

Elbaum, B. and W. Lazonick (eds) (1986), *The Decline of the British Economy* (Oxford: Clarendon Press).

Jessop, B. (1988), 'Regulation Theory in Retrospect and Prospect', International Conference on Regulation Theory, Barcelona, June 1988, subsequently published in 'Printed-Serie' der Zif-Forschungsgruppe 'Staatsaufgaben' 1, University of Bielefeld, West Germany, Zentrum für interdisziplinäre Forschung, Bielefeld.

Lipietz, A. (1984), 'Imperialism or the Beast of the Apocalypse', *Capital & Class* 22.

Lipietz, A. (1985), *The Enchanted World* (London: Verso).

Lipietz, A. (1987), *Mirages and Miracles* (London: Verso).

Weeks, J. (1988), 'The Contradictions of Capitalist Competition', International Conference on Regulation Theory, Barcelona, June 1988.

7 Learning to Bow: Post-Fordism and Technological Determinism*

Eloína Peláez and John Holloway

After the horrific defeat of the socialist movement in Germany by fascism, Walter Benjamin commented that 'nothing so corrupted the German labour movement as the belief that it was swimming with the current, a current that it located in the dynamic of technological development' (1973, p. 260).

Today once more, the same belief is at work in the labour movement: the belief that there is a strong current flowing, a current so strong that the only option is to swim with it. 'Adapt' we are told, 'adjust to the New Society, adapt to the New Reality!' The cry echoes through the Labour Party, the Communist Party, the trade unions, through workplaces, through universities. The image of the New Society is a mish-mash of elements, from Japanese industrial relations to the power of the banks, from government control of research funding to the electronic tagging of prisoners. But, however it presents itself, we are told: 'this is the New Reality: adapt!' And at the core of this New Reality stands the figure of New Technology, usually identified as the 'microelectronics revolution'. It is the power of the concept of Technology which seals the inescapability of the New Reality.

'POST-FORDISM'

In the past few years, the argument that capitalism is developing into a New Reality has acquired a new theoretical solidity, with the development of the concepts of Fordism and post-Fordism. It is argued that we are in a phase of transition from an 'old order' (Fordism) to a 'new order' (post-Fordism). The 'old order' is generally seen as having been characterised by mass production based on the assembly line principle adopted so successfully by Ford, by rising wages which provide the basis for an articulation of mass consumption and mass production, by large factories, a high degree of state intervention based on Keynesian principles, the development of the welfare state, a central role for the trade unions both in institutionalising regular pay increases through collective bargaining and in the formulation of state policies. The new order, 'post-Fordism' or sometimes 'neo-Fordism', is seen as characterised by new methods of production based on microelectronics, by flexible working practices, a much reduced position in society for trade unions, a new and sharper division of the working class between core and peripheral workers, a greater degree of individualism and social diversity and the dominance of consumption over production.

The political significance of the post-Fordism thesis lies most obviously in the fact that it is frequently used to bolster the argument that it is necessary to 'rethink' the concept of socialism, to abandon many of the traditional conceptions of the labour movement and to develop a strategy for the Left which is appropriate to the 'New Times'. The implications of the argument were most strikingly illustrated in the closing stages and aftermath of the miners' strike. Rats only too eager to desert a ship they thought was sinking, the proponents of the New Times approach were already putting forward the argument, as soon as the impetus of the strike began to weaken, that the strike was anachronistic and macho, the swan song of a dying age.[1] More recently, the idea that we have emerged into a 'new order' which demands a new politics has been proclaimed with smug optimism both by the Communist Party in its draft programme, 'Facing Up to the Future', and by the Labour Party's policy review.

The theory of post-Fordism is presented as a modern, sophisticated theory, in tune with the modern sophistication of *Marxism Today*. A long way removed, it would seem, from the old Stalinist traditions with their odour of economic and technological determinism. The key issue in discussing a 'new order' or a 'new reality' is of course the question of how to understand social change. Within the Marxist tradition, there have long been two currents: the tradition which sees change in terms of class struggle and the tradition which sees social change as the result of economic and technological development. The implications of the two traditions are well known: the one emphasises life, the other kills, often only too literally, as can be seen in the bloody history of Stalinism. The strange thing is that the new Marxism of the New Times, for all its post-Eurocommunist, post-structuralist, post-modernist post-Fordism, is firmly rooted in the economic and technological determinism of the (bad) old times. Underlying the post-Fordist thesis, in nearly all its versions, is the assumption, not that people make their own history through struggle, but that social development is subject to 'inescapable lines of tendency and direction established by the real world', as Stuart Hall puts it (1985, p. 15). This is expressed in the very title of the Communist Party's draft, 'Facing Up to the Future', as Richard Gunn points out:

> But why facing *up*? Facing up to something means acknowledging, reluctantly, an entity that at least in principle already exists . . . Facing *up* to the future implies a predetermined future. *Facing the future* permits the future to be an open space. The title's foreclosure on the future accurately reports a technological determinism which runs through every paragraph of the draft.
>
> [Gunn 1989a, p. 83]

Not only in *Facing Up to the Future*, but in most of the literature on post-Fordism, there is an implicit or explicit technological determinism. Hall's 'inescapable lines of tendency and direction' are assumed to have a technological basis in the microelectronics revolution. This is not a crude technological determinism which argues that every detail is predetermined: on the contrary, the argument is in favour of political intervention. This is a sophisticated, modified determinism, but no less determinist for all that. Hall's phrase expresses the point well: the determinism is one of 'lines of tendency and direction', so there is room for influence; at the end of the day, however, these lines are 'inescapable'. Political intervention is seen as being possible only within a certain framework, within a span of predetermined possibilities. 'Modernisation' is taking place anyway, whether we like it or not: the only question is said to be whether we want it to be a 'reactionary' or a 'democratic' modernisation. As Gunn says: 'The pudding that we have to eat is already cooked, and all that is allowed to us is the choice of sauce' (Gunn 1989a, p. 83).

TECHNOLOGY

Technological determinism embodies both a theory of how society develops and certain assumptions about the nature of technology. Inevitably, discussions about post-Fordism intersect with concepts of technology and technological change, and thus with the debates among those who are involved in research on technological development. Hence the reflections which gave rise to this article: discussions about technology have important political implications; and theories about the general development of society have very practical effects in shaping the framework of those of us who work on specific issues of technological development.

This intersection can be seen particularly clearly in some of the recent discussions about patterns of technological change. It has been argued by a number of authors[2] that the pattern of technological change is closely connected with long waves of economic development, that each new upswing or prolonged period of prosperity is associated with the introduction of a 'new technological system' (Freeman) or a new 'techno-economic paradigm' (Perez). The spread of the new technological system is said to be the stimulus which provides the basis for accelerating accumulation during the upswing. The long period of prosperity comes to an end when the technological trajectory has run its course. The downswing, or period or relative decline is characterised by experimentation in new technologies and the first steps in innovation. The new technology does not really take off, however, until the socio-institutional environment is brought into harmony with the new techno-economic paradigm, until the general organisation of politics and society is reshaped to fit the requirements of the new model of technological development.

In this discussion of technology we can already see some of the ideas put forward by the theorists of post-Fordism and, in more popular form, by the Communist and Labour Parties. Thus, the regulation theorists who first launched the post-Fordism thesis in France argue that a renewed period of capital accumulation depends upon establishing a 'harmonic complementarity' or 'correspondence' between the dominant technology and the social environment. On all sides, there is an assumption that it is both inevitable and desirable that society should adapt to fit the new technology. The main difference between the regulation theorists and Perez is that the explicit focus on technology makes the underlying technological determinism more obvious in the case of Perez. She herself denies that this is a technologically determinist approach since the way in which the socio-institutional environment is adapted to the techno-economic paradigm can take a wide variety of forms, and the precise outcome will depend on social conflict (1985, p. 446). But this is precisely the modified determinism of the post-Fordism approach: we can tinker at the edges, but basically the force of the technological trajectory drives society forward and establishes the limits within which we are free to choose.

Within recent discussions on technology in this country, one of the main criticisms of technological determinism has come from the Edinburgh 'social shaping' approach (MacKenzie and Wajcman 1985; PICT 1988). The argument put forward in this approach is that it is not sustainable to speak of an autonomous technological trajectory, because if we examine technological development we can see that it is shaped at every step by social considerations — considerations of gender, race, class and professional groups. In this sense, focusing discussion of technology on its impact is misplaced: what we need to examine first is the way in which society shapes technology.

This approach potentially opens up a more political understanding of technology. By showing that the course of technology is not pre-determined, that the whole technological process, from invention to implementation, is full of choices, conflicts and negotiations, the approach demystifies technology and does away with the notion that there is an implacable logic of technological development. If technology is socially shaped, it is possible to play an active part in its shaping.

But once the black box of technology has been opened, what are the political implications? The paradox of the approach is that, while it explicitly raises questions about the nature of technology, it leaves implicit both the nature of the society and of our work (as researchers on technology). This has two consequences. On the one hand, society is taken as it presents itself, as a society composed of pressure groups, specialists and professional bodies. The problem with this fragmented view of society is that, although it can throw light on particular aspects of technology, when all the fragments are added together, the result is a picture of society in which there is no room for radical change, in which the continuance of existing social relations is simply assumed. The second consequence is that, since the nature of our work is not made explicit, the fundamental question, for any socialist researcher on technology, namely our relation to the establishment of the 'new order' is not posed. Leaving these fundamental questions unexpressed means in effect swimming with the stream, floating in the current of social development. Determinism, the main object of this approach's attack, thus enters in by the back door and we return to the vision of the future in terms of a span of opportunities.

There are, of course, very material reasons for leaving these basic questions unexpressed. At one level, these have to do with the inherent difficulty of making the connection between the detail of technological research, say on the development of parallel computers, and the general nature of society. At another level, most of this research takes place within universities and the nature of the university imposes sharp constraints on research: time, the pressures of funding and questions of academic status all combine to make it much easier to leave the 'social' part of social shaping undefined. The 'social shaping' is socially shaped. These constraints are real and powerful, yet to leave the constraints unchallenged is the logic of defeatism.

Determinism, gradualism, ultimately and above all: defeatism. The 'Left' has learned to see the future as already existing, a highway where you can drive on the left or the right, but from which it is impossible to deviate. The appeal of the post-Fordism thesis is that it makes defeatism more comfortable.

The defeatism has a material basis. It is clear that capital has inflicted major defeats on the working class internationally over the past 15 years. It appears that capitalism has regained its stability, that there can be no other future, that it is impossible to leave the highway of history.

WHAT IS THE ALTERNATIVE?

It is clearly not enough to criticise the New Reality view for being determinist or defeatist. The crucial point is that the new reality of post-Fordism is fantasy.

Two distinct arguments have been made to criticise the post-Fordism thesis. The first has been to argue that the post-Fordist thesis is empirically false: the changes said to be taking place simply are not happening. In this view, all the elements pointed to by the post-Fordist thesis as being the new emerging trends either do not exist or, if they do exist, are quite untypical of current developments. The proponents of the post-Fordist thesis are said to have fallen prey to the hype of New Right ideology, to have mistaken the desires of the Right for their actual fulfilment in practice. Thus, for example, in the area of changes in the organisation of work and trade union practices, it has been argued that little has changed since the 1970s: the role of trade unions and shop stewards has not diminished, single-union agreements and no-strike agreements are not new, there is little evidence to support the segmentation of the workforce along new core/periphery lines.[3]

Such arguments are important but unsatisfactory. They are important because, by implication at least, they indicate the enormous gap that exists between the projects of capital and their actual implementation in practice, a gap that can be understood only in terms of the continuing strength of labour, despite apparent and real defeats. They are unsatisfactory because the argument that little has changed in the last ten years or so is difficult to reconcile with most people's experience and what we know both of our own working and living conditions and the working and living conditions of others. They are unsatisfactory because to say 'no change' is just as undialectical as to say 'total change': both arguments leave out of consideration the social conflicts (that is, class struggle) through which social change occurs. Although the post-Fordist thesis greatly exaggerates the strength of current trends, these trends are undoubtedly significant: the danger of simply saying that there has been no change is that, in denouncing those who cry wolf, we blind ourselves to the real and threatening movements taking place. The crucial point is not to deny that there are important changes, but to think about how those changes should be understood.

It is the issue of how we understand social change that is central to the other line of criticism.[4] An extraordinary feature of the post-Fordist thesis is that, although it is an argument based on the transition from an old order to a new order, surprisingly little attention is paid to the question of why and how such a change is taking place. In almost all accounts, from the more popular to the more academic, the emphasis is not on change, but on the juxtaposition of two models, the old and the new, and on working out the implications of those models. What appears to be a theory of history is, on closer inspection, a static, structural-functionalist analysis of society. In many of the accounts, the New Times are simply treated as having 'emerged' from the failure of the old system.

Once the focus is shifted from the juxtaposition of two models and crisis is placed at the centre of the analysis, the picture changes completely. What has been seen in the last 15 or 20 years is the crisis of a particular mode of capitalist domination and the struggle by capital to create another. The key element in the post-war mode of domination (Keynesianism, Fordism, call it what you will) was that it was based on the explicit recognition of the power of labour and the attempt to contain that power through the institutionalisation of industrial relations and the state management of (working-class) demand. The basic idea was to harness the power of labour in the hope that it could act as the motor force of capitalist development. Keynes was right in seeing labour as the driving force of capitalism, but over-optimistic in thinking that it could be harnessed, that the demands of the working class could long be reconciled with capitalist accumulation. The crisis of Keynesianism in the mid-1970s marked the failure of that project, the assertion of the power of labour not only within but against capital.

The implications of the breakdown of Keynesianism are enormous. In Keynesianism capital had recognised the power of labour and had tried to contain it through the institutionalisation of class struggle. This attempt failed. The struggle by capital since that time has been to reimpose its domination, to create a new order. It is on the creation of a new order, a new stable base for capital accumulation, that capitalism's survival depends.

Such a stable basis has not (yet) been created. The New Reality is a façade, no more real than the images of yuppidom purveyed by advertisements or television sitcoms. The façade, such as it is, has been constructed on the basis of an explosion of credit during the 1980s more than on any fundamental restructuring of capitalist production relations. The enormous fragility and vulnerability of that façade was indicated by the crash of 1987 and is evidenced by the continuing saga of the international debt crisis. Historical parallels suggest that the creation of a 'new order', a new stable basis for capitalism, may require an absolutely horrific degree of destruction. And yet here are the proponents of the post-Fordist thesis blithely suggesting that the new age is dawning and that we should join in its construction with a will! Such blind optimism is both oppressive and unreal: we live not in a New Order but in the midst of an intense and frightening struggle, of which we are inevitably part.

Technology is part of this struggle. It does not shape society, and it is not shaped by society. 'Shaping' suggests an external relation, whereas the relation between society and technology is not external. As part of society, technology displays all the contradictions of social development. Technological development, like all other aspects of social development, is marked by the always contradictory attempt by capital to harness human creativity. The 'microelectronics revolution' is not an external event which imposes a certain development upon society: at its core is the attempt to programme, to reduce complex social processes to minute rules, to render society computable: the inherent resistance which such a project encounters is expressed as technological crisis, above all as software crisis.[5] The New Technology which appears to provide such a firm basis for the New Order is no less contradictory than the New Order itself, no less a vulnerable, fragile façade, as the now widespread experience of software failure, viruses and sabotage make clear.

The New Order is a New Disorder.

NOTES

* This article was published originally in *Science as Culture* 8, Summer 1990.
1. See, for example Hall 1985; Campbell 1985; Esser 1985; Carter 1986.
2. See, for example, Freeman *et al.* 1982; Perez 1983, 1985; Blackburn *et al.* 1985.
3. See, for example, Batstone 1988; MacInnes 1987; Pollert 1988.
4. See, for example, Holloway 1987a, 1987b, 1988; Bonefeld 1987, 1988; Gunn 1989a, 1989b; Clarke 1988a, 1988b.
5. For a discussion of the software crisis, see Peláez 1988.

REFERENCES

Batstone, E. (1988), *The Reform of Workplace Industrial Relations* (Oxford: Clarendon Press).

Benjamin, W. (1973), 'Theses on the Philosophy of History', in W. Benjamin, *Illuminations* (ed. H. Arendt) (London: Fontana).

Blackburn, P., R. Coombs, K. Green, *Technology, Economic Growth and the Labour Process* (London: Macmillan).

Bonefeld, W. (1987), see Chapter 3 in this volume, 'Reformulation of State Theory'.

Bonefeld, W. (1988), 'Class Struggle and the Permanence of Primitive Accumulation', *Common Sense* 6, Edinburgh.

Campbell, B. (1985), 'Politics, Old and New', *New Statesman*, 8 March.

Carter, P. (1986), *Trade Unions — The New Reality* (London: Communist Party Publications).

Clarke, S. (1988a), *Keynesianism, Monetarism and the Crisis of the State* (Aldershot: Edward Elgar).

Clarke, S. (1988b), see Chapter 5 in this volume, 'Overaccumulation, Class Struggle and the Crisis of the State'.

Communist Party of Great Britain (1988), 'Facing Up to the Future', *Marxism Today*, September.

Esser, J. (1985), 'Britischer Bergarbeiterstreik ohne Perspektive', *Links*, März.

Freeman, C. *et al.* (1982), *Unemployment and Technical Innovation: A Study of Long Waves and Economic Development* (London: Francis Pinter).

Gunn, R. (1989a), 'Facing Up to the Communist Party', *Common Sense* 6, Edinburgh.

Gunn, R. (1989b), 'Marxism and Philosophy', *Capital & Class* 37.
Hall, S. (1985), 'Realignment for What?' *Marxism Today*, December.
Holloway, J. (1987a), 'The Red Rose of Nissan', *Capital & Class* 32.
Holloway, J. (1987b), 'A Note on Fordism and Neo-Fordism', *Common Sense* 1, Edinburgh.
Holloway, J. (1988), see Chapter 6 in this volume, 'The Great Bear: Post-Fordism and Class Struggle'.
MacInnes, J. (1987), *Thatcherism at Work* (Milton Keynes: Open University Press).
MacKenzie, D. and J. Wajcman (1985), *The Social Shaping of Technology* (Milton Keynes: Open University Press).
Miles, I. (1988), 'On Technology', Paper for Edinburgh PICT Network Conference.
PICT Edinburgh (1988), 'The Social Shaping of Technology', revised draft.
Peláez, E. (1988), *A Gift from Pandora's Box: The Software Crisis*, PhD thesis, University of Edinburgh.
Perez, C. (1983), 'Structural Change and Assimilation of New Technologies in the Economic and Social Systems', *Futures*, Vol. 15, 5, October.
Perez, C. (1985), 'Microelectronics, Long Waves and World Structural Change: New Perspectives for Developing Countries', *World Development*, Vol. 13, 3.
Pollert, A. (1988), 'Dismantling Flexibility', *Capital & Class* 34.

8 Polar Bears and Class Struggle: Much Less than a Self-Criticism

Bob Jessop

This paper is intended neither to secure the simple reproduction of old debates on state theory nor even of new debates on post-Fordism: its aim is to expand them.[1] Its starting point is two recent attacks on regulation theory by John Holloway (1988) and Simon Clarke (1988a). Both insist on the primacy of the class struggle in the dynamic of capitalism rather than that of its institutional forms or so-called objective laws. I will not try to defend regulationism by adopting the opposite position but instead will present a third view which is truer to the regulation approach (hereafter RA) as well as to Marx's own analysis. This alternative has obvious implications for research on post-Fordism but, since these have already been noted in my earlier reply to Bonefeld, they will get only brief mention here (see Bonefeld 1987; Jessop 1988).

INTRODUCTION TO THE DEBATE

John Holloway's reply first affirms Bonefeld's dual criticism of recent West German state theory and French regulation theory as follows: (a) they either treat class struggle as constrained and limited by so-called 'objective' laws of capitalist development or else, at best, regard it simply as the channel through which these laws are realised; and (b) they consider the working class as nothing but a passive object of history and thereby encourage workers to accommodate or submit to the new face of capitalism (Holloway 1988). He then adds that much work on Fordism and post-Fordism has rewritten the history of capitalism, affirmed the inevitability of capitalist recovery due to its objective laws, and thereby helped to suppress the class struggle (Holloway 1988). He argues that this errs theoretically since 'the relation between class struggle and "the objective laws of capitalist development" has always been the central issue of Marxist theory' (1988). And it leads to political errors by conspiring in working-class resignation in the face of capital's crisis-induced offensive to restructure the capital relation.

This critique rests on the claim that 'the "laws of capitalist development" are nothing other than the movement of class struggle. The categories of *Capital* are categories of struggle' (Holloway 1988). Indeed Holloway argues that the class struggle is mentioned throughout Marx's masterpiece and is considered from both sides. Thus *Capital* is pervaded by the metaphor of the dominance of the dead over the living ('the most violent antagonism of all') and is also replete with specific references to the presence of the working class as an antagonistic force inside capital (Holloway 1988).

Clarke develops a slightly different line of attack in arguing that the RA treats the structural reproduction requirements of capitalism as primary. The RA, according to his critique, sees the chief function of modes of regulation as securing a proper balance between different departments or branches of production so that the circuit of capital is integrated and stabilised. This does not imply as Clarke is happy to admit, that capitalists can just impose their will. But it does mean that regulation is seen as being targeted on capitalist structures rather than on the changing balance of forces in a struggle for class domination (Clarke 1988a). Clarke counters that modes of regulation should be analysed as the product of capitalist strategies to manage the balance of class forces: their primary purpose is to reproduce class domination rather than secure balanced growth. Given this concern, they can prove as problematic for capital as for the working class (Clarke 1988a, 1988b, *passim*). For example, far from containing the class struggle and stabilising the Fordist regime, Keynesian welfare state policies intensified that struggle, stimulated new forms of struggle, and precipitated a crisis of the state (Clarke 1988b, pp. 77, 79; see 1988a, *passim*).

CAPITAL IS MORE THAN CLASS STRUGGLE

The crux of these criticisms is that the RA errs in separating capital's laws of motion from the class struggle and suggesting that the development and impact of class struggle are confined within limits set by these laws. They counterpose a different premiss: that capital is class struggle (Holloway 1988). I share this premiss but am unconvinced that it is always interpreted correctly. For the moment I will concentrate on how Holloway develops its implications; in a later section I will note some problems with Clarke's account of class struggle.

In tracing the implications of this premiss, Holloway advances two rather different claims: first, 'the economic and the political are (superficial) forms of a historically specific form of class domination'; and, second, 'capital is not external to class struggle, but is the historical form assumed by class struggle' (1988). Despite their apparent similarities, these claims have very different implications. Whereas the former permits us to analyse the dialectical interplay between the form determination of class struggle (especially the 'doubling' of forms of domination into separate economic and political spheres) and its transformation in and through class struggle, the latter reduces capital to the unmediated effect of class struggle and gives the form of that struggle no independent effect. Indeed the second claim seems to suggest that there can be pure exploitation, pure domination, and pure class struggle — pure antagonism with no mediation through social forms, apparatuses, asymmetrically distributed resources, particular techniques of exploitation and domination (see Balibar 1985, p. 512). This would reduce the statement 'capital *is* class struggle' to the tautology: 'class struggle is class struggle'. I cannot believe that this is what Holloway intends to argue.

Holloway might have elided these two claims because he posits a false and biased choice: *either* distinguish structure and struggle and thereby suppress the historical effectivity of the latter *or* reduce capital to the historical form assumed by class struggle and so affirm the primacy of this struggle as the motor of history. This apparent dilemma is false because other options can easily be identified. And it is biased because, in restricting the choice in this way, Holloway clearly invites us, as Marxists, to opt for the second alternative. Indeed, if we take a closer look at Holloway's own arguments, they actually support a third alternative: an account of the forms in which dead labour dominates living labour and their implications for class struggle. In developing this third alternative it should be possible to map some basic ideas common to Bonefeld and Holloway, state reformulation theorists, French regulationists, and myself.

FROM METAPHOR TO METAFORM

Holloway develops his critique of capitalism from the standpoint of the working class: he sees capitalism essentially as 'the rule of death, of untruth, the denial of our identity' (Holloway 1988). These are powerful and evocative metaphors and they clearly invite us to take sides with life, truth, and working-class identity against the dead hand of capital. Moreover, as he notes, they also appear in *Capital*.[2] But, for all his literary skills and his love of metaphor and simile, it was not Marx's intention to give a metaphorical analysis of capitalism from a proletarian viewpoint. Nor was he offering us a metaphysical analysis of the struggle between life and death as reflected in the dynamic of capital accumulation. He was undertaking a critique of political economy on the basis of a scientific analysis of its laws of motion. Holloway begins to recognise this when he treats capitalism as a specific mode of exploitation and domination; and, in this context, finds the 'struggle between life and death' expressed in the law of value.

Yet, faced with the choice between grounding the metaphor of life and death in the actual *forms* of capitalist class domination or merely asserting that capital *is* class struggle, Holloway takes the latter path and thereby loses the chance to explore the dialectic of class struggle. He cannot see how this struggle is inscribed within the forms of the capital relation and how these forms shape the forms and outcome of class struggle. Nor can he show how bourgeois class domination involves much more than capital's ability to impose its will on the working class. Indeed he cannot see that even the capitalist class itself is subordinated to the domination of dead labour over living labour and, to continue the metaphor with Marx, through the impersonal forces of competition, 'one capitalist always kills many' (Marx 1867a, p. 715).[3]

Marx himself did not treat capital's success in its struggle with labour as the ultimate basis for the dominance of the capitalist mode of production (or CMP). Indeed he actually disclaimed the credit for discovering the existence of classes or class struggle as such (phenomena long familiar to bourgeois economists and publicists).[4] He described his own claim to originality as the discovery of the real secret of capitalist production: 'the specific economic form, in which unpaid surplus labour is pumped out of the direct producers' (Marx 1894, p. 791). For this provided the innermost secret, the hidden basis of the entire social structure, the key to deciphering the anatomy of civil society and the form of the state. This specific economic form was surplus value. It is the dominance of the value form (or, better, since it has several different moments, meta-form) in a system of generalised commodity production which determines the conceptual identity of classes, the nature of class relations, the forms of class struggle, and the totalising dynamic of class struggle and competition within the capitalist mode of production. In short, rather than beginning with the class struggle, he showed how the logic of abstract labour was imposed on workers *and capitalists* alike.

Marx argued that the CMP is unique because it is governed by quasi-autonomous forms of social relations and a logic which operates behind the backs of the producers rather than depending on direct and explicit relations of extra-economic coercion and domination. Thus the capital relation is not just one form which class conflict happens to take — as if class struggle exists as such throughout history and merely takes this or that indifferent form. Capital is a particular form of social relations and has an institutional logic and directional dynamic of its own. Once commodity production has been generalised (so that labour-power itself assumes the form of a commodity)[5] and relative surplus-value is the dominant form of surplus-value, capitalist domination is realised through an emergent, impersonal and quasi-natural network of social connections (see Marx 1867, pp. 733, 1024). This network is reproduced through human agents and could never be understood without referring to their actions. But the dynamic of the capital relation is also beyond their control in at least two respects. First, at any given moment, the capital relation pre-exists these actions as their unacknowledged or fetishistically perceived condition of existence and action. And, second, it operates 'behind their backs' in a systematic manner to produce unintended consequences with major implications for accumulation. The form of the capital relation dominates the actions of individuals: it is, as Marx said, *anarchic*.

MARX ON CLASSES AND CLASS STRUGGLE

Holloway notes that the class struggle is often mentioned in Marx's *Capital* but he does not discuss exactly how Marx handles it. A closer examination reveals that class struggle is not the starting point for Marx's critique. In fact Marx could only consider its role in accumulation *after* he had introduced the categories of political economy to define class relations and the interests at stake in class struggle. He first employed the category of class to establish a conceptual identity and only later used it to analyse conflicts between specific forces, whatever their self-identity and forms of organisation: it is never a name given to some pre-given, self-knowing 'class agent' (see Balibar

1985, p. 520; and Rosenthal 1987, p. 29). Class struggle is not the starting point but one of the mediations in and through which capital accumulation is analysed. Thus, if we are to analyse the nature and dynamic of class struggle, we need objective criteria which establish the class-relevance[6] of social antagonisms and struggles whether or not the forces involved are subjectively organised and conducted in terms of class identities and/or interests. These in turn must be derived from the nature of the capital relation and its implications for class antagonisms.

Schematically we can summarise Marx's references to class struggle in *Capital* as follows:[7]

The active subject in Marx's critique is capital viewed as the self-valorisation of value. For value is an 'automatic subject' which becomes active as the 'self-movement' of capital, as it adds surplus-value to itself in its continual, alternating metamorphosis into commodities and money (Marx 1867, p. 255). Thus we can either see capital itself as the subject or else treat it as a 'process without a subject'.[8] Marx himself always stresses that capital is the subject and he sees its independence expressed most adequately in the money form (Marx 1867, p. 255; this view is also powerfully stated in Clarke 1988b).

Marx typically refers to capitalists (individually or as a class) as the personification of capital or the conscious bearers of the self-movement of capital. The objective content of capital's endless and limitless metamorphosis, that is, its self-valorisation, is the capitalist's subjective purpose. But he stresses that 'it is only in so far as the appropriation of ever more wealth in the abstract is the sole driving force behind his operations that he functions as a capitalist, that is as capital personified and endowed with consciousness and will' (Marx 1867, p. 254, see p. 990). It is in this capacity that capitalists seek to increase the surplus-value extracted in the labour process.

When Marx refers to actual capitalists rather than character masks, it is usually in two contexts. Sometimes he refers to them to exemplify general tendencies in the antagonism between capital and labour (for example, reports on over-working in individual factories). And sometimes he discusses competition among individual capitals as the form in and through which the law of value in its capitalist guise is realised. In both cases it would be more accurate to conclude that class antagonism arises because of the inherent qualities of the capital relation than that this relation is antagonistic because of the contingent occurrence of class struggle and/or competition. In the latter regard, Marx clearly argues that the immanent laws of capitalist production assert themselves as the coercive laws of competition and therefore enter into the consciousness of the individual capitalist. He does not derive the immanent laws from the nature of capitalist competition but says that 'a scientific analysis of competition is possible only if we can grasp the inner nature of capital' (Marx 1867, p. 433). Likewise he notes that 'the struggle between the capitalist and the wage-labourer starts with the existence of the capital-relation itself' (Marx 1867, p. 553). He does not write that the capital relation begins with the struggle between capitalists and wage-labourers. And, of course, he concludes that the limit to capital accumulation is capital itself — not the class struggle (Marx 1867).

The *bourgeoisie* is mentioned only in giving capital some historical individuality as a political force in the genesis of capitalism (in the process of primitive accumulation) and/or in conflicts to reproduce the capital relation. References to the bourgeoisie and its various fractions and tendencies are much more common in Marx's political studies and commentaries but these are also frequently presented without any clear account of the mediations involved between function or place in the circuit of capital and the specific stance adopted in political struggle (see Cutler *et al.* 1978).

When Marx mentions the working class, it is not in opposition to capital — he does not juxtapose capital and the working class as though they were two terms external to each other. Instead labour (and thus all the working-class practices tied to the sale, use, and reproduction of wage-labour) is seen as an internal element of the movement of 'capital' (for example, Marx 1867, pp. 718–20). This is clear in his analyses of 'everyday struggles' over the length of the working day; the 'moral and historical elements' in the 'value' of labour-power; or the sources of relative surplus value. In each case he first identifies the *space* for struggle in terms of its underdetermination through value categories and also establishes the stake of this struggle in terms of the antagonistic class identities embedded in the structure of exploitation. In this sense Marx treats both the scope and the interests at stake in struggle over surplus-value as form-determined but he is equally insistent that they are not fully determined at the level of form. He writes, for example, that: 'the working day is . . . capable of being determined, but in and for itself indeterminate'. Or, again, that: 'the nature of commodity exchange itself imposes no limit to the working day, no limit to surplus labour' (Marx 1867, pp. 341, 344). In short, the full determination of value categories in his analysis must await Marx's account of the class struggle.

The form of the 'everyday' struggle between capital and labour within the capital relation is conditioned by the distinctive *commodity* form assumed by labour-power under capitalism. This gives the encounter between capital and labour in the sphere of circulation the form of an antinomy, a clash of right against right. In turn this shapes their class identities and demands. Thus Marx notes that, whereas the capitalist 'takes his stand on the law of commodity-exchange', the worker, just as every other seller, demands the best price for his commodity. Moreover, between equal rights, as Marx notes, force decides (1867, pp. 343–4, see 1069–71).

On the few occasions when Marx refers to the *proletariat*, he oscillates between viewing it as a class and as a mass — seeking both to describe a typical class structure and to show how a proletarian condition is transformed into a *mass* movement (see Balibar 1985, pp. 516–18). In this latter context the proletariat is better understood 'in the great historical sense', that is, as the gradual, spontaneous, historical development of the working-class movement as a whole, including each and every manifestation of its organisation and any and all of the alliances involved in this movement.

These conclusions suggest that the class struggle in capitalist society plays the role it does because that society is organised as it is (see Postone 1988, IX, p. 19). Class conflict is a driving force of capitalist development only because it is structured by, and embedded in, the social forms of the commodity and capital. Class antagonisms exist because capital is an inherently antagonistic relationship of class exploitation and domination; capitalism is not antagonistic because conflicts occur between forces which identify themselves as 'class' forces. The dynamic and totalising character which Holloway attributes to class struggle *as such* actually depends on the *forms* which structure this struggle and determine its directional and dynamising effects 'behind the backs' of active class forces. This means that we cannot take class subjects, subjective class identities, and class-conscious demands as our only reference point in interpreting the significance of class struggles. The most significant subjects, the most important identities, and the most crucial demands need not be expressed in 'class' terms. What is really crucial is their repercussions on the expanded reproduction of capital, on capital's ability to continue its self-valorisation, on the whole complex of conditions necessary for continued accumulation. And this is why we must start out with categories such as commodity, value, money and capital and their articulation before we can even begin to grasp the significance of particular class struggles.

VALUE FORM AND CLASS STRUGGLE

We can explore this point by considering the value form itself in more detail. This comprises various elements organically interlinked as moments in the overall reproduction of the capital relation. In the sphere of circulation, we find the commodity, price and money forms through which the exchange of goods and services is mediated. Capitalist production is organised as a process of valorisation and is subordinated through competitive pressures to the requirements of reduced costs and/or increased productivity. In turn labour power is commodified, subordinated to capitalist control in the labour process, and remunerated and reproduced through the wage form. More generally, the value form is linked to the law of value. This governs the allocation of labour-time among different productive activities according to the fluctuations of market prices around prices of production, which are determined by the socially necessary labour-time embodied in different commodities. In capitalist economies this law is mediated through fluctuations in profits (market price less cost price) and the uncoordinated decisions of competing capitals about the opportunities for profit associated with different patterns of investment and production (see Jessop 1985, pp. 337–8).

Assuming that these different forms are reproduced so that the continuing dominance of the value (meta-)form is secured (which is no mean historical accomplishment and depends on success in the class struggle), they define the *parameters* for capital accumulation and also delimit its possible crisis forms.[9] However, even when this form is dominant, it does not itself fully determine the course of capital accumulation. Indeed, as *formal* moments of the capital relation, value categories are underdetermined. Their full meaning emerges only when more substantive categories are added — categories which can also be analysed at levels of abstraction ranging from the fetishised forms of appearance of the objective categories through to specific modes of calculation and strategic action. Precisely how these forms are overdetermined and acquire a specific content depends on the balance of class forces engaged in economic and economically-relevant struggles within the limits set by the value (meta-)form.

Moreover, it is only in and through class struggle that the various moments of the value (meta-)form itself are reproduced (see Jessop 1985, p. 338). In this context the stake of class struggle is not so much relative (dis)advantage within value parameters as it is the dominance of the value (meta-)form itself. Referring to different stakes of class struggle in this way does not mean that struggles (or, indeed, sites of struggle) are neatly separated in reality into those affecting the value form as such and those whose impact is confined within this form. But there is an important analytical and political distinction to be drawn here. Holloway does not make it. He is thereby led to confuse resistance to specific aspects or consequences of the value (meta-)form with resistance to the capital relation as a whole. And he can also falsely accuse leftist 'political scientists' and regulation theorists alike of conspiring to defeat the working class struggle against capital because they do not share his assessment of the extent of radical resistance to post-Fordist restructuring relative to 'new realist' currents in the labour movement.

Yet it is quite possible to analyse class struggles in and against the value form and/or the fetishised separation between the economic and political spheres. Indeed Clarke has recently stressed the need to struggle 'in and against the institutional forms of the capitalist mode of production' (Clarke 1988b, p. 16; see Holloway 1980). In applying this distinction we would be much better placed to consider just what it means to argue that 'capital *is* class struggle'.

Nonetheless, although class conflict is an essential moment in the expanded reproduction of capitalism, it does not as such create the totality nor does it give rise to its dynamic trajectory (see Postone 1988, IX, p. 19). Indeed, if we focus too much on conflict between class conscious forces, other essential features of the capital relation will be missed. For the conceptual identity of class relations is given by the capital relation itself rather than being constructed by the classes which shape the capital relation. As Postone puts it:

> In addition to class exploitation, capitalist production, according to Marx, is characterised by a peculiar dynamic, rooted in the con-

> stant expansion of value which is a central moment of capital, and by the various inversions of the valorization process outlined above, which . . . become materialized in the concrete form of the industrial labour process. Marx grounds these characteristic features in the value form of wealth and, hence, of the surplus. They cannot be grasped adequately only with reference to the circumstance that the means of production and the products belong to the capitalists and not to the workers. In other words, Marx's conception of the social relations constituted in the sphere of production cannot be understood in terms of class relations of exploitation alone.
>
> [Postone 1988, VII, pp. 27–8]

To argue otherwise would be to reduce Marx's critique of political economy to a sociology of class struggle from the viewpoint of the working class. It is this sort of critique (and not, as Clarke seems to think, the regulation approach) which runs the risk that it 'stop short at a sociological critique of economics and fails to develop the Marxist critique of political economy' (1988a). In its most extreme form this reduction would treat the conscious, wilful conduct of classes acting for themselves in struggle not only as a source of evidence for class exploitation and domination but also as the only explanatory principle for all the phenomena arising from these class relations. I would not want to attribute such views to Holloway or Bonefeld. But it is not enough to repeat that 'capital *is* class struggle' as though the various sites and the forms of struggle, the complex emergent tendencies and counter-tendencies of capital accumulation, the modes of calculation and strategic orientation, and the organisational forms assumed by different forces made no difference to the course and outcome of class struggle. If one accepts that these make a difference, however, then 'capital accumulation is a form-determined outcome of class struggle'. How this form itself is reproduced, whether and in what respects it has extra-economic preconditions, how much scope there is for under- and over-determination would still be unresolved. But at least there would be a basis for debate.

HOLLOWAY AND PICCIOTTO ON FORM AND CONTENT

We can take this debate a little further by considering how Holloway actually develops his thesis that capital is class struggle. He correctly notes that Marx's approach contradicts claims that the historical movement of capital is simply the product of objective laws mediated through class struggle. So far, so good. But then he attributes this latter view to regulation theorists. This is plain wrong. For their approach also denies that there are pre-given, objective laws which are mediated in and through a secondary, subjective class struggle. Instead regulation theorists explore the dialectic of form and content in the capital relation in the same way as Marx before them — thereby attributing effectivity both to class struggles and to the forms which they assume. This is well put by the pioneering regulation theorist, Aglietta, who affirms that the general import (leçon) of historical materialism is 'the development of the forces of production under the effect of the class struggle, and the transformation of the conditions of this struggle and the forms in which it is embodied under the effect of that development' (1979, p. 16).

Holloway's critique of the RA implies that the only way to avoid prioritising objective laws is to assert that 'capital is class struggle'. His own work actually takes a different path, however, which, whether he realises it or not, anticipates RA methods just as much as it follows Marx. Thus he and Picciotto argued that the development of the capitalist state is determined by the dialectic between the enduring economic and political *forms* of class struggle and its changing *content* in both areas. The particularisation of the state is said to produce a form of class domination which is distinct but nonetheless correlated with the dominance of the commodity form within the economy. It provides the material basis for bourgeois political and ideological practices which fetishise the economic and political as wholly independent spheres and thus helps to drive a wedge between workers' economic and political struggles so that it is harder for them to challenge bourgeois domination. Given this general separation of the economic and political forms of class struggle, the content of specific struggles will reflect the inherent contradictions and crisis-tendencies of the capital relation. It is in and through this dialectic between form and content that the historical complex of economic, political, and ideological preconditions of capital accumulation as a social relation of exploitation is continually renewed and reorganised (Holloway and Picciotto 1977, pp. 79–85, 94; and 1978, pp. 14, 17–18).

Holloway and Picciotto started out from the capital relation as a whole and treated the economic and political spheres as different moments of that relation. Their account of *form* was limited to the fetishistic separation of the economic and political struggles of the working class; and this was explained in terms of capital's efforts to maintain the illusion that the capitalist state was neutral and independent of the economy. There is some merit in this analysis but it ignores the plurality of social forms within each of the two spheres. These also affect the nature of economic and political class struggles so that there is also a dialectic of form and content *within* each sphere. Thus a full account of economic struggle would need to take account of the money form, wage form, industrial relations systems, the tax form and so forth (see Clarke 1988b); and, on the terrain of political struggle, one would need to consider the representational regime, the 'inner state' (or articulation of state apparatuses), and forms of intervention. Once this is conceded, however, it becomes less clear where the RA and Holloway really differ.

CLARKE ON CLASS STRUGGLE

Clarke criticises the RA for structural functionalism and argues that modes of regulation are primarily concerned to manage the balance of class forces. But his own approach rests on unstated assumptions about the dynamic of capital accumulation which make it less distinct from regulationist studies than Clarke implies. I will show this in two stages: through a brief account of his own account of Fordism and a comparison with Aglietta's analysis of the same phenomenon.

First, Clarke's account of Fordism rests on a form-analytic view of capital. He argues that the rule of capital is not embodied in the person of the capitalist but derives from the dominance of the money form (Clarke 1988b, p. 17); he adds that it is the capitalist form of the state that underlies the political influence of capitalists, rather than vice versa (Clarke 1988b, pp. 120–1). This does not mean that these forms emerge spontaneously, function automatically, and magically guarantee both capital accumulation and class domination. For these forms are themselves the products of class struggle, cannot stop class struggles from flowing beyond their limits, and impose barriers on the ability of capitalists as well as workers to pursue their class interests (Clarke 1988b, pp. 15–16). It follows that these institutional forms can never comprise a stable, unified, functionally integrated totality but must always express the provisional, antagonistic and contradictory logic of the capital relation.

However, whilst the class struggle retains primacy, it is always articulated to the contradictory logic of accumulation inscribed in the capital relation. Clarke is well aware that something more than a succession of capitalist victories in the class struggle is required to secure capital accumulation: their outcomes must also be congruent with the changing technical and material conditions for capital accumulation. He also explores the particular forms assumed by the contradictory logic of accumulation under predominantly extensive and intensive accumulation regimes; and systematically examines the ensemble of institutional forms which are presupposed by specific accumulation patterns. Thus, despite his criticisms of regulation theory, the similarities between Clarke's analysis of the typical cycles and crises of nineteenth-century capitalism (based on extensive accumulation, limited mass consumption, and undeveloped banking and credit systems) and that given by Aglietta are quite startling (Clarke 1988b, pp. 167–8, 189).

Even more striking, given the main thrust of Clarke's critique of Aglietta, are the similarities in his analysis of the postwar boom. Thus he informs us that it was 'initially based on the generalisation of 'Fordist' methods of production of consumer goods and the associated steel, power, and machine tool industries' (Clarke 1988b, p. 267); that it involved monopolistic pricing and economies of scale, the amortisation of obsolescent capital through pricing and depreciation policies, institutionalised plant-level collective bargaining, relatively high and rising wages sometimes directly linked to productivity or profits, consumer credit, social insurance and social welfare provisions, and Keynesian credit creation (Clarke 1988b, pp. 269–70); and that it was sustained by the Keynesian welfare state — a state form involving 'the state, directly and indirectly, in the regulation of the reproduction of the working class through the wage, social insurance and social security, on the basis of a generalised expectation of rising wages, a guaranteed minimum subsistence, and a political commitment to full employment' (Clarke 1988a). Moreover, although he does not examine them in such detail, he also refers to the structural forms (in education and industrial training, financial institutions, industrial relations, social insurance and welfare arrangements) which are presupposed in an integrated Fordist system (1988a). Such similarities clearly reflect the fact that Clarke started on his book to provide a more adequate typology of accumulation regimes (Clarke 1988b, p. 89). That he subsequently came to emphasise the class struggle should not blind us to the form-analytic context in which class struggles are explored.

Conversely, Aglietta stresses the inherently antagonistic relation between commodified wage-labour and capital.[10] Thus he treats Taylorism and Fordism as capitalist responses to working-class struggle and resistance in the labour process and beyond it (1979, pp. 114–17, 162) and notes how class struggle limits capital accumulation (1979, pp. 67, 119–21, 168, 356). More generally he defines structural forms in terms of 'the complex social relations, organized in institutions, that are the *historical products of the class struggle*' (Aglietta 1979, p. 19, my emphasis). Thus any harmony in the labour process and working-class reproduction derives from capital's success in canalising the class struggle in all fields (notably for control of state power) in ways compatible with accumulation (Aglietta 1979, pp. 19, 22, 32, 66–7, 72–3, 197–8, 243, 383). This does not mean that the class struggle can ever be fully confined within a given mode of regulation. For Aglietta emphasises that the class struggle itself is beyond any 'law': it is not governed by any metaphysical determinism and overflows all limits placed upon it (1979, pp. 67–8). This must be so for two reasons. First, structural forms can only mediate and institutionalise class antagonism to the *extent that they remain in contact with its sources*; and, second, new conflicts can develop which are tangential to those codified and canalised through established structural forms (1982, p. x). Aglietta concludes that crisis tendencies are generic to capitalism and must be treated as primary. Thus, if integrative tendencies tend to prevail in periods of expansion, this does not mean that class conflict has disappeared (1982, pp. x–xi).

This brief review has revealed more in common between the RA and Clarke's approach than he concedes. But there are also obvious differences in theoretical strategy, preferred research topics, and analytic method. Thus, while RA theorists are more concerned to specify the inherently limited range of institutional patterns which can sustain relatively balanced capitalist economic growth, class-theoretical analysts are often more interested in the wide variety of class conjunctures — whether or not these are really consistent with long-run capital accumulation and/or capitalist class domination. Second, while regulation theorists attempt to periodise capitalism in terms of the serial alternation of more integrated phases of capital accumulation with more disorganised transitional phases, class theorists distinguish 'modes of regulation' in terms of stages in the class struggle and refuse to treat them as involving qualitatively different 'regimes of accumulation'. And, third, while regulationists often operate with stylised forms of reasoning and/or econometric modelling, their opponents' approach prefers detailed historical analyses of specific modes of growth and patterns of institutionalised class compromise. But these contrasts could prove complementary rather than contradictory as long as a form-analytic account of class struggle is adopted. The research agenda implicit in Clarke's analysis of Keynesianism and monetarism, for example, does not seem all that different from an RA account which emphasises the strategic selectivity of structural forms and their class-contested nature.

THE DIALECTIC OF FORM AND CONTENT

The issues at stake in this debate might become clearer if I make a couple of methodological points about regulation theory. For, in line with the arguments of Marxist scientific realism, it works on different levels of abstraction and its key concepts change as the analysis becomes more concrete. Thus, although form-analytic questions receive pride of place at more abstract levels of analysis, class-theoretic concepts gain in centrality at more concrete levels of analysis. Two points need stressing here.

First, since the labour process as a unity of material production and valorisation lies at the heart of the circuit of capital, the analysis of 'capital' as the self-valorisation of value necessarily refers to the class struggle between capital and labour. In this sense any analysis of the 'iron laws' of generalised commodity production already expresses the tendencies of class struggle and competition at the heart of the circuit of capital. Their treatment as 'objective laws' is not intended to separate them off radically from the realm of 'subjective action'. Instead they are treated as 'objective' to emphasise their emergent, quasi-natural and independent operation 'behind the backs' of the producers: without the conscious actions of producers, there could be no such emergent effects.

Second, at such high levels of abstraction, 'class struggle' can only be introduced in terms of the fundamental interests at stake and the typical forms of conflict. Thus we know that class struggle occurs in the sphere of circulation between owners of labour-power and owners of money capital over the price of labour-power and that it is conducted in terms of the exchange of commodities and freedom of contract. Equally we know that, in the sphere of production, the money-owner becomes a capitalist and the possessor of labour-power becomes a worker. The conflict is no longer conducted in terms of the 'innate rights of man'. Instead it is focused around capital's ability to control its workers in a system of factory despotism organised to minimise the amount of socially necessary labour time embodied in any given commodity and to maximise the total amount of socially necessary labour time expended in producing commodities. Here it is the distinction between absolute and relative surplus value and the struggle over socially necessary labour time which define the fundamental interests at stake. Knowing these typical forms of antagonism and conflict can tell us nothing, however, about the specific strategies or outcomes of struggle in any given conjuncture.

In short, since the value (meta-)form is substantively indeterminate and just defines broad tendencies and counter-tendencies in capital accumulation, it must be more fully determined at more concrete levels of analysis. The various moments of the value form must be given some institutional specificity (cf. Marx's comments on simple cooperation and the division of labour, manufacture and machinofacture, different forms of wage, different forms of money, and so on). Likewise the character masks represented by capital and labour must be removed to reveal more specific modes of calculation and strategies (cf. Marx's contrast between hoarding by misers and re-investment by capitalists or his various comments on absolute and relative surplus-value, strategies to overcome obstacles to the free movement of capital, or trade union strategies in relation to minimum wages).

In specifying these institutional forms and their associated modes of calculation and strategic conduct one is just fleshing out the formal structure of capitalism and defining the modalities of class struggle. This no more introduces a radical distinction between 'objective' laws and the 'subjective' class struggle than the same line of approach does at more abstract levels of analysis. Instead we are much better placed to explore their dialectical interaction. For abstract social forms and fundamental tendencies and counter-tendencies are too indeterminate to explain the actual course of capital accumulation. They can only explain its general dynamic and directionality. Thus regulation theorists have not broken with the general logic of Marxist explanation when they try to specify the institutional forms and modes of struggle within a given stage of capitalist development. They are actually located firmly within the Marxist tradition.

Thus Marx explored the implications of the transition from manufacture to large-scale industry for the dynamic of capital accumulation. Likewise the regulation school has been concerned with the implications of the transition from the dominance of Department I (capital goods) over Department II (consumer goods) to balanced growth between them in a system in which mass production and mass consumption predominate. In turn this means exploring the specific institutional forms assumed by the wage relation, the labour process, price formation, competition, money, credit, and so on, and the accumulation strategies and patterns of working class resistance with which these forms are associated.

There is no more reason *in principle* to analyse the course of capital accumulation at this level of abstraction in terms of 'iron laws' which operate totally independently of class struggle than there is to do so at the level of capital in general. Nor, in reply to the charge of voluntarism in my concern with 'accumulation strategies' (for example Clarke 1983), is there any reason on this level of abstraction to argue that capital somehow gains the capacity to realise any strategy it cares to pursue even though it lacks this power as capital in general. To suggest that regulation theory must inevitably prove 'structuralist' (the unstoppable onward march of objective laws) or 'voluntarist' (the unstoppable onward march of wilful capitalists) is to neglect the basic continuity between the regulation approach and the basic method of Marx's *Capital*. But this continuity does not, of course, mean that the regulationist approach has always been applied successfully.

Thus what both Marx's *Capital* and the regulation approach have in common is a concern with the dialectic of form and content. This dialectic should not be confused with the mechanical juxtaposition of 'objective laws' and 'subjective struggle'. Nor should it be equated with a simple contrast between enduring structures and the strategies which reproduce them. Indeed the approach presented in my reply to Bonefeld operates with a very different conception of both structure and strategy. It neither subordinates struggle to objective laws nor treats struggle simply as the medium through which pre-given laws are realised. Instead it emphasises the double dialectic in the interaction between structure and strategy. For it changes the terms of analysis from the simple dichotomy implicit in 'structure versus strategy' to the complex relation between the 'strategic selectivity' inscribed in structures and the 'structural transformations' produced in and through strategic interaction. The same approach is evident in Marx's account of the value form (for example, his contrast between the logic of exchange in the labour market and the logic of valorisation in the sphere of production) and in his account of how capitalist strategies influence the dynamic of accumulation (for example, on the changes entailed in capitalist pursuit of relative surplus-value).

In this sense the dialectic of structure and strategies involves a complex process of mutual historical conditioning and reciprocal recursive transformation. Their dialectic is nothing more (but also nothing less) than the structural conditioning of strategies and the strategic transformation of structural ensembles. Structures condition strategies both as explicit reference points for strategic calculation and as a partly and partially unacknowledged set of structural constraints and conjunctural opportunities on those strategies. Conversely strategies transform structures both through deliberate, if often unsuccessful, attempts to modify them and through the unanticipated consequences of interaction among patterns of strategic conduct with other objectives. In short the structure/strategy dialectic does not separate struggle from structures but shows their complex forms of interaction. This is also the method implicit in Marx's *Capital*.

THE PRIMACY OF POLITICS IN THE RECEPTION OF REGULATION THEORY

The overlap between early regulation theory and its critics' views suggests that we should look elsewhere to explain the controversy between them. There is no secret here. For Bonefeld, Holloway and Clarke all claim that regulation theory leads to pessimistic political conclusions and thereby weakens the class struggle by suggesting that capitalism will inevitably emerge stronger from the current crisis. Even if this holds for some regulation theorists and/or those who use regulationist concepts to justify their political positions, it is not intrinsic to the regulation approach itself. To reject regulation theory because it is sometimes tied to unpalatable political conclusions would be like rejecting Marxist political economy because it was once invoked to justify Stalinism. One could equally well reject theories based on the primacy of class struggle because they have sometimes been used to justify ultra-leftist strategies. It is surely far better to criticise theoretical work because it fails to meet criteria of theoretical adequacy.

Once we turn to theoretical rather than political differences, however, it is not clear that regulation theory is inconsistent with an emphasis on class struggle. Certainly early regulation theorists (such as Aglietta and Lipietz) as well as more recent regulationist theoretical currents (such as the Amsterdam school) have emphasised the primacy of class struggle in securing capital accumulation. But they refuse to see class struggle as related to class domination alone. This would imply that class domination is purely an issue of asymmetrical power relations and thus totally separated from the material preconditions for the reproduction of the circuit of capital. Instead they analyse the dialectic between form and content, structure and strategy, in the overall reproduction of capitalist domination.

Presumably Clarke had this in mind when he wrote that 'the regulation approach is very valuable in drawing attention to the systematic character of the regulation of capital accumulation, relating the forms of regulation of capitalist production to the forms of regulation of accumulation by money and the state'. But he also claimed that the regulation approach is inadequate in part 'because it has no theory of money and the state as the dual forms of capitalist power nor any conception of the contradictory character of capitalist regulation' (Clarke 1988a).[11] Without necessarily affirming the validity of this criticism, we can certainly note that it rests on a form-analytic account of class domination. It does not privilege a formless class struggle but seeks instead to explain class domination in terms of money and the state as interlinked forms of the social power of capital. They reproduce capitalist domination by separating the economic and political spheres and imposing distinct logics on them: market rationality and electoral competition respectively. In this sense Clarke develops a form-determined account of class struggle and shows how a failure to contest the imposition of these forms necessarily subordinates the working class to the rule of capital. When working-class struggles challenge these forms, however, the social power of capital is thrown into crisis. The same sort of logic underlies regulationist work and also has long informed my own approach.

CONCLUDING REMARKS

This chapter is a response to the continuing criticism in *Capital and Class* of the regulation approach. I have argued that regulation theory is broadly faithful to the principles of Marxist political economy in its form-analytic account of both capitalism and the class struggle and that there are affinities between the regulationist and

CSE approaches which have gone unremarked by CSE critics. I have suggested that the theoretical disputes hinge upon an overly simplistic opposition between the correct but elliptical claim that 'capital is class struggle' and the indefensible thesis, wrongly attributed to regulation theory, that there are objective laws of capitalist development which are mediated (but nothing more) by the class struggle. When we unpack the former claim and compare it with the regulationist account of form-determined class struggle, there is little left to dispute. In turn this suggests that something else is at stake in the debate and my own hunch is that the critics actually object less to the regulation approach than to its reformist misappropriation by social and political commentators on the current transition to post-Fordism. That such reformist reading exists (notably in the columns of *Marxism Today* and the policy reviews of the Labour Party) should not be denied. But the critics' hostility seems to have been reinforced because Bonefeld and Holloway have their own idiosyncratic, 'workerist' reading of Marxist theory.[12] I do not share this reading of Marxism but there is certainly some common ground in our joint emphasis on seeing class struggle as an integral element of the capital relation. We differ in so far as I believe that Marx always related the class struggle to the basic forms and dynamic of capital as the dominant force (*uebergreifendes Subjekt*).

Two conclusions seem to follow from this account. First, we will be misled both theoretically and politically if we focus on class struggle without regard to its specific forms and modalities. In practical terms this means looking closely at (a) the specific forms and modalities of class struggle which helped to reproduce Fordism and (b) the strategies which might have destabilised it by challenging the parameters involved in Fordist accumulation regimes and modes of regulation. It also means taking seriously the specific forms and modalities of struggle involved in the transition to post-Fordism. This cannot be confined to the forms of working class integration into the transition but must extend to the various forms of resistance. If and when a post-Fordist regime is established, we will also need to define the forms and modalities of struggle which complement it and those which might disrupt it. In all three cases we need to distinguish carefully among different types of struggle: marginal struggles which can acquire class-relevance, struggles within the parameters of a regime which help to reproduce it, and struggles whose effect is to disrupt and transform it. General references to class struggle are unhelpful here.

Second, errors will also occur if the issue of class subjects and subjectivities is emphasised at the cost of the class-relevance of specific forces, strategies and actions. Calculating class-relevance requires us to develop criteria which do not depend on subjective class identities and refer instead to the interests entailed in alternative economic strategies. For, once we turn our attention from the expanded reproduction of capital in general to the particular direction and rhythms of accumulation (or the transition to socialism), we must give some substance to the formal indeterminacy of the capital relation. The particular trajectories of capital accumulation (whether examined in global, national, or local terms and/or in relation to specific firms, branches or circuits) depend on which emergent strategies and alliances come to prevail in the course of competition and the class struggle.[13]

Finally, we must consider the Great Bear. In a footnote to his paper Holloway cites Tony Negri's witticism that it sometimes seems that intellectuals and workers see capital as a Great Bear: whereas the intellectuals regard it as though it were a distant constellation, the workers confront it daily as a wild and savage animal. In substance this remark resembles Aglietta's comments on new realist illusions, which 'do not deceive the working class, who daily confront the concrete realities of exploitation' (1979, p. 112; see pp. 122–3). But its effect is different. For it polarises positions for polemical or political purposes in a diversionary manner. Holloway treats the work of theorists such as Poulantzas, the regulation school, or the state reformulation theorists as poles apart from 'real Marxism' with its steadfast commitment to the primacy of the class struggle. He seems to think that the Great Bear confronting the workers is located in the Arctic region (where polar bears can indeed be found) whereas the intellectuals are hunting for their Great Bear in the Antarctic (where there are none) and, in thereby dividing the forces opposed to capital, are weakening the attack on the common enemy. But, as I have tried to show, this contrast is exaggerated. The theorists he attacks share some common ground with those who argue that 'capital *is* class struggle'. They also have some specific differences regarding the best way to interpret this highly elliptical statement. Rather than polarising debate (and even seeming to imply that some fellow Marxists are a new breed of 'social fascists' and thus a greater class enemy than those forces mobilised around Thatcherism) might it not be better to explore the common ground more carefully? There are enough real theoretical issues at stake in a continuing debate between RA theorists and their opponents without adding to the controversy with charges of 'social Thatcherism'. If we spend our time hunting imaginary polar bears, post-Fordism (if such is the next regime of accumulation) will certainly catch us all unawares.

NOTES

1. In writing this paper I owe a special intellectual debt to Moishe Postone. His book on *Time, Labor, and Social Domination* and several discussions with him have helped me to sharpen my ideas on the value form. But I have combined his arguments with my own and take full responsibility for the form in which they appear here. The paper was written during my stay at the Centre for Interdisciplinary Research (ZIF), Bielefeld, and my tenure of a personal research grant from the ESRC. I would like to thank both organisations for their support.
2. Although nowhere near as often as Holloway implies — unless we read every mention of objectified and/or constant capital as a reference to dead labour.
3. I am not so much arguing that Holloway does not see these points as that, if one takes class struggle to be the truth, the whole truth, and nothing but the truth about capital, they cannot be theoretically apprehended.
4. See his letter to Joseph Weydemeyer, 5 March 1852; he went on to claim a triple credit — for revealing the necessity of class struggle within capitalism, of its culmination in a dictatorship of the proletariat, and an eventual transition to a classless society. Only in his later critique of political economy, however, did Marx finally disclose the hidden necessity and dynamic of class struggle within capitalism.
5. Although, of course, it is not really a commodity.
6. See the distinction between class-conscious and class-relevant actions presented in Jessop 1982, pp. 242–3.
7. In formulating these points I have not only drawn on my own re-reading of *Capital* but also on earlier analyses of this text by Balibar (1985) and Postone (1988); the fifth point is also informed by Rosenthal (1987).
8. From their use of this latter phrase Bonefeld wrongly concluded that regulationists deny there are (class) subjects in capitalism. But it only means that the totalising dynamic of the capital relation works 'behind the backs' of these subjects.
9. It is worth distinguishing between crises whose causes are endogenous to capitalism and those provoked by exogenous events (such as earthquakes); even in the latter case (and assuming that we can really determine today how far events such as drought or famine are truly exogenous), the value (meta-)form will still shape the ways in which they are worked out in capitalist societies.
10. It is worth recalling that Aglietta developed his account of Fordism centred around the wage relation in opposition to the then dominant communist analysis of state monopoly capitalism — an analysis centred on changing

forms of competition. In this context the wage relation (*rapport salarial*) encompasses far more than forms of remuneration: it involves an ensemble of antagonistic capital-labour relations.

11. It is certainly not true that Aglietta lacked a theory of money as a form of capitalist power; but he did concede the need to work on the role of the state if the theory of capitalist regulation were to be completed (Aglietta 1979). He also emphasises the contradictions in regulation. Whether or not state reformulation analyses of regulation are adequate is, of course, one of the points at issue in my replies to Bonefeld and Holloway.

12. By 'workerist' I understand an emphasis on class struggle coupled with an emphasis on the primacy of the working class.

13. Space is too short and patience too limited to repeat my arguments on the significance of accumulation strategies for identifying class interests or those concerned with the difference which time horizons make to any attempt to calculate strategic interests. See Jessop 1983.

REFERENCES

Aglietta, M. (1974), *Accumulation et regulation du capitalisme en longue periode. Exemple des Etats-Unis (1870–1970)* (Paris: INSEE).

Aglietta, M. (1979), *A Theory of Capitalist Regulation: the US Experience* (London: NLB) (first French edition, 1976).

Aglietta, M. (1982), 'Avant-propos à la deuxieme edition', *Regulation et crises du capitalisme: l'experience des Etats-Unis* (Paris: Calmann-Levy).

Balibar, E. (1985), 'L'Idée d'une politique de classe chez Marx', in *Actes du Colloque Marx* (Paris: Editions de l'École des Hautes Etudes en Sciences Sociales).

Bonefeld, W. (1987), see Chapter 3 in this volume, 'Reformulation of State Theory'.

Clarke, S. (1983), 'Comment on Jessop', *Kapitalistate 10/11*.

Clarke, S. (1988a), see Chapter 5 in this volume, 'Overaccumulation, Class Struggle and the Regulation Approach'.

Clarke, S. (1988b), *Keynesianism, Monetarism and the Crisis of the State* (Aldershot: Edward Elgar).

Cutler, A. *et al.* (1978), *Marx's 'Capital' and Capitalism Today* (London: Routledge & Kegan Paul).

Holloway, J. (1988), see Chapter 6 in this volume 'The Great Bear: Post-Fordism and Class Struggle'.

Holloway, J. and S. Picciotto (1977), 'Capital, Crisis and the State', *Capital & Class* 2.

Holloway, J. and S. Picciotto (1978), 'Introduction', in *idem*, *eds*, *Capital and the State: a Marxist Debate* (London: Edward Arnold).

Holloway, J. (1980), 'The State as Class Practice', *Research in Political Economy*, Vol. 3, Jai Press.

Jessop, B. (1982), *The Capitalist State* (Oxford: Martin Robertson).

Jessop, B. (1983), 'Accumulation Strategies, State Forms and Hegemonic Projects', *Kapitalistate 10/11*, pp. 89–112.

Jessop, B. (1985), *Nicos Poulantzas: Marxist Theory and Political Strategy* (London: Macmillan).
Jessop, B. (1988), see Chapter 4 in this volume, 'Regulation Theory, Post-Fordism and the State: more than a Reply to Werner Bonefeld'.
Marx, K. (1857), 'Introduction to the Critique of Political Economy', in *idem*, *Grundrisse: Foundations of the Critique of Political Economy*, trans. M. Nicolaus (Harmondsworth: Penguin, 1973).
Marx, K. (1867), *Capital: a Critique of Political Economy, Volume One*, trans. B. Fowkes (Harmondsworth: Penguin, 1976).
Marx, K. (1867a), *Capital: a Critique of Political Economy, Volume One*, trans. S. Moore and E. Aveling (Moscow: Progress, 1970 edn).
Marx, K. (1894), *Capital: a Critique of Political Economy, Volume Three*, (Moscow: Progress, 1966).
Norton, B. (1988), 'The Power Axis: Bowles, Gordon, and Weisskopf's Theory of Postwar US Accumulation', *Rethinking Marxism* 1 (3), pp. 6–43.
Oakley, A. (1984), *Marx's Critique of Political Economy: Intellectual Sources and Evolution*, Vol. 1 (London: Routledge & Kegan Paul).
Postone, M. (1988), *Time, Labor and Social Domination*, mimeo.
Rosenthal, J. (1987), 'Who Practices Hegemony? Class Division and the Subject of Politics', *Cultural Critique*, Spring, pp. 25–32.

9 Capital *is* Class Struggle (And Bears are not Cuddly)

John Holloway

Bob Jessop should be congratulated, perhaps, on shaking regulation theory to its foundations by exposing it in all its stark theoretical nudity. However, since that was not his intention, this paper will concentrate on trying to sort out the theoretical differences between us.

The basis for the discussion will be Jessop's paper on 'Polar Bears and Class Struggle', Chapter 8 in this volume, which is in part a reply to my earlier paper, 'The Great Bear: Post-Fordism and Class Struggle', Chapter 5 in this volume. The merit of Jessop's paper is that, although there are many layers of confusion and misunderstanding, he does point to basic theoretical issues which divide us and which have important political implications. Rather than try to follow all the twists and turns of Jessop's argument in its labyrinthine complexity, I shall focus on what he correctly singles out as the central issue: the assertion that capital *is* class struggle.

CAPITAL *IS* CLASS STRUGGLE

The purpose of emphasising that capital *is* class struggle is to attack the separation so often made between class struggle on the one hand and capital (or 'the objective laws of capitalist development') on the other. This separation, which has so long plagued the Marxist tradition, leads to a deterministic understanding of social development in which obeisance may be paid to the centrality of class struggle, but what really counts is 'the inescapable lines of tendency and direction established by the real world', in Hall's revealing phrase (Hall 1985, p. 15). The separation may, of course, be taken in the opposite direction, to an interpretation which emphasises class struggle without reference to the peculiar forms which class struggle assumes under capitalism: voluntarism and determinism are theoretically complementary, both expressions of the separation between class struggle and capital.

The thrust of the assertion that capital *is* class struggle is thus twofold. Against the determinism which is so prevalent within the Marxist tradition, it insists on the antagonistic nature of the capital relation. The key to the understanding of any class society, as Marx points out in a passage quoted by Jessop, is 'the specific . . . form in which unpaid surplus labour is pumped out of the direct producers' (*Capital* III, p. 791). The core of capitalism (as of other class societies) is antagonistic, the daily repeated struggle by the dominant class to pump surplus labour out of the direct producers. Capital is a relation of exploitation, of the daily renewed struggle to extract surplus labour from the direct producers. That is class struggle: grinding, everyday, unspectacular class struggle, so unspectacular that it is not even seen by bourgeois theory, so everyday that the simple assertion that capital is class struggle seems inexplicable even to some within the Marxist tradition. The point is a simple one, but it has important implications: if struggle is at the core of society, then there is no 'objective' social reality other than the inter-subjective class struggle: the live antagonism between the 'pumpers' of surplus labour and the direct producers, an antagonism which, by definition, is open and unresolved.

The other face of the critique implicit in the statement that capital *is* class struggle is already given in the passage quoted from *Capital*. Essential to an understanding of any given class society is not simply the realisation that the society is based on a struggle-to-exploit but an understanding of the 'specific form' which the pumping of surplus labour out of the direct producers takes in that particular society. Under capitalism, for example, the relation of exploitation (the struggle-to-exploit) assumes a specific form, the form of the capital relation. It is important to understand not only that capital *is* class struggle, but that, conversely, class struggle assumes the form of capital in the society in which we live. Class struggle does not appear as such under capitalism: it appears as capital, as an objective reality with its own inescapable laws of motion. It is refracted through so many 'things' such as money, profit, rent, interest — the particular forms of the capital relation analysed in Marx's *Capital*. These are not mere forms of appearance: they are the contradictory modes of existence of the class antagonism, modes of existence which deny the reality of the class relation as class relation, or, as Richard Gunn puts it, the class relation exists in the mode of being denied (Gunn 1987). Class struggle is not a formless, to-and-fro, biff-baff sequence: it develops in-and-against these historically specific forms and cannot be understood in abstraction from them.

ON FORM AND FORM-PROCESSING

At this point, Jessop may feel that the differences between us are merely semantic. To make it quite clear that that is not the case, it is necessary to take another step.

Value, money, rent, state are forms of social relations: that is a formulation that would presumably be accepted by Jessop and by most regulation theorists. However, when one bears in mind that the social relations here are the social relations of an inherently antagonistic society, and hence antagonistic social relations, it is clear that the phrase 'forms of social relations' is intensely contradictory. Social relations are not easily detained in forms. The 'sheer unrest of life', as Hegel calls it (*Phenomenology*, §46), is not easily bound within the alienated, fetishised forms of capitalist social relations. The alienated forms contain within them their own antithesis.

Value, money, rent, state and such forms are not simply forms of social relations: they are specifically capitalist forms of struggle. They are form-processes: processes of forming social relations into a pattern compatible with the reproduction of capitalist relations of exploitation. Value, for example, is the dominant form through which our need for the useful products of other people's work is satisfied. However, value is not simply given. It is a form that is (more or less) imposed and re-imposed on our desire for access to the useful products of others. The imposition of value as a form of social relations is achieved, to the extent that it is achieved, only through the working of an immense apparatus of education and coercion. Value, as a form of domination, inevitably gives rise to resistance, resistance which, inevitably, is a struggle in-and-against value, without there being any clear dividing lines between struggle in and struggle against, between 'conscious' and 'unconscious' action. The forms of capitalist social relations are not simply forms into which struggle is subsumed: they are forms through which the struggle of capital is fought, forms in-and-against which labour resists (see Holloway 1980/1991, 1991).

This makes all the difference in the world to our understanding of

Marx's categories and of capitalist development. Value and the other fetishised forms of capitalist social relations are not established *faits accomplis*, but are constantly at issue, constantly the object of struggle, and therefore constantly open, un-predetermined (see Clarke 1991; Bonefeld 1987). It is precisely the fact that these forms are constantly at issue in struggle that gives meaning to the Marxist critique of value and money: it is not an academic critique that comes from outside, but an integral part of the constant struggle against capital.

The importance of this distinction can be seen by returning to Jessop's argument. Although he understands value and the other fetishised forms as forms of social relations, he sees these relations as being firmly established and having acquired an autonomous (or 'quasi-autonomous') logic of their own. Thus, 'capital is a particular form of social relations and has an institutional logic and directional dynamic of its own. *Once commodity production has been generalised* (so that labour-power itself assumes the form of a commodity) and relative surplus-value is the dominant form of surplus-value, capitalist domination is realised through an emergent, impersonal and quasi-natural network of social connections' (see p. 149, above); and '*assuming that these different forms are reproduced so that the continuing dominance of the value (meta-)form is secured (which is no mean historical accomplishment and depends on success in the class struggle)*, they define the *parameters* for capital accumulation and also delimit its possible crisis forms' (p. 153, above my italics). This is not the crude functionalist determinism of old Communist Party orthodoxy: it is a sophisticated, back-door functionalism, but it is no less functionalist and determinist for all that. Class struggle is effectively relegated to the origins of capitalism, to a period of primitive accumulation understood as a historical phase long past (see Bonefeld 1988). For the present, capitalism develops according to its 'quasi-autonomous logic'. The existence of class struggle in modern capitalism is not denied, but it takes place within the framework constituted by this 'quasi-autonomous logic'.

The result is that Marxism is understood not as a theory of struggle, but of the structural framework of struggle, a framework set firmly in place, apparently, at the dawn of capitalism. Once it is assumed 'that these different forms are reproduced so that the continuing dominance of the value (meta-)form is secured', then obviously Marxism becomes a theory of the reproduction of capitalism, rather than of its rupture. The working class is understood simply as the *object* of capitalist development, rather than as the pole of an inter-subjective antagonism. The revolutionary transformation of society, in so far as it has any place within this theoretical framework, can only appear as an exogenous event. The functionalism of the approach expresses itself in a very sharp dualism between reproduction and revolution, reflected also in the sharp distinction which Jessop insists on making between unconscious and conscious action, and between struggles in and struggles against the institutional forms of the capitalist mode of production (see p. 154, above). The theoretical assumptions thus reproduce the Leninist distinction between reform and revolution, between trade union and revolutionary consciousness. The only difference is that, in the absence of a revolutionary party, revolution has been postponed *sine die* and Marxism has become quite simply a new, more sophisticated theory of capitalist equilibrium, a theory of capitalist regulation.

ON BEARS, GREAT, POLAR AND TEDDY

As in all academic debate, there is an element of play in my reply to Bob Jessop. I enjoy arguing with him as I would enjoy playing chess or cards with him. Because there is no decision to be taken, it is all too easy to see the argument as a game, as though there were no real issue at stake. Unfortunately, that is not the case.

It is not a question of dismissing Jessop (or anyone else) as a 'social fascist', but of recognising that the theoretical approach which he adopts has significant political implications. These implications seem to me very harmful, in at least two respects. Firstly, because of the separation which it makes between Marxism and struggle, Jessop's theory contributes to the evisceration of Marxism which has been a feature of 'left' academic writing in recent years and which is exemplified not only by regulation theory, but by other currents such as rational choice Marxism and scientific realism (see Gunn 1991). This is harmful because it gives Marxism a bad name: it makes Marxism seem irrelevant, if not oppressive, to those actively engaged in struggle.

The second reason why the approach of Jessop and other regulation theorists seems to me harmful is that the theoretical suppression of class struggle on which they are based gives support to those currents within the labour movement (in its broadest sense) which seek to suppress open struggle both in their rhetoric and in their practice.

It is thus with regret that I reject Jessop's invitation for us to be cuddly teddy bears together. The world is not a cuddly place and there are theoretical and political differences that should be clearly stated. Now more than ever, when so much that has been done in the name of Marxism is collapsing in the east and when the categories of Marxism are being used to justify a reactionary restructuring in the west, it is important to reassert that Marxism makes sense only as a theory of struggle, a theory of anger, a theory of hope.

REFERENCES

Bonefeld, W. (1987), 'Open Marxism', *Common Sense* 1, Edinburgh.

Bonefeld, W. (1988), 'Class Struggle and the Permanence of Primitive Accumulation', *Common Sense* 6, Edinburgh.

Clarke, S. (1991), Introduction to *The State Debate* (London: Macmillan).

Gunn, R. (1987), 'Marxism and Mediation', *Common Sense* 2, Edinburgh.

Gunn, R. (1991), Chapter 11 in this volume, 'Marxism, Metatheory and Critique'.

Hall, S. (1985), 'Realignment for What?' *Marxism Today*, December.

Hegel, G.W.F. (1977), *The Phenomenology of Spirit* (London: Oxford University Press).

Holloway, J. (1980/1991), 'The State and Everyday Struggle', in S. Clarke (ed.), *The State Debate* (London: Macmillan).

Holloway, J. (1991), 'Crisis, Fetishism, Decomposition', in W. Bonefeld, R. Gunn, K. Psychopedis (eds), *Open Marxism* (London: Pluto).

Jessop, B. (1991), Chapter 8 in this volume, 'Polar Bears and Class Struggle'.

Marx, K. *Capital* (Moscow: Progress, 1965/71).

10 Crisis of Theory in the Contemporary Social Sciences

Kosmas Psychopedis

The set of questions which will be developed in the text which follows refers to the crisis in social theory as an expression of the crisis in society. The crisis in society is defined as a disruption of relations between the socio–economic aggregates which ensure the continuation of social reproduction. Similarly, the expression of that crisis on the theoretical level — the crisis in theory — consists of a neglect for the internal relational nature of the social object and of the disconnection of coherent conceptual frameworks, as well as of an attempt to restore, *a posteriori*, an external relationship between them.

This first approach to the problem of the crisis in theory already makes it explicit that there is a connection between analysis of the theories in which this crisis manifests itself and a methodological line of thought oriented towards the critique of those theories. By means of critique it is possible to restore, in the theoretical/conceptual framework, constitutional relations of the social object which appear to have been separated, and to reveal the contradictory nature of these relations, against which is set the practical and axiological ideal of their transcendence. These critical connections, which render visible the unity-in-contradiction of the social object, involve a concept of the unity of social science, while negation of this unity suggests precisely the crisis which exists in social theory.

The critical dimension to which we have referred clarifies the fact that the idea of unity among the social sciences which is presupposed whenever we talk of a crisis in theory does not coincide with the organic nineteenth-century idea of unity between science and values, between theory and practice, an idea which was overthrown in the twentieth century as it degenerated into positivism, structuralism, decisionism and so on (in which case the practical maxim would be, 'back to unity'). It does, however, coincide with the insistence on the critical disclosure of those relations which are characteristic of the essence of the historical and contradictory nature of contemporary social formations, relations which theory in crisis disrupts, making it impossible to understand and even question them. The crisis, then, lies not in the loss of some original unity but in the sense which we have given to the positivisation and extenuation of criticism.

The idea of the unity of social science is formulated in the classical theories of bourgeois society, in pre-Marxist dialectical theory and in Marxism, within the framework of a concern for a binding theory of society, the state and politics, a concern which manifested itself in the idea of a methodical exposition (*Darstellung*) of categories. As soon as classical theory was shaped, this concern found itself immediately faced with the relativistic theories about society and politics developed by historicism.

The historical evolution of social theory can be reconstructed as the relativisation of the claim for a binding social theory, a relativisation which is inherent in the modes of social reproduction of ideological consciousness. As already noted, this relativisation takes the form of the violent disconnection of certain dimensions which in their constitution have been of a relational and, in the relationship between them, integral nature. Among such disconnections — which constitute forms of the crisis of theory — are the disconnection of the axiological from the descriptive elements of theoretical analysis, the disconnection of the conceptual constitution of the historical object from the idea of the historicity of the conceptual framework, the disconnection of the empirical element from the social theory which concerns its constitution and, lastly, the disconnection of the structural from the spontaneous elements in social action.

In our day, the most recent endeavours within what is known as Western Marxism to develop a dialectical theory capable of restoring the inner relations between these dimensions are connected with the attempts which have been going on since the late 1960s in the so-called 'derivation of the state' (*Staatsableitung*), taking as its starting-point the discussion on the classic work of Rosdolsky and of more recent work by Backhaus, Reichelt and others.

These attempts were stillborn, and their initial conclusions have not been adequately exploited by Marxist theorists. The so-called 'left' social sciences were invaded by structuralist and spontaneist paradigms, many of which have today developed into dominant paradigms in the academic social sciences.

STRUCTURALISM AND METHOD

Among the characteristics of structuralist approaches is the distinction between particular 'regions' of analysis within a socio–economic object, and particularly the identification, next to a field of 'fundamental economic relations', of distinct 'regions' of institutions of political society, political and social superstructures, and so forth. With regard to these 'regions', such approaches raise a methodological demand that they should be analysed in their specificity and then be connected to the results produced by narrowly 'economic' analyses. This manner of analysis is ascribed by some theorists to Gramsci, largely without justification, since Gramsci was interested in stressing the problems which practical politics ought to take into account and not in developing a methodological model for research into socio–economic problems, as post-Gramscian structuralism has attempted to do.

The separation of the social object into regions, followed by the dominance of structuralism, has resulted in the distancing of research interest from problems of relations, that is, from problems of modes of relationships or modes of movement, to use Marx's term, and of an invocation of the 'relative autonomy' of these individual regions, together with a search for typical manners of articulating them. The fragmentation of the unity of the social object which has been achieved by structuralism was expressed in Nicos Poulantzas' *Political Power and Social Classes*. In this work, Poulantzas introduces a classification of social theory on three levels, specifically:

(a) the historico–materialist general theory of modes of production;
(b) the particular theory of the capitalist mode of production;
(c) an analysis of the specific 'region' of the political: the theory of the capitalist state.

This very distinction undoubtedly creates certain methodological problems. More specifically, the distinction into general theory of the modes of production, on the one hand, and particular theory of the capitalist mode of production, on the other, overlooks the conceptual attraction of categories which refer to more than one society (bourgeois, pre-bourgeois) for the theoretical question of the 'anatomy' of bourgeois society. This idea, which had already been developed by Marx in the introduction to the *Grundrisse*, discloses the historicity of the so-called trans-historical concepts and anticipates a criticism against the trans-historical teleological theories of the periodisation of the modes of production. The second distinction which Poulantzas attempts, that between the theory of the capitalist mode of production on the one hand and the theory of the capitalist state 'region' on the other, a distinction typical of the structuralist, 'articulationist', mode of thought, appears problematic as well. Poulantzas attempted to develop this theory by relying on some 'external' elements of Marxist methodological thought (questions developed by Gramsci, Lenin and Engels and in the 'French' writings of Marx) rather than on the 'internal' connections between the political and the economic on the basis of the labour theory of value. He was thus led to a theory of the state marked by functionalist elements, such as, for instance, that the state maintains the 'cohesion' of the class-divided social formation, and lost sight of the methodological idea that the cohesion of the social formation is maintained through the processes of reproduction themselves and through the division of labour in the capitalist formation, and that it is possible, taking precisely this division of labour as a starting-point, to understand both the relationship between society and state and the problem of the state functions. The functionalist elements in Poulantzas' theory were connected with an over-emphasis on the significance of the legal and institutional framework. In this connection, Poulantzas developed the problem of individualisation in bourgeois society, and through that he was led to an examination of problems in the theory of social class (for example, he writes that the state impedes the attempts of the oppressed classes to overcome fragmentation and isolation while at the same time itself working to overcome the fragmentation and isolation of the ruling classes; in other words, he understands the problem of individualisation in relation to the institutional aspect and has no access to it by abstracting from the institutional aspect). Later in his work, Poulantzas emphasised a theory of state functions in the contemporary interventionist state; however, he connected this theory not with a theory of the division of labour in bourgeois society but with a theory of conflicts between social classes and social groups.

After Poulantzas, many theorists believed that they found in his work features which could be used as a starting-point for the foundation of a Marxian descriptive sociology. After some hesitation, they linked up with the French 'regulation school' (Aglietta 1976, 1979) and made particular use of the concept of Fordism, believing that with the concepts worked out by the debate in France and by structuralism they could make more concrete the abstract Marxian concepts which were discussed in the debate on the derivation of the state during the 1960s and the early 1970s. What these theorists failed to discern with sufficient clarity was that with the concretisation (according to Hirsch) or the complementation (according to Jessop) of Marxian concepts on the level of structuralist models, a threat arises for the relational nature of the concepts, particularly for the essential concept of exploitation and the corresponding practical demand for exploitation to be transcended and for autonomy to be actualised, and that analysis becomes non-binding and eclectic.

The position adopted by Jessop (1983) is typical. He argues that the missing link between the labour theory of value, on the one hand, and the specific terms under which the socio–economic struggle takes place, on the other, are supplied by the concept of 'accumulation strategy' and goes on to supply examples of historical forms of accumulation strategy, including Fordism, Hitler's Grossraumwirtschaft, the social market economy, the domination of the City in Britain, the development of Japan into a 'rich country with a strong army', the import substitution/export promotion economy, the concepts of the Pax Britannica and the Pax Americana, various forms of Keynesianism, and so on. It is clear that these concepts on which Jessop works under the heading of 'accumulation strategies' involve the most diverse methodological spheres and that they are unlikely to provide a satisfactory answer to the question of how to adapt Marxist concepts originating in the labour theory of value to specific historical societies.

Particular problems arise with the concept of Fordism, which is used in different ways by different theorists. To take one of the most cohesive definitions, that of J. Hirsch (1983), Fordism is deemed to be characterised by: (a) an intensive mode of capitalist accumulation and exchange in the production of relative surplus value (as we can see, Hirsch uses concepts from the labour theory of value); (b) the mass production, on a Taylorist production base, of consumer durables; (c) high wages; (d) polarisation between skilled and unskilled labour; (e) the organisation of labour on a Taylorist basis; (f) extensive state intervention, which expands into social security, health and education. It is characteristic that this analysis constructs a list of features which refer to different problems and different levels of analysis. In reality, these problems refer us to questions whose relationship still remains to be investigated. It is clear that their mere co-existence, as a numbered list, in a complete entity cannot make them into a theoretical concept; in fact, they constitute a pretheoretical concept. However, in the particular case of Fordism, it is equally clear that the features assigned to this concept are not linked merely by numbering them but follow the lines of a model, the model of the 'Fordist enterprise'. In other words, a concept which refers to one single enterprise is here being transferred to society as a whole, cutting the analysis off from the idea of the social conditions which make possible the formation of Fordist enterprises. At the same time, this concept proves to be ideological, since it converts the entrepreneurial ideology of increasing consumption on the part of the workers and of cooperation between employers and employees, into a theoretical formula concerning unfettered reproduction on the level of society as a whole in conjunction with the results of Keynesian policies.

Methodological problems corresponding to those which arise with the Fordist model are generalised in the mode of thinking which articulates 'norms of consumption' and 'state intervention' (regulation models) and which is regarded as being capable of serving as a basis for the theoretical analysis of individual capitalist societies and for a reconstruction of capitalist development. One particular feature of this articulationist rationale is the preceding disarticulation of the aggregate of social labour from its relational involvement in a Marxian labour theory of value. This disarticulation takes the form of replacing the Marxist category of variable capital (through the analysis of which the Marxist theory of the relationship between social classes and exploitation is formulated) with concepts of norms of consumption and regulation intended to adjust the conceptual framework to the 'new' socio–economic relations as they appear historically (for example class relationships, society/state relations). In other words, the conceptualisation of the historically 'new' takes place with a dissociation of the analysis from the relational framework by which the new is incorporated into the development of the division of labour in the specific historical formation. By substituting for the political and economic analysis of relations the positing of a current norm of consumption, a mode of regulation, the rational social scientific argument is in effect being replaced by an irrational one. It is from the difficulty encountered in predicting the direction in which political and economic relations will be modified, that theory in its irrationality derives legitimation for the denunciation of the very theoretical discourse which informs those relations at the level of the social formation. In this way, the contemporary 'articulationist' and 'regulationist' argument forms part of a tradition of fragmentation and transposition of elements in the relational whole, which is typical of historicism and which found its most classic expression in the works of Max Weber, such as *The Protestant Ethic* and *The Sociology of Law*, although the theories under criticism here fail to approach the theoretical profundity and reflection which are characteristic of Weber's analysis. Characteristic of the historicist argument in *The Protestant Ethic*, for example, is that it fragments and transposes the essential theoretical elements which concern relations of constitution of the formation under analysis into the historical past. In particular, it understands the problem of analysing capitalism as principally a problem of the processes of its emergence, thus excepting it from reflection designed to expose its essential features in a binding model for analysis in the contemporary social sciences. (This structure reappears, in a simplified form, of course, in modern neo-liberal concepts of the type advanced by Hayek concerning the 'traditional' nature of the relations of property.) A further characteristic of historicism, as manifested, for example, in Weber's *Sociology of Law*, is that it fragments the structure of the 'new' from the very possibility of approaching it rationally, that is, by referring to the division of labour and to the overall framework of relations of the formation within which this 'new' arises, and thus prepares the way for methodological irrationalism. This structure we find once more in neo-liberal theories, which delude themselves as to the real limitations which constitute the structure of the future, and also, as we have seen, in 'left-wing', 'articulationist' theories.

These structures of disarticulation and irrational reconstruction of the social scientific argument are encountered in a characteristic manner in the contemporary theories of periodisation of the stages of development in capitalist production and labour organisation. Such theories assign to each stage of 'evolution' a corresponding 'mode of regulation', 'norm of consumption', 'norm of intervention', and so forth. Three types are normally advanced: the pre-Fordist model, the Fordist model and the post-Fordist model. Similarly, models are constructed for the organisation of the working class and for the tactics and strategy of emancipation (on the basis of the methodologically problematic concept of Fordism).

Of course, there is nothing new about such schematically formulated periodisation of the social formation; as early as the 1960s, the schematically formulated periodisation of capitalism appeared as the forerunner of the structuralist approaches, emphasising the emergence of 'state monopoly capitalism' as the 'final stage', and so on.

This trend, which we might call 'late dogmatic', can be found in theorists such as Boccara and also at many points in the work of Poulantzas. Poulantzas made an attempt to polish up the methodology of the monopoly capitalism theory, incorporating it into disarticulated Marxian conceptual frameworks, such as that of absolute surplus value, which appears to correspond to the competitive stage of capitalism, and that of relative surplus value, which he introduces during the stage of monopoly capitalism. Poulantzas' analysis is led into schematic presentations and the concealment of essential relations, since he overlooks the central position occupied by the production of relative surplus value in Marxian theory which, as a main issue in the analysis of the capitalist mode of production, cannot be separated from the concept of competition.

In Poulantzas' *Classes in Contemporary Capitalism* (1974), the periodisation is associated with the new role of the interventionist state, against which is set a vague claim for rupture (the class struggle). In the more recent structuralism of the 'regulationists', periodisation refers to the concept of Fordism, and at the same time stresses the existence or not of Keynesian policies, norms of consumption, the degree of consensus, and so forth, while the claim for rupture is replaced by an emphasis on the spontaneity of the labour element. The problems concerning the concept of relative surplus value are analysed within the concept of a 'classificatory and identificatory logic' of the social, of the 'systematic institutionalisation of society' (Aglietta, 1979), of the state's penetration into political society and of the fracturing and recombination of social elements — in other words, it is replaced by an abstract functionalist conceptual framework.

STRUCTURALISM AND SPONTANEISM

One typical expression of the methodological problems in the contemporary crisis in theory to which we have been referring is M. Aglietta's *Theory of Capitalist Regulation*, whose considerable appeal is indicative of the kind of dominant science in 1980s. For this reason we shall deal with certain types of concept formation in that text, which describes itself as a Marxist perception of the capitalist system. In a manner typical of structuralism, Aglietta understands the Marxian notion of the capitalist system as a mode of articulating the laws of capital accumulation and the laws of competition. Of course, this distinction between two types of 'laws' is already problematic from the methodological point of view, since it disconnects the internal relation existing between the processes of competition and the processes of accumulation, which Marx refers to as the 'inner nature' of capital. But the structuralist–articulationist logic permeates all the development of Aglietta's concepts, revealing a *sui generis* method of exposition of categories. I believe that it is possible in the logic of this method of exposition to detect traces of elements which express the current crisis in theory, that is, structuralism and its transition into spontaneism.

Aglietta's analysis is divided into two parts which correspond to the distinction between the two types of laws which we noted above. In the first part, in which the production of capital and the general tendencies in the accumulation of productive capital are developed, the focus of the analysis shifts on to the problem of transforming the labour process (such as Taylorism, Fordism), of the 'working day' and of the formation of the labour union movement. This shift in the method of exposition of categories means that capitalist relations of production can be understood by starting from transformations in the living conditions of wage-earners, that is, in the last analysis from the formation and evolution of a norm of social consumption. Thus social relations are 'explained' by means of the norm of consumption (for example the scope for providing the working class with cheap housing and cars), which is regarded as a primary and irreducible category of analysis. Similar shifts are also to be found in the second part of the book, which analyses, as laws of competition, the processes of concentration and centralisation of capital. Giant firms and financing clubs are identified as the forms of centralisation, and questions of the realisation of surplus value under conditions of perfect and monopolistic competition or of price formation, are also examined.

In both parts, there is a clear and systematic attempt to destroy the conceptual links which permit a theoretical approach to essential social relations in contemporary societies. The concept of capital as an exploitative relationship of production and as a process of accumulation is destroyed. The 'aspect' of the productive nature of capital is perceived, in effect, as 'organisation of labour', which is thematised independently of a rational theory of the historical division of labour and of the development of technology; such a theory would deal with both the dimension of labour constitution and the dimension of the constitution of processes of real subsumption of labour under capital as a single problem. Similarly, the capital concentration processes are analysed as phenomena of competition: in a dialectical exposition of categories those phenomena presuppose the development of a theory of the accumulation, concentration and centralisation of capitals. This avoids a disclosure of the internal relations between social phenomena on different levels of abstraction, that is, it avoids the full development of the critical dimension of the dialectical argument. Aglietta's analysis is permeated by an understanding of the state as a vehicle for social cohesion (a goal whose nucleus can already be identified in Poulantzas) and by an understanding of institutionalisation as an expression of two relations which are seen as fundamental: the money relation and the wage relation. These relations are connected with the evolution of mass consumption. In all the relations which are analysed we can recognise as a 'founding element' that of the 'wage' or the 'norm of consumption' which, in turn, is founded on nothing except itself. The fixing of wages is not seen as a commodity relation and it is regarded as lying outside the logic of the labour theory of value. A wage relation:

> denotes the dispossession suffered by a class in a society dominated by private property. . . . It is the logical contrary to a commodity relation, for it does not involve any exchange of equivalents. It is curious that Marx maintained the classical fiction of labour-power as a commodity in his own conceptual system, even though his decisive pages on primitive accumulation abundantly proved that it was the very opposite.
>
> [Aglietta 1979, p. 31]

The transposition — so typical of historicism — of the labour theory of value, which refers to a constituted capitalist system, into a theory of the emergence of social relations is quite clear here. The labour theory of value is reduced to problems connected with primitive accumulation and these to an abstract element of political violence and class struggle, which precedes the value relationship and is maintained unaltered in it. On the basis of this, the theory of constituted bourgeois relations is conceived of as the analytical continuation of the theory of their emergence; the political element is stressed as fundamental. Similarly, the element of class struggle, too, is seen as impossible to incorporate into any approach whatever: 'At our present level of knowledge of the problems of social transformation, we can accept here that if the class struggle produces norms and laws which form the object of a theory of social regulation, it is itself beyond any law' (p. 67). The class struggle which permits a theoretical approach to economic relations lies beyond any rational explanation. 'Even though it is rooted in existing conditions, the class struggle goes beyond them in producing social institutions and procedures that are not re-arrangements of these conditions. It is a process of creation in the strong sense' (p. 68). The idea of the 'creation' of an institutional framework by a process of struggle which cannot be approached rationally permeates all the analysis of the regulation school. It is characterised by a shift of interest from the object of critical analysis of contemporary society, that is, the division of labour and class relations, to the thematisation of a spontaneous practice, whose conditions defy analysis. Precisely this constant shift which we have already noted, from structuralism to spontaneism, is the principal feature of the crisis which is afflicting the social sciences.

One consequence of the fact that spontaneistic theories have constructed their concepts using mystified ideas about 'creation' as a starting-point is, on the methodological level, the rupture between them and the idea of the 'method of exposition' of categories and dialectics. Thus they have joined the tradition of romantic criticism of rationalism, which stresses the importance of the imaginary, of lived experience (*Erlebnis*), as it manifested itself in the inter-War irrational theories of Juenger and Heidegger. This shift in the direction of the imaginary and the foundation of an argument which relativises rationalism by reducing it to spontaneism, results on the political level in the disconnection of politics from a framework of rational analysis, bringing it into dangerous proximity with Carl Schmittian patterns. It is characteristic of the degree to which this mode of thinking has penetrated the left that, in the name of the spontaneity and self-determination which ought to be features of the revolutionary project, the rational is located exclusively in the 'bad' rationalisation of an alienated society which is destined to be transcended, while 'revolutionary subjectivity', in its pure form, resorts to the spontaneity of the imaginary, which is given precedence over institutionalisation in all forms. Castoriadis' theory of the imaginary which crystallises into institutionalisations is typical of this tendency. It is clear that this approach leads to a form of historicist relativism, according to which any institutionalisation is possible while the 'preference' of the theorist for institutions of autonomy and freedom is the outcome of the decisionism typical of theory. I believe that the analyses of Negri and Cleaver risk incorporating themselves into this tendency, stressing the 'non-systematic' aspects of the Marxian work and aiming at a 'rupture' with method — that is, at an interruption of the conceptual continuity of the exposition of categories and a direct juxtaposition of the particular analyses with a nuclear emancipatory element reducible to 'struggle' (in this sense, Aglietta's reference to Negri is not surprising). By way of contrast to these views, it is clear that the roots of revolutionary subjectivity cannot lie in some creativity divorced from the presuppositions and achievements of social practice as it stems from the system of division of labour and of political/class relations. Nor can these presuppositions and results be analysed as *creatio ex nihilo* by taking the 'creative' element in action as a starting-point; they must be analysed as social relations within which human creativity is shaped historically under alienating and exploitative forms. The 'creative' element in human action becomes abstract and ideological if it is separated from that relation and given precedence over it so as to provide a foundation for it.

If we search for a logical form of this social relation, we will be led into problems of the foundations of the rationalism and radicalism in social theory. As early as the *Theses on Feuerbach*, Marx had begun the search for this logical form, starting with the distinction between the intuitive and the rational as it manifests itself in the theory of knowledge. His aim was to make the distinction comprehensible as a redoubling and covering of the 'self-cleavage' in the social base itself. This 'self-cleavage' was the central problem in Marx's inquiries right down to his very last works. Human creativity was seen as developing within this social relation, which is the object of analysis by means of the dialectical theory (which grounded its axiological and practical claims in reference to it). The theory treats the social relation as rational, that is, as governed by a characteristic and reconstructable mode of movement, and as non-reasonable, that is, as acting against the axiological framework which can be produced, in practical terms, by that relation. Rational reflection on the irrationality of the social relation accompanies the action directed to its change and to replace it with a new relation which will transcend the exploitative form of society, thus also transcending the ideological reproduction of the abstract segregation between spontaneous action, on the one hand, and alienated conditions, on the other.

REMARKS ON A NEW DEBATE ABOUT THE STATE

The theoretical positions which are discussed above appear to have particularly important consequences for an understanding of the crisis in state theory today. We may now be witnessing the beginning of a significant debate about problems of method in the theory of the state, in which a critical argument against structuralist theories of the state is taking shape in work such as that of S. Clarke, J. Holloway and W. Bonefeld. To this debate I should like to contribute some remarks concerning a central methodological misunderstanding and the epistemological affinities of structuralism, together with an observation on the position adopted by criticism.

To begin with the methodological 'turn' in the so-called 'Reformulation' of state theory, its explicit goal was the need to overcome 'abstract academicism' and the lack of political consequences ('*politische Folgenlosigkeit*') of the state derivation debate (J. Hirsch). In reality, however, the interest of the theorists engaged in this tendency was of an analytical character. Their acceptance of descriptive terms drawn from Gramscian structuralism, such as accumulation strategy, hegemonic structure, popular programme and Fordism, responded to their need to develop conceptual frameworks which would allow the acquisition and systematisation of new and more knowledge about the specific development of capitalism and about the specific historical forms it has taken. Precisely at this point, however, is the central methodological misunderstanding on the part of those theorists: it lies in the understanding of the question concerning the 'derivation of the state' as an abstract theory which refers to general structural features of capitalist societies and is not in a position to take account of fundamental historical changes at the level of surplus value, production, class relations, internationalisation of capital or societalisation. It is exactly because 'Reformulation' understands theory as an abstract structure that the demand arose for the structuralist categories of the 'derivation of the state' to be combined with a theory of the historical development of capitalist society, which it attempts to approach with concepts such as Fordism. We have already analysed the problematic nature of Fordism and similar concepts. In general, we should note that in view of its inability to formulate a logically powerful generative theory for the production of each new phenomenon, the 'reformulation' school resorts to articulationist alternatives, thus isolating the 'new' phenomenon from the mode of movement of the real and reconnecting it in an external manner and *a posteriori* with an abstract theoretical structure. Characteristic of this external mode of connection is the analysis of the 'new social movements' (such as ecologists), which are presented (see Hirsch) as contingent and which are not developed in a relational reference to the social division of labour. These movements were initially developed as 'defences' of pre-capitalist relations against the expanding capitalist relation. They subsequently evolved into movements *within* that relation. The appearance of such movements is not a mere empirical datum capable of being combined with other data or with general structures; it can, however, be approached theoretically within the framework of a dialectical theory of politics. Such a theory would refer back to the Marxist idea of the preservation of social substance whenever the latter is threatened, actualising, thus, the presupposed and latent general conditions of reproduction (starting, for example, from the Marxian analysis of *Capital*, Vol. I, Chapter 10). This materialist and dialectical idea about the 'positing of the precondition' (*Setzung der Voraussetzung*) was implicitly raised in the issues posed by the analyses of the *Logic of Capital* (Rubin, Wygodski, Rosdolsky) on which structuralism turns its back. The structuralist–articulationist logic is fully expounded by Bob Jessop, first in his work on the capitalist state, where he develops a methodological framework — in which he discusses a state theory without reference to the labour theory of value, and also in his other works (see Jessop 1983) where he attempts to incorporate the labour theory of value into his argument. The way in which Jessop has conceived the structuralist argument is conspicuous for its formalism and idealism, as in his concept of accumulation strategy (which we have already subjected to criticism in this paper). This strategy is understood as a 'subject' which, in Jessop's own words, 'must take account' of the circuit of capital, international conjunctures, the balance of power and which 'must consider' the relation between the classes. (In other words, we have here a reappearance of the Hegelian idealistic subject so disliked by the structuralists.) These constructs are linked with a form of methodological individualism and also with historicist relativism (understanding of culture as a mode of variation of patterns).

Jessop, true to his articulationist line of argumentation, denies (as do the theorists of 'reformulation' and 'regulation') that 'there is a single objective logic of capitalist development which transcends all particularities', while he deduces from this denial the separation of abstract theory, on the one hand, from empirical data, on the other:

> The development of capitalism is always mediated through historically specific institutional forms, regulatory institutions and norms of conduct, for example, wage relations, forms of competition, monetary emission, the state, the international commercial and financial system and the norms of conduct and modes of calculation which correspond to these institutional forms, etc.

On the transition to a new phase, Jessop accepts that this 'depends on class struggle', but he emphasises that there is no 'objective developmental logic of capital that inevitably and painlessly ensures passage from one regime to another'. These positions make clear the empiricism and relativism of Jessop's analysis. The element of the class struggle is separated from the problem of its mode of movement and degenerates into a factor in the contingency and relativity of historical development. The real is, finally, understood to be indeterminable, given that it is seen as mediated by an infinite number of empirical factors. As a whole, Jessop's methodology displays the epistemological form so typical of theories of 'regulation' and 'reformulation', that is, the form of construction of the concrete as a combination of 'mechanisms' and 'abstractions', which are not, in their conception, connected with each other, in such a manner that the concrete may be produced as a 'contingent'. This epistemological form is characteristic of the so-called 'realist' epistemologies, which do not accept the dialectical position that views particular 'mechanisms' as abstractions from essential relations and understands the concrete as necessary and determinate (for a critique of 'realism' see Gunn 1989).

To counter these regulationist, articulationist and other views of the social sciences, the *criticism* which has begun to be formulated has identified significant weaknesses in their tendencies. I believe, however, that this criticism has not yet been completed and in this sense it should also question some of its own assumptions. The fundamental idea of this criticism focuses on the fact that Reformulation makes use of concepts such as 'regulation' which stress the structural dimension and the aspect of the 'objective laws' of capitalist development, thus failing to refer to social relations as 'relations of struggle'. This criticism against objectivism is accompanied by an accurate critique of functionalism, particularly of the structuralist view that the state ensures the functional cohesion of society ('politicism'). Lastly, the criticism is correct in identifying the voluntarism and methodological eclecticism which accompany the structuralist constructs. At the same time, however, the critical argument raises certain methodological problems concerning the positions it itself adopts, and particularly in relation to the introduction of the concept of 'struggle'. One methodological problem for the criticism emerges to the extent to which it retains the separation between structure and struggle, demanding simply that the element of the struggle not be subordinated to that of the structure but that the structures should be understood as 'mediations of struggle itself'. This view of mediation has its roots in the separation between structure and struggle, instead of demonstrating that the separation itself and the divided concepts are expressions of fetishism in theory. The element of the struggle thus risks being understood as an irrational primary and spontaneous act regardless of the historical and social relation and the social division of labour. Over-emphasis on the element of struggle as a distinct element may lead the criticism to the unfortunate position of underestimating the fact that structuralism constructs fetishistic concepts and merely turning the foundation upside down, demanding that these concepts be approached as 'mediations of struggle' (see Bonefeld 1987). Thus, as we have already noted, it is a mistake to retain concepts such as Fordism and post-Fordism, and to demand that their foundations be located on the side of struggle, since a materialist reconstruction of contemporary social and political relations also leads to the identification of the ideological nature of these concepts. The concept of 'class relations', in particular, which is so central to the materialist analysis, should not be reduced to an abstract element of 'struggle' (since then we should be led to a pre-critical view of the class struggle such as that to be found in Marx's *Poverty of Philosophy*). This concept should instead be analysed within its historical and political forms, in the struggles for the reappropriation of the social product on the part of the workers, as well as in the struggles for the preservation of social life and the establishment of democratic institutions.

REFERENCES

Aglietta, A. (1979), *A Theory of Capitalist Regulation, The US Experience* (London: New Left Books).

Bonefeld, W. (1987), see Chapter 3 in this volume, 'Reformulation of State Theory'.

Castoriadis, C.L. (1975), *L'institution imaginaire de la societe* (Paris: Seuil).

Clarke, S. (1988), see Chapter 5 in this volume, 'Overaccumulation, Class Struggle and the Regulation Approach'.

Cleaver, H. (1979), *Reading Capital Politically* (Brighton: Harvester Press).
Gunn, R. (1989), 'Marxism and Philosophy: A Critique of Critical Realism', *Capital & Class* 37.
Hirsch, J. (1983), 'The Fordist Security State and New Social Movements', *Kapitalistate* 10/11.
Hirsch, J. and R. Roth (1986), *Das neue Gesicht des Kapitalismus. Vom Fordismus zum Post-Fordismus* (Hamburg: VSA).
Holloway, J. (1988), see Chapter 6 in this volume, 'The Great Bear: Post-Fordism and Class Struggle. A Comment on Bonefeld and Jessop'.
Holloway, J. and S. Picciotto (eds), (1978), *State and Capital: A Marxist Debate* (London: Edward Arnold).
Jessop, B. (1982), *The Capitalist State* (Oxford: Martin Robertson).
Jessop, B. (1983), 'Accumulation Strategies, State Form and Hegemonic Projects', *Kapitalistate* 10/11.
Negri, A. (1984), *Marx beyond Marx, Lessons on the Grundrisse* (Massachusetts: Bergin & Garvey).
Poulantzas, N. (1973), *Political Power and Social Classes* (London: New Left Books).
Poulantzas, N. (1978), *State, Power, Socialism* (London: New Left Books).
Rosdolsky, R. (1977), *The Making of Marx's Capital* (London: Pluto Press).
Rubin, I. (1972), *Essays on Marx's Theory of Value* (Detroit: Black Rose Press).
Wygodski, W.S. (1968), *Die Geschichte einer grossen Entdeckung* (Moscow, Leipzig).

11 Marxism, Metatheory and Critique

Richard Gunn

Quite often, major political differences can turn on apparently technical and esoteric conceptual points. Inasmuch as there is no such thing as 'brute' or sheerly immediate politics any more than there is a 'brute' fact, this should be unsurprising: how we see the world is bound up intrinsically with what we do. Nonetheless Marxists eager to address first-order social and political questions have been perhaps too ready to consign questions of concept-formation to a hinterland of 'methodology', whose problems are always on the agenda for tomorrow but which is never discussed today. Of course it was not always so: from Lukács's 1923 declaration that Marxist 'orthodoxy refers exclusively to *method*' — a declaration which Lukács's subsequent discussion proceeded to undermine[1] — there developed a Marxist tradition according to which methodological concerns were prioritised over debates of a first-order or 'empirical' kind. A split arose between what Isaac Deutscher termed 'political' and 'philosophical' Marxism (Deutscher 1972). An exciting feature of debates in the 1960s and 1970s was that there emerged a promise that this split could be healed. But in the pragmatic Thatcherite 1980s Marxist theorising has too often taken a sheerly empiricist turn. Understandable political urgency has tended to marginalise conceptual questions, despite the circumstance that these questions are as political as may be. Thus it is more than welcome that Bob Jessop contends that 'only by re-examining . . . methodological assumptions' (Jessop 1988, p. 8) can a discussion of state theory proceed.

The 'methodological assumptions' upon which Jessop claims to rely are those of the 'Critical Realism' advertised by Roy Bhaskar in, most recently, two flagship-style articles summarising presentations to the UK Socialist Conference and published in the journal *Interlink* (Bhaskar *et al.* 1988, 1989; see Jessop 1988, pp. 8–14 and footnotes 15–18). Bhaskar offers a realism which is *critical* inasmuch as it challenges the fetishised claims of social appearances, and a criticism which is *realist* inasmuch as it turns upon identifying 'enduring structures and generative mechanisms' which underlie and produce 'observable phenomena and events' (Bhaskar *et al.* 1988; the opening paragraphs of the 1989 version reproduce the same views). The more complex statement of Critical Realism which Jessop invokes turns on a distinction between '*real* mechanisms', '*actual* results' and '*empirical* indicators' (Jessop 1988, p. 9). For the purposes of the present discussion I set these complexities aside. Instead my topic will be the conceptual status of Critical Realism *per se*, this being a topic which raises quite directly the question of Marxist concept-formation and which therefore extends well beyond a discussion of Critical Realism's specific claims.

Bhaskar opens his 1988 article by stating that 'the left needs to take philosophy seriously', which is certainly and uncontroversially the case. Throughout its two-thousand-years history philosophy, arrogating to itself the programme of a unique lust after wisdom, has reserved questions of concept-formation and concept-validation to its own discourse. The more modern the philosophy, the more hubristic has this arrogation become. From Descartes and Kant onwards, philosophy has devoted itself to evaluating the categories — the terms or truth-criteria — in and through which first-order discourse proceeds. Its quite reasonable entitlement for doing so is that vicious circularity is the outcome whenever first-order discourse, on its own behalf, lays claim to this role[2]: and so a second-order discourse (viz. 'philosophy') is wanted to carry the epistemological can. This gives rise to both a narrowing of philosophical concerns[3] and a problem. The problem is that the terms of a second-order discourse require, according to the same programme, to be validated by a third-order discourse . . . and so on, without hope of halt. In place of vicious circularity, infinite regress is called in to do the job. The twentieth-century philosopher who sees this consequence most clearly, and who most naively and engagingly accepts it, is Bertrand Russell (in his Introduction to Wittgenstein's *Tractatus* and in his theory of logical types). But naive acknowledgement by no means amounts to resolution. And so 'the left needs to take philosophy seriously', brute facts and romanticist politics-of-immediacy being a nonsense. But — given the problems of infinite regress — it can only take philosophy seriously in the form of critique. It has to reappropriate philosophical questions (those of category-formation and category-validation) and avoiding the Scylla and Charybdis of vicious circularity and infinite regress, it has to do so by reopening the question of the relation between first-order theorising and theorising of a higher-order (or 'metatheoretical') sort. The difficulty with Bhaskar's 1988 pronouncement is that he appears to construe the left's need to take philosophy seriously to mean that the left *needs a philosophy*, namely, his own. The roots of Critical Realism lie in precisely the philosophy of science — the philosophy which claims to be able to demarcate natural-scientific truth-claims from others — which Russell's Theory of Types inaugurated. In the old days, Critical Realism used to be termed 'transcendental realism' (Bhaskar 1975), thereby more directly indicating its Kantian source (which Russell and philosophy-of-science share). Quite apart from the question of the internal complexity of Critical Realism's statement, there is a question about the conceptual — and political — status of Critical Realism itself.

If indeed the left *needs a philosophy* (whether Critical Realist or otherwise) in order to address the issue of its concept-formation then, substituting infinite regress for vicious circularity, it professes itself willing to ascend a ladder of metatheories whose top rung rests nowhere but upon clouds. It is in the light of problems regarding this kind of idealism that, I suggest, Marx's critique of philosophy in the 1840s is to be understood. Sometimes, to be sure, the Marx of the 1840s advises us simply to 'leave philosophy aside' (Marx 1975, 5, p. xxx) and devote ourselves to the study of the empirical world. But such passages — veering back into vicious circularity from infinite regress — are atypical. The strength of Marx's critique of philosophy is that it advertises a mode of theorising which, because it is at the same time *both* first-order *and* higher-order (both 'theoretical' and 'metatheoretical'), escapes the dilemma of vicious circularity versus infinite regress.

In order to see how Marx achieves this, we have to turn to the thesis of *the unity of theory and practice* which his texts of the 1840s announce. Marx posits an internal relation as between theory and practice, and accepts (or rather stresses) that just such a relatedness obtains in the case of his own thought. In other words Marxist theorising is not just *reflexive* but *practically* reflexive (Gunn 1987a). Two definitions help to clear my argument's way.

Theorising is reflexive when, and insofar as, it asks after the validity of its own categories, concepts, truth-criteria and/or terms. Theorising is practically reflexive when it does this *in the course of* asking after its practical — its social or historical — situatedness. The phrase 'in the course of' reports the *internal* relatedness of theory to practice for which Marx contends. Were theory merely to ask after its conceptual validity and, separately, to reflect upon its social preconditions (as in bourgeois 'sociology of knowledge') then — as reported in the conjunction 'and' — it would regard theory and practice as linked merely in an external way. Practically reflexive theorising unites not just theory with practice but first-order theory with metatheory because (a) in reflecting upon society (its first-order object) it reflects upon itself, and because (b) in reflecting upon itself (upon its own categorial validity) it reflects upon the social practice which it challenges and within which it inheres. Its first-order object includes itself as a second-order object, and comprehension of itself as a second-order object involves comprehension of its relatedness to social practice as as a whole (see Lukács 1971 first essay; Horkheimer 1972, p. 229). Another way of stating this point is to say that practical situatedness impinges on theorising not just in a third-person — as in 'sociology of knowledge' — but in a first-person way. Yet another way of registering the argument is to say that practical reflexivity is by no means a 'methodology' discussion which might be confined to the introduction of a text which is informed by it; rather, it is the mode of practice of a practically reflexive text itself.

In sum Marxism, *qua* practically reflexive, is *neither* first-order *nor* sheerly higher-order because it is both together and in the same breath. The same body of theory (or movement of theorising) plays now a theoretical, and now a metatheoretical, role. Even the word 'now' in the preceding sentence is problematic, because the role played by any particular conceptual shift is a function only of the questions which, in relation to it, are posed. In other words instead of a dualism ('theory' contraposed to 'metatheory') we have a totalisation. Marx's 1840s critique of philosophy is not a matter of turning away from the questions philosophy has reserved to itself towards empiricism, but of enunciating a mode of discourse which retains purchase on 'philosophical' issues (such as those of category-validation) while hurling the philosophical carapace of these same questions aside. It has good reason to do so since, as discussed above, nothing but stones and whirlpools — infinite ascent and circular regression — await the theoretical traveller who confronts either metatheory or first-order empiricism on their own, reciprocally distinguished, set of terms.

The argument just presented can be taken a stage further or, rather, it can be set into reverse gear. Sheer metatheory (philosophies and methodologies of science, for example) and sheer empiricism (positivism, sociology) are discourses which take in one another's washing. Each relies upon the other to substantiate it:

empiricism calls for the metatheoretically-prescribed demarcation criteria (for example, Popper 1972, p. 249) which might prise it away from mysticism, while philosophy of science is forced to humble itself by undertaking an 'underlabourer' role in relation to the theorising it claims to legislate for in order that it have something substantive to discuss. Russell, a philosopher by no means famous for his self-effacement, conceded this latter point when he remarked that any metatheory whose implications clashed with the results of physics could only be false.

All this said, two crucial theses are in order: (a) whenever theory and metatheory are prised apart then only on the one side positivism and, on the other, infinite ascent through metatheories ('idealism' in one sense of that term) can obtain. And (b) unless practical reflexivity is the condition of theorising the course of thought reported in my first theses is inescapable. To be sure this 'unless' awaits rigorous proof. But notice its conditions: to avoid it we have to be able to unite first- and third-person discourse and theoretical and metatheoretical discourse *minus* practical reflexivity. Not a single utterance in the two-thousand-years-old tradition of Western philosophy suggests that this can be done. Practical reflexivity therefore appears as the catharsis of theoretical truth and of practical emancipation (involving demystification) alike.

Perhaps my argument may strike a reader as a top-heavy condemnation of what Bhaskar and Jessop have to say. Perhaps neither of them distinguishes theory from metatheory in so rigorous a fashion as to qualify as a 'philosopher' in my above-criticised sense. Possibly practical reflexivity lurks somewhere within their works. In fact the opposite is the case; in demonstration of which I shall discuss a passage from each in turn.

Firstly, Bhaskar *et al.* (1988) reports that 'social theory and social reality are causally interdependent' in the sense that 'social theory is practically conditioned by, and potentially has consequences in, society'. This sounds like practical reflexivity until we notice the causalism by means of which each of these two citations establishes the connections upon which they rely. What is missing is the in-the-course-of condition which, in my definition, allowed the thesis of an internal relation as between theory and practice to stand. And it was through this internal relatedness that first-order theory and metatheory were enabled to form a unity. Causal relations *can only* be external relations. Bhaskar's hostage to causalist fortune severs first-person from third-person reflexivity and supplies exactly the conceptual gap within which sociologies of knowledge thrive. In other words a unity of theory and metatheory is far from being Bhaskar's profferment. What obtains even in such encouraging formulations as the one just quoted is faithfulness to his philosophy-of-science (his Russellian and ultimately Kantian) roots.

Secondly, Jessop (1988, footnote 18) turns instead to the notion of a 'double hermeneutic' as developed in Anthony Giddens's work. 'A hermeneutic framework about a reality,' says Jessop, is 'already pre-interpreted by its participants' (loc. cit.). Here too something like practical reflexivity appears to be signalled: interpretations arise from reality and inform reality (or practice) in their turn. However, if causalism undermines practical reflexivity so too — from as it were the opposite direction — does a sheerly hermeneutical approach. From a third-person standpoint (that of causalism) we are translated over into a first-person standpoint (that of meaning). Practical reflexivity for its part requires a totalisation of these standpoints in such a way that, reflecting on the presence of our theory in our practice and of ourselves as subjects in society (our object), we can see ourselves as socially conditioned ('causalism') and as socially conditioning ('hermeneutics') in, once again, the same breath. To draw two breaths here instead of one is to sever sociological from categorial self-reflection; thereby, it is to sever first-order from higher-order theorising and theory from practice itself.[4] The 'dialectic between structure and strategy' announced by Jessop (1988a) signifies his endorsement of just such a dualistic approach. Jessop, like Bhaskar, writes 'and' where practical reflexivity writes 'in-the-course-of'. External relations supplant internal relations, as is usual when sociology (or indeed any other first-order discourse) calls for metatheoretical — methodological or philosophical — support.

Thus I conclude that it *is* fair to tax Bhaskar and Jessop with missing the point of practical reflexivity and so reproducing, in different fashions, a theory/metatheory split. And a further point in this connection is to be noted: such a split has consequences not merely for the conceptual status of, but *within*, the first-order dimension of theorising itself.

In regard to Jessop something of this has already been indicated: hermeneutics distinguishes itself from causalism, and methodology from sociology, in the same movement as structure *and* strategy become first-order truth-claims controlling terms. In Bhaskar's work it appears that the theory/metatheory severance is so severe that there is *no relation at all* between Critical Realism as a metatheory and the first-order political prescriptions Critical Theorists wish to raise. Bhaskar *et al.* (1989) opens with a summary of the philosophical claims set forth in Bhaskar *et al.* (1988) and then offers a list of political desiderata which he and his associates would like to see the left endorse: the connection between the first and the more lengthy second part of this article remains thoroughly unclear. *Arbitrariness* within first-order theory seems to be the primary consequence of Critical Realism's theory/metatheory split. On closer inspection, however, an interrelation between the levels of Bhaskar's discussion can be discerned at least in regard to *the form* of the first-order political theory his 1989 article presents. What this first-order theory amounts to is a defence of certain 'models' of democratic socialism held to be praiseworthy. Model-building is of course a central activity of social theory, from neo-classical economics through Weberian sociology, which understands itself as independent of philosophical dictats-from-above. Models, unlike philosophies, can be built and torn down in and through first-order theorising itself; they (or something like them) become needful under the sign of a theory/metatheory severance inasmuch as guidance has to come *from somewhere* in the matter of which categories first-order theory is to employ. In other words, a totalisation as between theory and metatheory *does* obtain in Bhaskar; but it is a totalisation which obtains only in the mode of being denied. It is a totalisation which goes forward behind the backs of the Critical Realists who are unconsciously its bearers. The theory/metatheory separation *has consequences* for, and within, both metatheory and theory: it constitutes the former as 'philosophy' or 'methodology' and the latter as a *positivism* which uncritically derives the models which guide it from the way of the existing social world. The model which it *makes most sense* to employ is the model in closest conformity to this world's ways.

This may seem an unfair charge since, after all, a re*modelling* of existing society might amount to confronting society with its failure to live up to the rationale which animates it: it might amount to immanent critique. To such an objection I have two replies. The first is that immanent critique has to challenge not just the content of social relations but their form, and, theory being seen as a moment within social practice, not just the content of first-order truth-claims but their form as well. That is to say, it cannot merely be a matter of the empirical or ethical accuracy of models: and in the end it is only some such notion of accuracy upon which model-building relies. To be sure Weber says that his models (or ideal-types) are not to be understood normatively; and to be sure Kant says that the regulative ideas (in effect the building-blocks of models) which control his ethics are not to be construed in an empirical way. In each of these cases, the qualifying clause is intrinsic to the coherence of the model-building programme. But in the case of immanent critique it would have to be an ethical-empirical *unity* which enabled it to go forward. In other words the 'models' supporting an immanent critique would have to be *in*accurate, empirical accuracy being infected with ethical desiderata and ethical accuracy being infected with empirical concerns. Precisely the is/ought distinction respected by Weber and Kant alike would have to be overcome. I suggest that the best way to resolve these conundrums is to say that immanent critique has nothing at all to do with model-building. And, on the basis of this suggestion, my charge of positivism against Bhaskar stands.

The second of my replies is *ad hominem*, but to the same effect. In fact Bhaskar understands the relation of metatheory (Critical Realism) to first-order theory in a way which precludes the notion of immanent critique. Bhaskar *et al.* (1989) announce 'a distinction between (a) *emancipatory* action or practice and (b) *emancipated* action or practice, which are often unwittingly confused . . . [This distinction] is the distinction between *socialism as a movement* (or programme) and *socialism as a society* (or way of life)'.

I leave aside, here, the question of the egregious and ultimately bureaucratic elision of 'programme' with 'movement'. Instead I should like to focus on the distinction between emancipatory action and its goal. And on this score I should like to confess myself as one who is confused, unwittingly or not, by the circumstance that Marx reported communism not to be a future ideal but as the real or actual movement of the working class. 'Communism is neither the teleology of the capitalist system nor its catastrophe. It is . . . a concept that we can only formulate within the form of transition' (Negri 1984, p. 165). Once emancipatory action is separated from its goal, the notion of *self*-emancipation which Marx celebrated throughout his life's work is undermined. The matter is all the more strange inasmuch as Hilary Wainwright, one of the signatories to Bhaskar *et al.* (1989), was a co-author of a work entitled *Beyond the Fragments* in which the notion of 'prefigurative' political organisation — or in other words political organisation which quite precisely refused to separate the goal of action from action itself — was deployed against Leninist vanguardists, male intellectuals and other rightly-or-wrongly identified riff-raff. Prefiguration (both theoretical and practical) is in the event necessary to critique if critique is to be *immanent*, inasmuch as such critique has to be able to discover a basis within the present on which an emancipatory future might be built. Bhaskar's '(a)'-and-'(b)' distinction severs action from the future towards which it aims and which (see writers as different as Hegel, Marx, Heidegger, Kojeve, Bloch and Sartre) self-determines and self-defines it. His distinction alienates action from itself and places the question of the rightness or wrongness of such action (I understand these terms both epistemologically and normatively, and in the face of positivism's is/ought distinction I would stress these latter terms' unity) in the hands of metatheorists who, *qua* metatheorists, perforce construe philosophy and methodology as a practice-independent 'realm of their own' (Marx 1975, 5, p. 447). Stated the other way round: the alienation of action — the severance of itself from its goal, and the undermining of its self-determination — *is a first-order consequence* of the theory/metatheory split, whose roots lie in the theory/practice split (the subversion of practical reflexivity) itself. Marx reports the same thing when, in the terminological formulae of *The German Ideology*, he traces the alienation of theory from practice and the consequent constitutions of philosophy on the one hand and positivism on the other to the division between mental and manual labour. For Marx immanent critique *turns upon* practical reflexivity, since otherwise neither the rootedness of present theory in past practice nor the internal ('prefigurative') relation between present practice and a theory of the future — this 'neither . . . nor' comprising once again a single totalisation — can be understood. Thus, once again, I conclude that my charges against Bhaskar *et al.* (in this case to the effect that model-building and immanent critique count as entirely different conceptual procedures) are indeed fair.

In the preceding paragraphs I have offered a discussion of the consequences of the theory/metatheory separation (stemming from a theory/practice separation) within first-order theorising in a more-or-less unsystematic way. However, it is easy enough to draw the threads together and to show that one central difficulty underlies all that has been said. Once theory is separated from metatheory, in such a way as to permit the latter to dictate terms to the former — despite all the modesty of philosophical and methodological 'under-labouring', and despite first-order theory's attempt to claw concept-formation back into its own domain through the idea of 'models' — *universals* are privileged over *particulars* in the constitution of first-order thought. Categories and terms are necessarily universals, in the sense that they amount to lenses through which a whole series of reciprocally distinct particular objects are to be seen. *All* thought proceeds in terms of universals so that a thought wishing to focus on particulars has to be a thought willing to encompass paradox, and (see Adorno 1973) to think against itself. On this score the basis for complaint against metatheory as a discrete discipline is not that it insists on the cognitive and normative-political role of universals — it could not do otherwise without succumbing to brute facticity and romanticism — but that it prioritises universals above particulars in such a way as to deny the latter a categorial and political voice. All that metatheory can prescribe to first-order theory is the set of spectacles (the universals or categories) which such a theorisation should wear, if its truth-criteria are to be defensible. Metatheory as separate from first-order theory constitutes the latter as a domain in which particularity has no rights. And yet it is particulars which first-order theory experientially encounters. I can stumble over an object in the dark, without my spectacles and half-asleep and before I can find the light-switch: that is, I can encounter it as a particular before (in terms of universal categories) I know what it is. Unsurprisingly, the history of philosophy records a debate between the cognitive roles of particularity and universality respectively. The universalism of Plato's Theory of Forms declares against the particularism of the Sophists in the ancient world, Plato (in his *Parmenides*) averring for reasons best known to himself that there are no universal Forms of such undignified materials as 'hair' and 'dirt'.[5] In the early-modern period, the same battle was renewed in the form of a struggle as between deduction (starting from universals: Descartes) and induction (starting from particulars: Bacon), deduction winning — as is consistent with the theory/metatheory severance upon which modern philosophy turns — the theoretical day. (Just this victory is celebrated in Karl Popper's notion of refutability.) In our own times, philosophically marginalised figures like Nietzsche, Bataille and indeed Adorno line up on the side of particularity as a reference-point against philosophers of science, from Russell onwards, comfortable in their purely metatheoretical role.

One point to note here is that a metatheory prescribing terms to first-order theory separates universals (which have priority) from particulars (which count as secondary) within first-order theory itself. The lens and its object, not to mention the optician and his/her client, are after all two different things. Hence the need for 'models' or ideal-types or regulative ideas — Kant in his *Critique of Judgement* was one of the first to see the difficulty clearly — to mediate between categories and the objects which categories claim to know. Returning closer to home, the invocation of 'intermediate' categories in Jessop (see ch. 4) belongs within the same problematic. The programme of mediating between universal categories (for example, 'capitalism') and more particular categories (for example, modes of regulation, Fordism and post-Fordism and so on) emerges in the light of the argument just presented as a function of theory's dissociation from practice by way of the theory/metatheory split.

Perhaps Jessop might reply to this that the problem of integrating general points with more specific ones inheres in the activity of theorising itself. Discussion of capital-in-general is a necessary rather than a sufficient condition for understanding the quite particular conditions of our 1980s capitalist world. Were he to say this his point about *specificity* should be well taken, but the terms in which his point is stated — a genus/species distinction as between capital-in-general and the modes in which it is articulated — would remain open to challenge in Marxist terms.

For it is not just a matter of universals tending to overshoot particulars, in the sense of different flowers being able to grow in any field universal categories might circumscribe. Nor (*pace* Adorno) is it just a matter of the uprooting of hedgerows undermining the survival-basis of flora and fauna although, to be sure (Adorno 1973, p. 362), the philosopheme of pure identity' connotes 'death'. Rather the question turns on the circumstance that universals can be particulars in their turn. More strongly stated: in social life, all universals are particulars (or potentially so). In the self-understanding of social life, therefore, a genus/species distinction can have no place. Nor can a theory/metatheory distinction, since if universals *are* particulars then there can be no question of prescribing to social theory the universal categories in terms of which particulars are to be seen. Nor, finally, can there be a theory/practice distinction — in the sense of an external separation between the two — since the very abstractions and generalities and universals in which theorising goes forward are ones which have a vivid social (a practical) mode of life.

It remains to clarify the claims which my preceding paragraph has raised. Jessop styles his conception of an interaction between 'structure' and 'strategy' dialectical, but an entirely different conception of 'dialectics' will be presented below. *Pace* Jessop, it will turn not just on the notion of an interrelation (in the end a causalist one?) but of mediation, understanding this latter term in the sense of *mode of existence*: two terms reciprocally mediate one another when each is the mode (or form) in which the other subsists. Once again internal rather than external relatedness: universality and particularity subsist in and through one another in the dialectic of social life. To be sure they can subsist through one another *contradictorily*, that is, in the mode of being (each of them) denied, and this is what Adorno's epigram concerning the 'philosopheme of pure identity' reports. Universality existing as particularity can countermand itself, and vice versa. For the present we can set these complexities aside, however, and confine ourselves to enunciating two theses: (a) an understanding of theory and metatheory as forming two discrete realms of conceptualisation — for example, philosophy and sociology — cuts the ground from under the idea of universals existing in and through practice while conversely (b) only practically reflexive theory can admit the possibility of universals existing in this way.

Practical reflexivity can admit this possibility inasmuch as its understanding of its own categories *in the course of* reflecting on its practical situatedness implies a similar understanding (an understanding in what I have called the 'first person') of the object, that is, society, upon which it reflects. *In the course of* theorising theories, or 'ideologies', it theorises practice as well. In other words it problematises not just theory *and* practice but the relation in which theory and practice stand. It unites its own subjectivity with social objectivity in the same movement as it construes ideology as a material existence while equally construing practice as shot through with potentially mystificatory ideas. Conversely, a sufficient condition of blinding oneself to the possibility of universals existing in and through practice (however contradictorily) is to remove metatheory from theory: once this is effected universals can only be *prescribed to* the understanding of particulars or, to state the same point the other way round, they can only be understood as *abstracted from* rather than as *inhering in* the particulars whose significance they claim to report. A comprehension of universals *as* particulars is precluded. Furthermore, if indeed as contended earlier a separation of theory from metatheory and practical reflexivity are mutually exclusive, it follows that my theses (a) and (b) report from two different viewpoints — those of theory and of practice — one and the same thing.

All this, it seems to me, was sharply perceived and registered by Marx. His 1857 Introduction to the *Grundrisse*, distinguishing as it does between labour as production-in-general, that is, as an activity upon which *all* social formations depend, and labour as an abstraction which *qua* abstraction obtains only in a society of generalised commodity-production (Marx 1973, Introduction; Gunn 1989, pp. 105–8) announces nothing else. Abstract labour (a universal) is practically real, and indeed murderous, as anyone whose life depends on the sale of their labour-power quite directly knows. But it is practically real only within a particular social formation (a capitalist one) and only as a particular condition of such a social formation (inasmuch as for example unsold and *unpaid* domestic labour is no less a condition of the reproduction of capitalist relations of production from day to day). Marx's critique of political economy turns on the refusal to elide abstract labour as production-in-general with abstract labour which, as a socially and practically existing category, appears in and through generalised commodity-production alone. To construe labour as a generally applicable category for all societies is to *abstract from* particular social conditions; to construe labour as a peculiarly capitalist abstraction, both in theory and in practice, is to approach it as an *abstraction in and of* the specific social world of the 'doubly free' labour whose historical preconditions the final section of *Capital* Volume I reports. To confuse these two senses of the category 'labour', and these two meanings of abstraction, is to render oneself complicit in the eternalisation of commodity production against which Marx, from the beginning to the end of his life's work, so tirelessly declares.

Abstraction from is compatible with all manner of genus/species, universal/particular, metatheory/theory and practice/theory distinctions and dislocations; it entitles all manner of models and intermediate categories, and in fact requires them so as to prevent the universality of theorising and the particularity of theorisation's object from floating reciprocally free. *Abstraction in and of* (otherwise known as 'determinate' or substantive' abstraction: see Gunn 1987b and Bonefeld 1987) is the preserve of practically reflexive theorising alone. Indeed practically reflexive theorising *has to* be able to construe its abstractions as determinate ones since, otherwise, it would require a metatheory standing outwith first-order theory as the court of appeal before which its 'abstractions from' were supposed to receive justification and make sense. Abstraction-from amounts to an *induction* which all philosophers of science from Plato ('Don't tell me which actions are virtuous; tell me what virtue *is*') to Popper ('Don't announce to me a logic of scientific discovery, but describe to me the methodology in terms of which one is able to refute a point') have agreed requires philosophical or methodological back-up of some sort. Abstraction-in-and-of confounds, no less than does Marx's refusal to separate emancipatory and emancipated action, the theory/metatheory distinction upon which such a back-up turns. And in fact it is the category of action, or practice, which is all-important. Once its moments, for example its project and its goal, are held apart from one another practical reflexivity's totalisation implodes. Categorial appeal to an alienated practice reproduces the alienation of practice rather than the (possible) practice which, to use an ancient Marxist expression, might stand alienation on its head. If the theory/metatheory split has its roots in practice, it has practical consequences as well. And these consequences are of a murderous kind.

Bhaskar and Jessop play off philosophy and sociology against one another, and in this play the notion of determinate abstraction — the understanding of a *universal* category such as labour as a *particular* category of social existence — finds no place. Practical reflexivity implies determinate abstraction and vice versa, and both (in other words the Marx of the 1840s and the Marx of 1857 onwards) are alike ignored by the external relation of metatheory to theory upon which Bhaskar and Jessop agree. Labour as a contradictory relation between use-value and value-production — between its particularity and its universality, each existing in a capitalist world *through the other* but only in what I have called the 'mode of being denied' — can never be made sense of on a Bhaskar/Jessop account, since once universality is construed as *genus* and particularity as something which lurks beneath the notion of *species* everything becomes properly ordered: contradiction is marginalised as incoherence, instead of being construed as the movement of the universal/particular relation itself.

Between them, in other words, Bhaskar and Jessop by allowing philosophy to complement sociology subtract class struggle from the categories of Marx's mature work (see Cleaver 1979; Negri 1984). One way of seeing Marx's intellectual development — Althusser's way — is to counterpose his youthful humanist zeal against the scientific historical materialism which he announced in his first exile and as he approached middle age. A quite different way — that which the argument of the present article suggests — is to regard his early *critique of philosophy* as being pursued through his later studies into a critique not just of political economy but of sociologism in all its guises: that is to say, in the name of practical reflexivity, he hunts down the consequences of a theory/metatheory separation to its (and his) end. First of all (the anti-philosophical polemics of the 1840s) comes his condemnation of metatheory as a 'realm of its own'. Subsequently, in positivist England and as announced in the 1857 Introduction, comes his critique of first-order theory (positivism) which blushes whenever metatheoretical claims are invoked. Hence a deepening of an original insight rather than an abandonment of it. What confuses this record is the 'historical materialism' — the general theory of historical and social change — enunciated in *The German Ideology* of 1845–46 and summoned to memory in the form of a 'guiding thread' in the famous or notorious Preface of 1859. Historical materialism can sound all-too-like the kind of sheerly first-order theory of society which Jessop (with complexities) wishes to apply and which Bhaskar (with no less a sequence of complexities but in a metatheoretical register) offers philosophically to underpin. Perhaps we should get used to seeing historical materialism as a temporary aberration on Marx's part. Nothing in his critiques of philosophy or political economy turns upon it, and indeed the notion of historical materialism as a *general* theory of society which awaits only its historically rich *application* reproduces the genus/species distinction against which the notion of determinate abstraction (the notion of the presence of the universal within the particular and vice versa) contends. Like any other sociology, historical materialist sociology is placed by Marx out of conceptual bounds.

This said, it would be wrong to conclude the present article on a textual note. I set out from the premise that apparently technical difficulties within concepts can carry potent political points. Marxists are used to seeing concepts pertaining to Taylorism (in the production process) and to market rationality as fatal to millions. My proposition is to the effect that concepts deriving from a theory/metatheory severance are fateful, and fatal, no less. If not the theory/metatheory split itself then, at least, the theory/practice split from which it arises can kill. *Self*-emancipation — initially a *particular* point within my article but now, construing my own points as practically reflexive, quite properly becoming a *universal* and conditioning one — counts as torpedoed at the moment when such a split occurs. In effect this is the débâcle of what used to be termed Western Marxism. The unity of theory and practice enunciated by Lukács in 1923 has fallen asunder; antiquaries with names like Bhaskar and Jessop peruse the ruins; and who it is that will reap the whirlwind remains to be seen.

NOTES

1. Lukács 1971, p. 1. Lukács goes on to argue that dialectical method is available only from the class standpoint of the proletariat, and that indeed an external relation between method (or form) and content is a bourgeois deficiency in Kant's thought.
2. See Althusser 1971, p. 59. Althusser announces that theoretical practice (science) is its own truth-criterion, but then adds that this thesis applies only to sciences which are 'truly constituted and developed' for their part. Let anyone make sense of this who can. I quote Althusser because, although I do not discuss structuralism explicitly in the present paper, so much of Jessop relies (*via* Poulantzas) on quite-rightly-unfashionable Althusserian thought. Notice, in the context of my later argument, the shiftiness as to the status of philosophy as between Althusser (1969) and Althusser (1976). It is by no means clear to me that contemporary Marxism has sorted out the difficulties which Althusser's intellectual demise left unresolved.
3. Philosophy used to reserve to itself questions not just of concept-formation (or 'metatheory') but of cosmology. These latter were both first-order and higher-order, and *could* be both because truth was seen as pre-inscribed in the very order of things. The ratchet-effect of enlightenment has (despite Green romanticism) once-and-for-all undermined any such programme, but — see below — it is far from clear that either sociology or philosophy-of-science (or both in combination) can perform the task which cosmological philosophy, as in Plato's employment of *mimesis*, undertook. Our reckoning has to be with the movement of contradiction rather than with any static and harmonious whole.
4. See Giddens 1981, pp. 53–5. Giddens's view is that we are *in some respects* conditioned by our circumstances and *in other respects* free. But unless I am *in one and the same respect* self-determining the notion of my freedom (my self-determination) falls. A bit of causalism and a bit of 'human action' undermines, through its eclecticism, the latter. Two breaths always prevent the necessary single breath when, from alienation towards freedom, we are required to totalise our resources and take just one leap.
5. Marx was less prurient. In a letter to Engels of the early 1850s he looks forward to having put paid to 'all this economic shit'. My suspicion is that Marx's shit (*Scheiße*) reports — even perhaps by way of classical allusion — Plato's dirt. In other words Marx was prepared to dwell, for decades, within the dirt — the particularism as opposed to universalism — which Plato categorically and categorially renounced. Which 'hair' Plato most mistrusted remains an open question, but already in this marginal encounter we can see the battle between universalism and particularism breaking out.

REFERENCES

Adorno, T.W. (1973), *Negative-Dialectics* (London: Routledge & Kegan Paul).
Althusser, L. (1969), *For Marx* (London: Allen Lane).
Althusser, L. (1976), *Essays in Self-Criticism* (London: New Left Books).

Althusser, L. and E. Balibar (1971) *Reading Capital* (London: New Left Books).
Bhaskar, R. (1975), *A Realist Theory of Science* (Leeds: Books of Leeds).
Bhaskar, R. *et al.* (1988), 'Philosophical Underlabouring', *Interlink* 8.
Bhaskar, R. *et al.* (1989), 'Philosophy: More Underlabouring', *Interlink* 13.
Bonefeld, W. (1987), 'Marxism and the Concept of Mediation', *Common Sense* 2.
Cleaver, H. (1979), *Reading 'Capital' Politically* (Brighton: Harvester Press).
Deutscher, I. (1972), *Marxism in Our Time* (London: Jonathan Cape).
Giddens, A. (1981), *A Contemporary Critique of Historical Materialism* (London: Macmillan).
Gunn, R. (1987a), 'Practical Reflexivity in Marx', *Common Sense* 1.
Gunn, R. (1987b), 'Marxism and Mediation', *Common Sense* 2.
Gunn, R. (1989), 'Marxism and Philosophy', *Capital & Class* 37.
Horkheimer, M. (1972), *Critical Theory: Selected Essays* (New York: Seabury Press).
Jessop, B. (1988), 'Regulation Theory in Retrospect and Prospect', International Conference on Regulation Theory, Barcelona, June 1988, subsequently published in 'Printed-Serie' der Zif-Forschungsgruppe 'Staatsaufgaben' 1, University of Bielefeld, West Germany, Zentrum für interdisziplinäre Forschung, Bielefeld.
Jessop, B. (1988b), see Chapter 4 in this volume: 'Regulation Theory, Post-Fordism and the State'.
Lukács, G. (1971), *History and Class Consciousness* (London: Merlin Press).
Marx, K. (1973), *Grundrisse* (Harmondsworth: Penguin)
Marx, K. (1975), *Collected Works* (London: Lawrence & Wishart).
Negri, T. (1984), *Marx beyond Marx* (Massachusetts: Bergin & Garvey).
Popper, K. (1972), *Conjunctures and Refutations* (London: Routledge & Kegan Paul).

Index

GPSR Compliance

The European Union's (EU) General Product Safety Regulation (GPSR) is a set of rules that requires consumer products to be safe and our obligations to ensure this.

If you have any concerns about our products, you can contact us on ProductSafety@springernature.com

In case Publisher is established outside the EU, the EU authorized representative is:

Springer Nature Customer Service Center GmbH
Europaplatz 3
69115 Heidelberg, Germany

Batch number: 08231819

Printed by Printforce, the Netherlands